*THE ENGLISH LANDED ESTATE*
*IN THE NINETEENTH CENTURY:*
*ITS ADMINISTRATION*

# THE ENGLISH LANDED ESTATE
# IN THE NINETEENTH CENTURY:
# ITS ADMINISTRATION

BY

## DAVID SPRING

THE JOHNS HOPKINS PRESS
*Baltimore 18, Maryland*

This book has been brought to publication with the
assistance of a grant from the Ford Foundation.

# ✍ PREFACE

THIS study is in the nature of a by-product. For some years I have been reading account books and estate and family correspondence belonging to English landowners in the nineteenth century. My aim has been to find what the English landowner looked like in the round—that is, in the exercise of his social, economic, and political functions. This book deals with but a part of this large subject, and views it more from the vantage point of agents and the central government than from that of the landowner. I hope, however, in the near future to publish studies in which the latter figures more prominently than he does here.

I owe much to the kindness of many persons. In particular I should like to acknowledge my gratitude to the following: to Mr. W. Corbett and the Bedford Estate Office, to His Grace the Duke of Northumberland, to Lord Lambton, to Sir Fergus Graham, to Earl Fitzwilliam and the Trustees of the Wentworth Woodhouse estate, to Earl Spencer, and to Mrs. M. C. Cruwys for making it possible to consult manuscripts in their possession; to the Guggenheim Foundation for a generous grant in aid of research in England; and to the editors of the *Durham University Journal* and the *Journal of British Studies* for allowing me to make use of material from articles published in their journals.

I should also like to thank Miss Lilly Lavarello, secretary to the Department of History, The Johns Hopkins University, for cheerfully bearing the burden of typing drafts of my manuscript.

My greatest debt—and one which I cannot sufficiently express—is to my wife, who worked alongside me in the research and writing of this book.

D. S.

*Baltimore, Md.*
*November, 1962*

# ↳ CONTENTS

# ⚰ INTRODUCTION

THE ADMINISTRATION of English landed estates in the nineteenth century had two aspects, a private and a public one. The first has received no systematic treatment apart from an essay by Professor Edward Hughes on the eighteenth-century land agent which provides an introduction to the subject.[1] The second, which concerns the role of the state in English agriculture, has also received little attention apart from some contemporary accounts of the functions of the Inclosure Commissioners.[2] It is hoped, therefore, that a useful purpose will be served by discussing at length both of these aspects of estate administration.

English landed estates were of many sizes, ranging from roughly 1,000 acres to 100,000 acres and more. Although the administration of the small estate will not go unmentioned here, it is with the administration (and the administrators) of the large estate that this study will chiefly deal. This emphasis is in part determined by the important role played by the large estate in the economy of the landed society. In part it is determined by the nature of the historical evidence, for in the course

[1] E. Hughes, "The Eighteenth Century Estate Agent," in *Essays in British and Irish History in Honour of James Eadie Todd*, eds., H. A. Cronne, T. W. Moody, D. B. Quinn (London, 1949).

[2] For example: J. Bailey Denton, "On Land Drainage and Improvement by Loans from Government or Public Companies," *The Journal of the Royal Agricultural Society*, 1868.

of its history the large estate is likely to have provided, and to have preserved, an ample archive of accounts and correspondence, thus disposing the historian to lean heavily on its experience.

This study will also tend to be limited chronologically. For the most part it will fall within the period of high farming, the period between the agricultural depression of the 1830's and that of the 1870's.[3] This was the last age—and a great age—of the landowner's predominance in English agriculture. Much of the initiative came from the landowner. State intervention was intended less to supplant him than to assist him. After the 1880's the landowner declined in importance, as the state gradually limited the sphere of his operations, giving its support to the tenant farmer and removing him from the landowner's tutelage.

This book will begin with a sketch of the administrative arrangements found on a number of estates, small and large. This sample of estates will not include all possible arrangements, but it may be representative enough to provide a general framework or anatomy of estate administration. The next three chapters will deal with the activities of the several administrators—landowner, lawyer, and land agent. It is hoped both to discuss the role of each as a class and to provide detailed portraits of a number of individuals. The final chapter will describe something of how the English state in the mid-nineteenth century entered the world of the landed society, making use of its administrators, and seeking to promote agricultural prosperity and efficiency.

[3] Although recent research suggests that the word "depression" conveys too much, the traditional outlines of English agrarian history in the nineteenth century will be adhered to in this study.

# CHAPTER I

# THE ANATOMY
# OF ESTATE
# ADMINISTRATION

ADMINISTRATIVELY LANDED ESTATES fell into two classes. The first comprised the numerous small estates. If they were very small they depended on the efforts of the landowner assisted by a bailiff. The latter, usually a farmer on the estate, was severely limited in his powers, and his responsibilities were normally confined to the big house and its grounds or farm. The collection of rents and the keeping of accounts were **normally not** the bailiff's responsibility, but would fall to the landowner himself. On the Duke of Northumberland's estate, a superior agent bore the title of bailiff, but this was a historical accident peculiar to that estate. A less rudimentary organization among the small estates employed in addition to the bailiff an agent from outside the estate who took over some of the land-owner's functions. Either a solicitor or a professional land agent, he probably acted in the same capacity for a number of estates.

The second class comprised large estates which themselves varied much in size. Their distinctive mark was the employment of a resident land agent to whom considerable authority was delegated. As such estates grew in size or complexity of resources, or where they comprised several properties, they were likely to employ a chief or supervisory agent who presided over one or more resident land agents with their subordinate staffs. The supervisory agent was often a lawyer, either a solicitor or a barrister; and he often bore the title of auditor, for one of his functions was the customary one of examining and verifying estate accounts. In the course of the nineteenth century it would seem that the auditing function fell more and more to professional accountants, leaving the chief agent with his general function of supervision. This last varied much in its comprehensiveness from estate to estate, depending on the degree of central control exercised. The resident land agent's functions, however, tended to be much the same everywhere. Not a lawyer, he gave most if not all of his working time to the administration of one estate, to the collection of rent, the keeping of accounts, and the management of the tenantry.

Estates of either class might be diverse in their resources, and might thus encompass nonagricultural enterprise such as mining and urban development in addition to agriculture. Such estates often needed the services of specialized agents. These were either permanently attached to them or called in as consultants, depending on the volume of nonagricultural business that was transacted. There were some land agents, however, who achieved a remarkable versatility in all kinds of estate business.

# I

Cruwys Morchard, the Devon estate of the Rev. G. J. Cruwys, about 1,000 acres in size, may serve as an example of the small estate where the administrative machinery was as simple as was to be found. The landowner received his own rents, the few large tenants bringing them in person to the big house and paying them into his hands; and he himself kept the only record of such transactions in the form of jottings in his pocket diary.[1] He did not receive the rents of the smaller tenants which were collected by the bailiff, Henry Beedell, who was himself one of the large tenants. Beedell paid the laborers, bought the corn and hay for the big house, arranged for repairs on estate farms, and sold off the timber.[2] Occasionally, as the Rev. Cruwys wrote in his diary, he would accompany Beedell about the estate: for example, Feb. 22, 1878, "I went with Mr. Henry Beedell to Gogland plantation to look at some poles"; or May 23 of the same year, "In the morning I walked with Mr. Henry Beedell to the Orchard Hill and found that the rooks were doing damage to the potatoes."[3] Apart from such supervision exercised by the landowner, Beedell's work apparently went unsupervised by any other agent. The Cruwys family, like every landed family, had its solicitor to transact its legal business and draw up its deeds. He happened to be the proprietor's brother, Arthur Cruwys Sharland of Tiverton. But Sharland, it would seem, had little to do with estate management.[4]

On an estate larger than Cruwys Morchard, the landowner left more of estate business to agents. As we have seen, he delegated some of his functions to an agent from outside the estate—probably a local solicitor or land agent who acted for other estates as well. This agent collected his rents, kept his accounts, and supervised the work of his bailiff. On an estate about 3,000 acres in size Sir Roger Gresley of Drakelowe in Derbyshire employed in this way his family solicitor, Mr. Mousley of Derby.[5] On an estate of similar size John Moore Paget of Cranmore Hall, Somerset, so employed a professional land agent and surveyor, Charles Wainwright of Shepton

---

[1] Cruwys Morchard MSS, Diary of the Rev. G. J. Cruwys, *passim*.
[2] *Ibid.*, Mr. Henry Beedell's Agreement for Agency, Sept. 29, 1874.
[3] *Ibid.*, Diary, Feb. 22, May 23, 1878.
[4] Obituary of Arthur Cruwys Sharland, *Tiverton Gazette*, Dec. 27, 1887.
[5] *The Law Reports*, Chancery, vol. 45, Gresley *v.* Mousley.

Mallet. Wainwright regularly visited the estate to find what was needed and to keep the bailiff instructed. Sometimes Paget accompanied him on his rounds, as in June, 1861: "Viewed the quarry road with Wainwright and marked out the site of two new cottages on the Bytham road—also inspected Harrison's new buildings." [6]

The agent might come from farther afield than the neighboring county town. When David Ricardo became a landed gentleman and purchased an estate in Gloucestershire, he hired as his agent Edward Wakefield, who as early as 1814 had set up office in Pall Mall, in London.[7] Wakefield described himself as a "general land agent for the sale and purchase of land; acting as steward, and in the receipt of rents, for several large estates; and a land valuer." [8] He regularly visited Gatscombe to collect the rents and oversee Walker, the bailiff.[9] It is not clear why Ricardo should have chosen not to make use of a local man; but it may be that he knew Wakefield earlier in life before becoming a landowner, or perhaps that Wakefield purchased the estate for him and remained in his service.

## II

It would seem that a landed estate of a size somewhere between 5,000 and 10,000 acres began to feel some inadequacy in this rudimentary organization. Burton, the sixth Lord Monson's Lincolnshire property, was about 7,000 acres in size,[10] and its administrative arrangements were at times something like those of a large estate. In the 1840's, for example, in the

[6] Paget MSS, Diary of John Moore Paget, June 6, 1861.
[7] I. O'Connor, *Edward Gibbon Wakefield* (London, 1929), p. 21.
[8] British Parliamentary Papers (hereafter designated B.P.P.), *Report from the Select Committee on the Petitions complaining of the depressed state of the agriculture of the United Kingdom* (1821, IX), p. 206.
[9] Ricardo MSS, *passim.*
[10] 6,892 acres in 1841–42; see Monson MSS, 8/64.

place of a bailiff it had a resident agent, a tenant farmer named Brown, who received the rents, kept accounts, dealt with his fellow tenants, and undertook estate improvements; in addition it had a supervisory agent, a London solicitor named Gem, who presumably was meant to oversee Brown. In the 1850's, having abused the authority delegated to him, Brown was removed, and his place was taken by another farming tenant on the estate. The new man, however, was demoted to the position of bailiff, and such functions as receiving rent were taken over by a local solicitor in Lincoln. No more was heard of Gem. That this arrangement proved unhappy may suggest that Burton needed something more than the administrative organization of a smaller estate.[11]

Keele in Staffordshire, the estate of the Sneyd family, was about 2,000 acres larger than Burton,[12] and its resources were more diverse. There was no question here of trying to make do with the administrative organization of a small estate. Keele thus employed a resident land agent, Andrew Thompson, who apart from acting as an Assistant Inclosure Commissioner served the Sneyds exclusively.[13] Keele also regularly employed an auditor, a Mr. Hartley of Birmingham, who was a professional accountant; and occasionally employed a firm of mining engineers to advise on the letting of the mines.

It would seem that an estate larger than Keele almost invariably employed a resident land agent. Netherby in Cumberland, owned by Sir James Graham, about 26,000 acres in size,[14] put most of its administrative burden on the shoulders of its resident land agent, John Yule; unlike Keele it does not seem to have regularly employed an auditor. Sometimes Sir

[11] Monson MSS, Lord Monson to his eldest son, Sept. 9, 1858.
[12] In the 1870's Keele was 9,232 acres, and was presumably about the same size in the 1840's and '50's.
[13] See D. Spring, "Ralph Sneyd: Tory Country Gentleman," *Bulletin of the John Rylands Library*, March, 1956.
[14] In 1845 the estate was 26,133 acres in size; see Netherby MSS, "General Statement of the Extent of the Estate of Netherby."

James acted as his own auditor; sometimes—how often it is
not clear—there was no auditor at all.[15] On the Lambtons'
estate in county Durham, however, an estate midway in size
between Keele and Netherby, there was usually to be found
both a resident land agent and a supervisory agent.[16] But the
Lambtons' estate put heavy demands on its agents since it was
the scene of a large colliery enterprise, one of the few estates
on which its owners mined rather than let coal. What was
more, its owners were less energetic in estate administration
than was Sir James Graham.

On a great estate, like that of the Percies in Northumberland
which was over 150,000 acres in size, or even on estates half
that size, every sort of agent was likely to appear—supervisory,
resident, and others. With organization so complex and on so
large a scale, one might expect to find some thought taken
about administrative arrangements. This happened, in fact, on
the Percy estate shortly after the fourth Duke of Northumberland succeeded in 1847. Practitioners of administrative theory
in the twentieth century will find the lucubrations of the Duke
and his agents disappointing. They were highly tentative and
pragmatic. But they may be briefly considered for what light
they throw on the administration of the Percy estate and on
that of great estates generally.

Traditionally the Percy estate had been administered by an
establishment of Commissioners (or supervisory agents) at
Alnwick Castle and of bailiffs (or resident agents) in the
localities. The former varied in number from one to three,
and the latter usually were twelve or thirteen.[17] Nine of the
bailiwicks, as the local estates were called, were under 6,000

---

[15] Netherby MSS, J. Yule to Sir James Graham, April 3, 1843: "I am
really desirous to have my accounts of last years affairs audited by yourself, or some other competent person, as soon as may be convenient."

[16] When the auditor retired in the 1850's it would seem that the
accounts were not audited by anyone. See Lambton MSS, H. Morton to
Lord Lambton, March 16, 1856: "I have often thought since Mr. S.[teph-
enson] retired that my accounts sh$^d$ be regularly examined."

[17] Alnwick Castle MSS, "Minutes on local Agencies of the Northumberland Estates," June 26, 1848.

acres in size, and four ranged from 9,000 to 58,000 acres.[18] The bailiffs were tenant farmers on the estate who held farms at nominal rents in return for their services which (it was understood) would be devoted to the Duke exclusively.

Traditionally the duties of the bailiffs were as follows.[19] They collected rents. They saw to the cultivation of the estate farms, reporting annually to the central estate office at Alnwick and recommending repairs and improvements. They kept a watch on estate boundaries and prevented encroachments. They settled disagreements between entering and outgoing tenants. They received applications for farms and reported on them to the central estate office. They attended the Commissioners and valuers on their rounds of the estate, submitting information about land values and about the capacities of tenants. In general, they were expected to send information of all sorts on request to Alnwick and to carry out all orders emanating therefrom.

Various proposals were put forward—some in criticism and some in commendation of the system of bailiffs. It was suggested, on the one hand, that there were advantages to be gained by consolidating the bailiwicks and replacing the bailiffs with fewer agents of a more professional calibre. Such men were likely to have a better education than the bailiffs, to be more intelligent, and therefore in a position to relieve the central office of some of its burdens. They were likely to have "a more general knowledge of business, though it cannot be expected that they should possess the same thorough practical acquaintance with Agriculture." They were also likely to be better acquainted with the scientific aspects of farming. Finally, not being tenants, "they may be considered more independent and less identified with the interests of the Tenants."

On the other hand, it was suggested that there were good reasons to keep the old system. The great extent of the North-

---

[18] See Appendix I.

[19] Alnwick Castle MSS, "Minutes on local Agencies of the Northumberland Estates."

umberland estate, with its various soils and its several kinds of
farming, almost demanded that "men should be born on the
property to understand it thoroughly." In the past fortunately,
each generation of farmers on the estate had produced enough
men to fill the ranks of the bailiffs. Their "thorough local
knowledge" was of great value, especially in the letting of
farms. Finally, being men born and bred on the estate, there
was really no question of their loyalty to the Percy family:
they were "peculiarly the Duke's own men, whose attention
has never been diverted from the Estate, and who are more
devoted to it than probably any others that might be appointed;
for the latter, not being fixed upon the property, would no
doubt seek for more lucrative employment and leave as soon
as they could meet with it."

Such were the considerations put forward for and against
the old system. After reviewing them, the Duke's Commissioner concluded that either the bailiffs or the professional
men would do well enough. In the end he recommended that
the Duke keep the old system—which in fact was done. He
had decided that among its virtues was, first, the fact that it
was proved; second, that it was no more expensive than the
untried system; and third, that it could be accommodated to
the needs of an extensive program of agricultural improvements. The contemplated improvements on the estate in farm
buildings and draining were to be administered from the central
office, and consequently "there is less necessity for a critical
knowledge on these subjects on the part of the Bailiffs." In
fact, as the Duke's Commissioner concluded, "the real com-
plexion of the Estate must be derived from the Noble Posses-
sor," from the Duke and the central office at Alnwick. "In this
point of view, the arrangements of Head Quarters are to be
regarded as the proper source of improvement and when these
are clearly determined, the perfect local knowledge possessed
by each bailiff of his own district, cannot be otherwise than
highly useful."

The central office during the regime of the fourth Duke of

Northumberland was in most respects a businesslike affair. It had behind it a tradition of business, going back at least to the beginning of the century. In 1806, the second Duke in drawing up a book of general instructions for his agents had desired them to know "that the Estate is mine, and that in the management of it, it is my peculiar province to Direct." [20] His successors ruled with the same sort of firmness, none more so than the fourth Duke. On coming into the estate he reproached one of his Commissioners for failing to put questions on which decisions were requested with sufficient clarity and adequate information.[21] This was soon remedied by what was known as the Weekly Business Minutes which were written accounts of each subject of business as it came up, providing on each page a margin for the Duke's comments and decision. The system saved the writing of innumerable letters, provided a detailed record of the estate business, and kept the Duke fully informed.[22]

Supreme among the ducal agents was the Duke's Commissioner. During the regime of the third Duke there had sometimes been as many as three Commissioners, one of whom had been known as the Chief Commissioner; usually they acted in concert, although each was responsible for some part of the estate. Under the fourth Duke there was but one Commissioner, Hugh Taylor, who had for a long time been the colliery agent; [23] in 1865, on the fourth Duke's death, he was warmly recommended to the next Duke as being "with his large local and *practical* experience in mineral and other property" [24] the best man for the position. Before the fourth Duke's time one of the Commissioners seems to have served as auditor of accounts; but this practice ceased under the fourth Duke when

[20] *Ibid.*, General Instructions to Commissioners and Auditors, 1806.
[21] *Ibid.*, J. Blackden to Duke of Northumberland, May 15, 1847.
[22] The Business Minutes were sometimes supplemented by Legal Minutes, i.e., memoranda drawn up by the Duke's lawyers.
[23] Alnwick Castle MSS, *passim;* see also R. Welford, *Men of Mark 'Twixt Tyne and Tweed* (London, 1895), 3 vols. III, 494–97.
[24] Alnwick Castle MSS, Report of Alfred Bell, March 2, 1865.

a London accountant, G. C. Begbie, was employed, who saw
to it that "the Duke of Northumberland knows periodically
to a penny, and without the slightest complication, how he
stands." [25] In addition to Begbie and Taylor among the Duke's
leading agents, there was the London solicitor, Alfred Bell,
who was in charge of the Duke's legal business, acting as his
local solicitor in Middlesex, superintending his local solicitors
in the North Country, attending to his parliamentary business, and generally offering advice on a great many subjects.
It was Bell who had recommended Hugh Taylor to the fifth
Duke.[26]

Apart from the Commissioner the principal agents in the
Alnwick Castle office comprised the colliery agent, the surveyor (that is, draftsman and architect), the clerk of works,
the draining surveyor, and the wood bailiff.[27] The colliery
agent was responsible for letting the mines, for assessing their
value and condition, and for negotiating wayleave as well as
colliery rents. The surveyors and the clerk of works were
among other things responsible for supervising the large improvements in building and draining which the fourth Duke
initiated. For all important purposes the estate office kept a
firm hand on estate affairs, and exercised a close supervision
over the bailiffs. The latter were seldom free to spend money.
They made written or verbal reports as to the requirements in
their respective districts which were reviewed in the estate
office by the clerk of works. Plans and estimates were then
drawn up and submitted by the Commissioner to the Duke
"either on the occurrence of any Special Case, or more generally set forth in an Annual Schedule of proposed buildings
and improvements." [28] Once undertaken, works were paid for
in the central office on the certificate of the clerk of works.
Monthly estimates of such expenditure were prepared in ad-

[25] *Ibid.*
[26] Bell seems to have specialized in North Country business, for he was
also Lord Eldon's solicitor.
[27] There was a staff of estate office clerks to assist these agents.
[28] Alnwick Castle MSS, Business Minutes, Feb. 28, 1865.

vance, as a guide to the Duke's London bankers who made the necessary remittances.

All in all, the Duke of Northumberland's administrative arrangements were probably as businesslike as any to be found among the great estates. The Duke had the advantage, of course, of being the owner of an estate largely concentrated in the county of Northumberland; huge as it was, it was not dispersed over the British Isles or located in various parts of England. At the same time, it would seem that the main strength of the Northumberland estate lay in the quality of its central management, in the administrative aptitude of the Duke and his leading agents. Even an estate much more dispersed than that of the Duke of Northumberland operated with reasonable efficiency if its central direction was energetic.

Such an estate was that of the Dukes of Bedford, about 80,000 acres in size, which comprised three main country estates and a London estate. The chief country estate, on which the main ducal house sat, was Woburn; it consisted of 33,488 acres, most of which lay in Bedfordshire. The second was the Thorney estate in the Fens, much of which had been reclaimed and improved by the Dukes of Bedford; it was 23,652 acres in size. The third was in the West Country, and included the town of Tavistock as well as a great copper and arsenic mine, Devon Great Consols, which was worked from 1844 onwards; this estate was 20,377 acres in size.[29] Finally there was the immensely valuable London estate, comprising 119 acres in the heart of London, most of it let to builders on 99 year leases. In the seventeenth century the Crown had granted to the Russells the right of holding markets on their estate; and by the nineteenth century Covent Garden Market was the chief produce market in the kingdom, and a substantial income was obtained from levying tolls on produce sold there.[30]

---

[29] There was also a detached estate in Dorset of 2,176 acres. The acreages for the Bedford estates belong to the year 1857.

[30] This information was derived from the Bedford MSS; see also Duke of Bedford, *A Great Estate* (London, 1897).

The local agencies on the Duke of Bedford's estate were almost invariably held by men of some professional standing, not (as on the Duke of Northumberland's estate) by tenant farmers.[31] Their salaries would indicate that they were among the best land agents to be had.[32] As the Duke of Northumberland's Commissioner had implied, such men could be managed with a looser rein than that used on the Northumberland bailiffs; and during the regime of the sixth Duke of Bedford (which ended in 1839) the local agents were in fact pretty independent. During the regime of the seventh Duke (1839–61), however, when an energetic owner and an equally energetic supervisory agent were in power, the reins were drawn tighter. The greater centralization under the seventh Duke consisted mainly of more detailed reporting by the local agents, and of closer and more frequent scrutiny of their activities and accounts from the center.[33]

The central estate office of the Dukes of Bedford was in London—appropriately so, given the importance of that estate. It was presided over by the Duke's auditor (as he was called), who rather resembled the Duke of Northumberland's Commissioner, except that he audited the Bedford estate accounts and was likely to be a lawyer. Under the seventh Duke he was a solicitor, Christopher Haedy by name. Haedy was in charge of all estate business. The local agents reported directly to him, and he in turn wrote innumerable letters to a Duke who was equally assiduous at letterwriting and hungry for information. The Duke of Bedford was not so close to the center of estate business as was the Duke of Northumberland; he was at Woburn more than in Bloomsbury; nevertheless he was in large part responsible for giving the estate its businesslike aspect. Much more will be said of him in the following chapter.

Another great estate, the Fitzwilliam estate, also dispersed

---

[31] Except for the agent on the London estate who was a solicitor.
[32] See Appendix II.
[33] The administrative arrangements on the Bedford estate are described in greater detail in the next two chapters.

like that of the Dukes of Bedford, was less tightly knit. It lay in three main blocks: in Ireland, in Yorkshire, in the east Midlands. The Irish estate was the largest, some 80,000 acres in extent, situated in county Wicklow. The Yorkshire estate was geographically two estates: the Malton estate in the North Riding, and the Wentworth Woodhouse estate in the West Riding. The Malton estate had no family residence, and was small and mainly agricultural, although among its enterprises it included the operation of a canal. The Wentworth Woodhouse estate, about 19,000 acres in size, was highly varied in its enterprise. In part a farming estate it sat upon the great Barnsley seam of coal, and the Fitzwilliam family mined coal and iron ore and at times manufactured iron. The east Midland estate, about 24,000 acres in size, with its center at Milton near Peterborough, was largely agricultural—although the Fitzwilliams owned a large part of the ground rents in the town.[34]

The local agents on the Fitzwilliam estates, unlike those on the two great estates just examined, were neither tenant farmers nor semi-professional land agents. On the English estates they were solicitors; on the Irish estate the agent, following local custom, was often a man of superior status, being in this case a kinsman of Earl Fitzwilliam and probably of no professional standing of any sort. This considerable reliance on country solicitors as local agents does not seem to have been questioned or discussed on the Fitzwilliam estate so long as the fifth Earl was alive (he died in 1858). The system went back into the eighteenth century, and was accepted by the nineteenth, some of the solicitor-agents perpetuating themselves dynastically. The West Riding solicitor gave orders to the Malton solicitor; otherwise all received instructions from the Earl alone. Once a year they took their accounts to Wentworth Woodhouse or to Milton House for auditing; apart from this they were under no obligation to keep in touch regularly with the central administration of the estate.

[34] The Fitzwilliam acreages belong to the 1870's; I have no figures for an earlier time.

By comparison with the ducal estates of Bedford and North-umberland, the Fitzwilliam estate cannot be said to have had much of a central administration. There was in fact no central estate office which gathered information from all parts of the estate, sifted it, and reported to the Earl. There was no Weekly Business Minutes, no annual report. For that matter, there was no one on the Fitzwilliam estate comparable to the Duke of Northumberland's Commissioner or the Duke of Bedford's auditor. Earl Fitzwilliam's chief agent served very largely in a consultative capacity and had no authority over the local agents. Even the Fitzwilliam estate accounts were wanting in centralization, there being no summary of them, apart from a sketchy record drawn up by the Earl himself, presumably annually at audit time. One must conclude that the Earls Fitz-william were not as businesslike as the seventh Duke of Bedford or the fourth Duke of Northumberland. It may be that the interests of the fifth Earl Fitzwilliam were more numerous than those of the Dukes of Bedford and Northumberland, and his attention to estate business therefore less singleminded. He is not to be charged with failing to look into his affairs, but it may be said that he was lacking in system. Yet whatever the defects of his estate management, it worked after a fashion.[35]

Finally, among the great estates to be noted here, there was that of the Duke of Buckingham. More dispersed than the others, it was far more ramshackle in organization. In 1837 it comprised 56,823 acres, of which 26,838 acres were in Bucking-hamshire, 17,282 were in Ireland, 9,225 in Hampshire (some-times known as the Avington estate), 1,836 in Cornwall, 1,640 in Middlesex, together with a plantation of unknown size in Jamaica.[36] Apart from some mines in Cornwall and some ground rents in Middlesex, neither of which amounted to a

[35] For a sketch of the Fitzwilliam estate and of the 5th Earl Fitzwilliam, see D. Spring, "Earl Fitzwilliam and the Corn Laws," *The American Historical Review*, Jan., 1954. Since writing that essay I have learned more about aristocratic landowners and have concluded that my account of Fitzwilliam's businesslike qualities in that essay is exaggerated.

[36] Stowe MSS, General Rental for 1837.

great deal, the estate was exclusively agricultural. The home estate in Buckinghamshire, of which Stowe was the principal seat, lay in three districts: one in the vicinity of the market town of Buckingham, another in the vicinity of the market town of Aylesbury, and the third (Wotton) on the Oxfordshire border about eighteen miles from Oxford. The land was chiefly in pasture, the produce being largely butter sold in the London and Oxford markets.[37]

The local agencies on the estate—or more precisely, those on the Stowe and Avington estates—were held by semi-professional and resident land agents. Some of these were competent, some were not; all went almost wholly unsupervised. Occasionally, when a financial crisis was blowing up, their affairs might be hastily looked into by some solicitor or man of business hired by the Duke or his trustees. Ordinarily, however, there was lacking a proper system of auditing their accounts. It was even said of the Stowe agent in 1832 that he did not "keep separate and distinct accounts for His Grace's Estates"; that he kept a record of daily receipts and payments, but nothing more.[38] The local agent on the Avington estate, Crawfurd by name, was sufficiently distressed by this laxity to admonish the Duke: "It is quite true," he wrote to him in 1826, "that Your Grace's concerns should be minutely looked into and undergo a rigid examination by men of business that will do their duty and establish a regular system of auditing, paying, and passing your accounts half yearly." [39]

This was not the only time that the first Duke of Buckingham was offered such valuable advice. Some years later, when his affairs were in a state of periodic crisis, the barrister and friend of the family, Sir Edward East, urged him to look into his estate business and keep regular accounts; such things, he assured the Duke, would give "him a pride and pleasure in looking into his own affairs, and feeling himself to be the real

[37] *Ibid.*, Mr. Newton's Report on value of Buckinghamshire estates, 1844.
[38] *Ibid.*, Memo. by Mr. Parrott, probably in 1832.
[39] *Ibid.*, Crawfurd to 1st Duke of Buckingham, June 15, 1826.

master of these and his family and servants." [40] For a while, finding that the Duke was auditing his steward's and banker's accounts, Sir Edward rejoiced in seeing his advice taken. But this show of industry on the Duke's part was short lived. Sir Edward's son, also a barrister, then strongly recommended that the Duke dismiss his solicitors, the Robsons, and find himself a lawyer who would manage both his legal business and his estates, "and by whom alone the secondary agents should be directed." [41] But this seems to have been too much for the Duke's chronic indolence. As he once said, in answer to the same advice, he could not at his "time of life begin new confidences with a new attorney." [42] It proved easier to stand down altogether and put his affairs in the hands of trustees. In the last year or so of the first Duke's regime (he died in 1839), some effort was made by the trustees to remedy the want of central control, but this ended with the Duke's death.[43]

The Duke's successor, his son, Lord Chandos of the Reform Bill, was a strange, unfortunate being who in a few years so mismanaged the estate that he bankrupted it. Designated the Farmer's Friend, he knew more about agrarian politics than about practical farming. Unlike many of his generation of English landowners, he seems to have taken relatively little interest in the new techniques of agricultural improvement. What mainly interested him was the figure he cut in the country, and if indolence was the father's chief failing, egomania was the son's. He had a great gift of self-deception which led him to avoid the paths of common sense. He soon broke with his father's trustees, surrounded himself with shady attorneys and moneylenders, and in quick time brought a great estate to the verge of ruin. There is in the Stowe MSS in the Huntington Library a personal account book which the Duke

[40] *Ibid.*, Sir Edward East to 1st Duke of Buckingham, n.d., probably 1832.
[41] *Ibid.*, J. B. East to 1st Duke of Buckingham, Aug. 15, 1835.
[42] *Ibid.*, Duke of Buckingham to Lord Chandos, May 3, 1828.
[43] The Minute Books of this trust are to be found in the Middlesex Record Office.

began at the time of his accession. He may have intended it as some kind of record of his finances, but it very quickly petered out in obscure scribblings. It is an appropriate epitaph to the second Duke of Buckingham as an estate administrator.[44]

So unbusinesslike a landowner was not, however, typical. In fact there was rather more aptitude for business, especially on the large estates, than is usually imagined, and it was to be found among landowners as among agents. So authoritative a Victorian as John Stuart Mill had little respect for the landowners of his day. He once observed, "The truth is, that any very general improvement of land by the landlords is hardly compatible with a law or custom of primogeniture. . . . Were they ever so much inclined, those alone can prudently do it, who have seriously studied the principles of scientific agriculture: and great landlords have seldom seriously studied anything." [45] But Mill was not the most reliable observer of society, especially aristocratic and rural society.[46] The next chapter will be devoted to the study of a single landowner, the seventh Duke of Bedford, who if not typical in all respects of the great landowners of the nineteenth century, still conveys much of their flavor.

[44] For studies of the 2nd Duke and his career, see F. M. L. Thompson, "The End of a Great Estate," *The Economic History Review*, Aug., 1955; D. and E. Spring, "The Fall of the Grenvilles, 1844–48," *The Huntington Library Quarterly*, Feb., 1956.

[45] J. S. Mill, *Principles of Political Economy*, ed. Sir W. J. Ashley, (London, 1929), pp. 231–32.

[46] For Mill's defects as a sociologist, see R. B. McCallum, "The Individual in the Mass: Mill on Liberty and the Franchise," in P. Appleman, W. A. Madden, and M. Wolff, eds., *1859: Entering an Age of Crisis* (Bloomington, 1959), p. 159.

# CHAPTER II

# THE LANDOWNER

THIS CHAPTER WILL ATTEMPT to provide some insight into the workings of a landowner's mind. As Dr. Kitson Clark once wrote, "we have all been content to describe far too much of the history of the nineteenth century in terms of the play of a few principal actors posturing before a back-cloth painted with conventional figures." [1] The landowner is one of these conventional figures—to all of which we are often ready to attach a neat, briefly inscribed, emotive label. It may therefore profit us to see in some detail how a landowner coped with the business of his estate.

## I

Francis, seventh Duke of Bedford (1788–1861), belonged to a formidable generation in the history of the English landed aristocracy; the generation of the fifth Earl Fitzwilliam, the fifth Duke of Richmond, Lord Althorp of the Reform Bill, and Sir James Graham; the generation which made a valiant attempt to protract aristocratic leadership into a new and increasingly unaristocratic age. On the political side of that

[1] G. Kitson Clark, "The Electorate and the Repeal of the Corn Laws," *Transactions of the Royal Historical Society* (London, 1951), p. 109.

effort, the Duke of Bedford played no great part in public. During the two decades after the Napoleonic Wars he made some stir as Marquis of Tavistock, and at times there had been talk of his becoming Whig leader in the House of Commons.[2] But nothing came of it. The reasons are not altogether clear, but perhaps ill-health and a retiring disposition were among the main ones; it was on grounds of health that he refused Lord Melbourne's offer of the Indian Viceroyalty in 1839.[3] In that year his father, the sixth Duke, died, and the responsibilities of great wealth, together with those of a large family of brothers and sisters, weighed heavily upon him. His retirement from public view became so complete that he never spoke in the House of Lords.[4] But privately he was a power behind the scenes, an indefatigable negotiator and a member of the highest Whig councils: brother to Lord John Russell, he made Woburn the headquarters of aristocratic Whiggism. Charles Greville found him one of his chief sources of political information; and believed that his correspondence, "whenever it sees the light, will be more interesting, and contribute more historical information than that of any other man who has been engaged in public life. The papers of Peel and of the Duke of Wellington may be more important, but I doubt their being more interesting, because the Duke of Bedford's will be of a more miscellaneous and comprehensive character." [5]

The Duke's Whiggism, like his estate, was a family inheritance. The house of Russell had long stood for rational liberty and popular rights against an oppressive Crown. In the nineteenth century this creed was transformed into something potentially anti-aristocratic, as it took more and more to championing the cause of government by public opinion. Like

[2] As in 1816; see Sir H. Maxwell, ed., *The Creevey Papers* (New York, 1903), 2 vols., I, 258.

[3] *Letters to Lord George William Russell from various Writers, 1817–1845* (London, 1915), 2 vols., I, 290–92.

[4] *Annual Register*, obituary, 1861.

[5] L. Strachey and R. Fulford, eds., *The Greville Memoirs 1814–1860* (London, 1938), 8 vols., VI, 409.

his father and his brother, the Duke took an active part during the 1820's in public agitation for a reform of Parliament. "I started in life a reformer," he wrote in 1829, "and every year's experience has confirmed me more and more in the opinion of my early days." [6] He was all for emancipating the Catholics and purging the Irish Church; and he was all for putting down Tory boroughmongers like the Duke of Northumberland who (unlike Whig boroughmongers, it would seem) obstructed the free flow of public opinion. A monument to Byron won his ready support: "I paid my tribute," he declared, "to his talents and public services in the cause of general liberty." [7] So experienced an observer of aristocratic politics as Charles Greville was startled and puzzled by the passion which could on occasion inform the Duke's Whig creed.[8]

But the Duke's enthusiasm for liberty did not always shine brightly. Once at least—during the 1830's—his mood darkened and his popular sympathies were strangely eclipsed.

> A social phenomenon [was] at hand [he declared], that the history of the world had never yet seen. That there was a canker at the heart of European civilization. That there was a destructive principle at work, that would cause the fabric of modern society to crumble, as effectively as the Alps did with the fire and vigour of Hannibal. . . . I thought the millions of this country were rotten to the core, but still associated, strong and gigantic from the hatred and wish to destroy.[9]

By the 1830's the Duke may have suffered disillusion. It may also be that what he once observed in himself—"my habit of mind is gloomy and exaggerates" [10]—had taken deeper root.

---

[6] *Letters to Lord G. W. Russell,* II, 137–39.
[7] *Ibid.,* I, 114.
[8] *The Greville Memoirs,* II, 207, where Greville remarks on the inflammatory nature of Macaulay's speeches during the Reform Bill agitation of 1831; "but how the Miltons, Tavistocks, Althorps and all who have a great stake in the country can run the same course is more than I can conceive or comprehend."
[9] *Letters to Lord G. W. Russell,* I, 244–47.
[10] *Ibid.*

It was to Christianity that the Duke turned as a barrier against the forces of social dissolution. "Christianity had built up the pile of modern civilization" [11]—without it civilization would crumble. It is not altogether plain what the nature of the Duke's Christianity was. Perhaps somewhat more evangelical than his father's: there is a note of self-scrutiny and doubt of his personal worthiness in the Duke's reflections which suggests this. It may be that he was not as horrified by his brother, Lord Wriothesley Russell, as was their father. Lord Wriothesley had turned enthusiast, and the sixth Duke protested bitterly against harboring such a viper in his bosom: "that class of the over righteous," he exclaimed, "these are an increasing and dangerous sect." [12]

By his father's standards the seventh Duke was something of a Philistine. The father had much of the eighteenth-century connoisseur in him. He was an indefatigable collector: Roman statuary, Egyptian sarcophagi, Canaletto prints, even a menagerie, all were gathered up avidly and stuffed into Woburn or its park. He had hoped to inspire his son with a similar taste for the fine arts, "so that [as he once wrote to another son] when I am dead and gone, the interesting pursuit may not be lost sight of at Woburn. It is not incompatible with those of hunting, shooting or politics." [13] The hope was vain. Although the seventh Duke's enthusiasm for hunting and racing declined, he never took up collecting. When he came into the estate, he observed drily "that in all those matters the chief pleasure consists in the collection," [14] and he reduced the menagerie, added nothing to the marbles and prints, and turned his attention to estate administration. Of his father's collection of prints he said, "Very little use is made of it. Indeed, it is seldom seen by anybody." [15]

Father and son differed also as managers of estate affairs. The

[11] *Ibid.*
[12] *Ibid.*, I, 107.
[13] *Ibid.*, I, 13.
[14] *Ibid.*, I, 350.
[15] *Ibid.*

sixth Duke was an agriculturist of some renown. Under him Woburn was, for a time at any rate, one of the chief centers of experiment and stimulation in the farming world. [16] But the son with some reason may have looked upon his father as a dilettante in agricultural affairs. In fact there was something of a literary flavor in the father's farming. His catalogue of Woburn marbles was matched by a treatise on grasses drawn up under his direction.[17] Coming across a paper on manures published by the Société Économique de Berne, he thought he might translate it.[18] More important, he blew hot and cold about agricultural improvements: in 1813 he brought the famous Woburn sheep shearings to an end,[19] and in 1821 resigned from the Smithfield Club publicly declaring that there was nothing more to be done in animal husbandry.[20] The seventh Duke, as we shall see, was less concerned to add to the literature of farming than to invest capital in its new techniques; and his enthusiasm for agricultural improvement never waned.

The father also spent more freely than the son—and this was sometimes especially distressing to the latter. When one of his daughters married, the sixth Duke presented her with a large gift for her trousseau. The son much resented this parental generosity: "I'll venture to say," he exploded, "that this is the first instance of the kind that ever occurred. However, it matters very little, for if my father goes on squandering and borrowing at the present rate there will be nothing left

[16] E. Clarke, "Agriculture and the House of Russell," *The Journal of the Royal Agricultural Society*, 1891; *The Dictionary of National Biography*, (hereafter designated *D.N.B.*), article on Lord John Russell.

[17] Entitled *Hortus Gramineus Woburnensis*.

[18] *Letters to Lord G. W. Russell*, I, 92.

[19] Brougham claimed to know the Duke's real reason, namely expense; but the Duke was not much given to economizing. See Lord Brougham, *The Life and Times of Henry Lord Brougham* (New York, 1871), 3 vols., II, 65.

[20] *The Times*, Dec. 19, 1821. According to the Duke: "It may gratify, perhaps, the personal vanity of some of us, to exhibit extraordinary animals; but the public derives no benefit from our bringing to a greater degree of perfection animals of a breed known to possess the highest merit."

soon for any of his family in a short time." [21] This petulant
outburst was largely, but not wholly, uncalled for. If the sixth
Duke left a large debt, a good part of it was incurred for
merely normal portions for his younger children; and it may
be that he himself inherited a sizable debt.[22] But it would be
true enough to say that the sixth Duke lived up to his great
income: he denied himself very little (Greville called him a
sensualist), [23] he saved nothing, and he was a careless housekeeper. And all these were for the son considerable sins.

The son was, as we shall see, a most careful housekeeper. His
propensity to save came close to miserliness. Sometimes this
had its amusing side, as when he made a habit of borrowing
Emily Eden's carriage while in London. As she observed, "It
is a great thing to assist the struggles of virtuous poverty. . . .
if in any future state of existence, I become Duke of Bedford
with £200,000 a year, I think I shall keep a one-horse fly of
my own in London." [24] Sometimes the Duke's pennypinching
seemed less amusing, as in his treatment of his brother, Lord
John Russell. At least one of the latter's biographers has
charged the Duke with a "meanness [that] . . . was almost
incredible." [25] This may be too strong: the Duke did not fail
to provide for Lord John, although it may be said that he
failed to do so in a sufficiently generous fashion—in spite of
his great attachment for him, and his pride in Lord John's high
place in the political world.[26]

It should be added that if the Duke made demands on others,

[21] *Letters to Lord G. W. Russell*, I, 183.

[22] So the 7th Duke told John Cam Hobhouse in 1814; see Lord Broughton, *Recollections of a Long Life* (London, 1910), 6 vols., I, 174.

[23] *The Greville Memoirs*, IV, 209–10. Greville's portrait of the 6th
Duke was most unflattering: "a more uninteresting, weak-minded selfish
character does not exist . . . a complete sensualist and thinks of nothing
but his own personal enjoyments."

[24] Sir H. Maxwell, *The Life and Letters of the Fourth Earl of Clarendon* (London, 1913), 2 vols., II, 194.

[25] A. Wyatt Tilby, *Lord John Russell: A Study in Civil and Religious
Liberty* (New York, 1931), p. 23.

[26] *The Greville Memoirs*, VII, 26–27.

he did not spare himself. There is a picture of him set down by Lord Clarendon that may give the flavor of the man. "[At breakfast] he is always in a very old dressing gown, scribbling the illegible letters that will be the death of him . . . he loves to think himself the centre to which information tends and from which advice radiates. . . . No man at his age, with a slender stock of health, can keep getting up through the winter at 4 or 5 in the morning, lighting his own fire and writing till 10 or 11 upon an empty stomach." [27] Some of these letters went to Charles Greville, some to the Queen and Prince Albert, some to Cabinet Ministers—and many went to Christopher Haedy, the auditor of his several estates.

## II

In 1839, on coming into the estate, the Duke announced his strategy for the future management of the family properties.

You are aware [he wrote to a brother] that the debts and incumbrances, created by my uncle and my father, are very great. Lord Torrington, who knew much of this world and had great wisdom, always said that a large estate might bear two extravagant possessors but that the third must be prudent, in order to save it. I am that third, in this case, and it must be my part therefore to repair the breaches that have been made, or the family importance and influence in this Country will sink into ruin. It is very easy to be generous at the expense of posterity, and to acquire a great name by it. . . . I do not mean to speak harshly of those who have gone before me, or to complain of anything they did. God forbid. They were in many respects greater and better men than I can ever hope to be. So far superior indeed that in one thing only can I ever expect to surpass them, viz., in prudence and care of the family estates.[28]

What did prudence dictate to the Duke? Many things, as this chapter will show; but some of them he particularly rel-

[27] Maxwell, *Life of Clarendon*, I, 320.
[28] *Letters to Lord G. W. Russell*, I, 308–11.

ished and these will be dealt with here. They were of varying importance: a better system of reporting estate business; the reduction of household expenditure and what went with it the reform of household accounts; and last the reduction of extraordinary expenditure.[29]

In 1842 the Duke proposed that Haedy keep a permanent record of the important decisions taken during his regime. "It would be very desirable," he explained, "that the Duke of Bedford should find in the office whenever you are removed from it (which God grant may be long distant) some record not only of what has been done by me, under your administration of the affairs, but also your opinions on any considerable questions that are likely to rise hereafter."[30] He likened such a document to Cabinet Minutes, implying that Haedy was a kind of ducal Prime Minister. Since the Russell estates constituted a kind of kingdom, this was not too far fetched.[31]

More important was the subject of household expenditure. It weighed heavily on the Duke's mind. He had several houses and one of them, Woburn, was among the greatest in the country. Lord Shaftesbury once noted in his diary, "It is not a palace, a house; it is a town, a municipal borough, a city."[32] Lord Broughton found a dinner at Woburn "pretty much in the Windsor Palace style; but, of the two, more formal."[33] And Prince Pückler-Muskau, that German nobleman who called himself a "parkomane" because he never had his fill of viewing English country houses and parks, sighed with envy at the sight of Woburn: that "accumulation of luxury and magnificence . . . far exceeding the powers of any private person in our country."[34]

[29] It will be seen that Haedy played a part in making up the Duke's mind on these matters.

[30] Bedford MSS, 7th Duke to Haedy, March 21, 1842.

[31] Greville likened the Bedfordshire estate to a kingdom; see *Memoirs*, V, 347.

[32] E. Hodder, *The Life and Work of the Seventh Earl of Shaftesbury* (London, 1886), 3 vols., II, 527.

[33] Lord Broughton, *Recollections of a Long Life*, VI, 86.

[34] Prince Pückler-Muskau, *Tour in Germany, Holland and England* (London, 1832), 4 vols., III, 97.

The cost of Woburn at first intimidated a Duke intent on making economies—especially as his father had died leaving behind him an accumulation of unpaid bills and expensive and unfinished projects. When Haedy suggested that Woburn be closed down temporarily, the Duke was inclined to fall in with the proposal. As if in justification he wrote to his brother explaining, "you will recollect that I am only following the example of many others who have succeeded to great debts and family charges. Lord Bradford closed Weston for two or three years, the Duke of Richmond, Goodwood, Whitbread, Southhill, etc." [35] Perhaps to his brother's relief—for younger sons often relied on the hospitality afforded by their elder brothers—the Duke soon changed his mind; and he chose to meet the problems of household expenditure in less drastic fashion.

He sought advice: not only from Haedy but from his brother, Lord John Russell, and from fellow landowners. Lord John warned him that at Woburn "there has not been sufficient check on subordinates," that "in the [government] departments everything is done on a far more economical plane than on a great nobleman's estate." [36] In the country houses that he visited the Duke pursued his inquiries: at Lord Jersey's, Lord Mount-Edgcumbe's, and the Duke of Rutland's. Country-house conversation, it would seem, was well able to accommodate so humdrum a subject. The Duke was told that Mr. Turner, a London solicitor, had reformed Lord Keith's household and was at work on Lord Willoughby d'Eresby's. And Lord Jersey told him that no household in England was better arranged than Belvoir, the Duke of Rutland's great house.[37]

On visiting Belvoir the Duke was much impressed by his fellow nobleman's system of household statistics. The Duke of Rutland's agent had quickly produced a return on the number of persons (including servants) who had dined at Belvoir in

[35] *Letters to Lord G. W. Russell*, I, 312.
[36] Bedford MSS, 7th Duke to Haedy, Nov. 7, 1859.
[37] *Ibid.*, 7th Duke to Haedy, March 14, 1841.

the past year. The number was 18,000.[38] He had also been able to calculate such matters as the average cost of feeding and lodging Belvoir's establishment and the average consumption of bread. The Duke thereupon set on foot his own statistics: the number of diners at his table in a year, at the steward's table, at the servants' table; the annual consumption of articles of food and drink—for example, the number of quarts of ale drunk in the servants' hall; the number of fires lit annually at Woburn; and the number of flues swept. He stopped short, regretfully it would seem, at keeping count of the fish in his ponds: "it must be very difficult, if not impossible," he concluded.[39]

Before going to Belvoir the Duke had already sought to reform the system of auditing his household accounts. Under his father, owing to a want of ready money, bills were not paid regularly and punctually; they accumulated for as long as eight months, and a harassed house steward, busy with the ducal entertaining, failed to scrutinize them adequately for price and quantity.[40] Haedy and the seventh Duke both insisted that "prompt payment and short accounts" was the best way to prevent exorbitant charges.[41] At first the Duke asked for monthly payment and accounting. But the new house steward at Woburn, one Palfreyman, was not a good man with accounts. He complained that they confused him—made him "low and nervous." [42] Moreover, the London office also found the monthly system too burdensome. Quarterly payments were therefore substituted for monthly payments; and the London office saw to it that the arithmetic of the tradesmen's bills was accurate, trusting to the Woburn steward to check on price and quantity.

The Duke accepted more readily than Haedy that there were limits to his surveillance. If Haedy had had his way, he

[38] Ibid.
[39] Ibid., 7th Duke to Haedy, July 27, 1841.
[40] Ibid., Haedy to 7th Duke, Dec. 18, 1839.
[41] Ibid., 7th Duke to Haedy, Dec. 26, 1839.
[42] Ibid., 7th Duke to Haedy, Aug. 8, 1842.

would have taken the further step of explicitly forbidding household servants to accept gifts from tradesmen: "which is," as he put it, "allowing the watchman to receive bribes from those he is to watch."[43] There was a good chance, according to Haedy, that such a regulation would work; the days were over "when perquisites and presents were looked upon by Servants so much their right as the wages they received."[44] The Duke, however, was sceptical. "Many have tried it," he said, "but few have succeeded in stopping it." Both Lord Sefton ("a most accurate man in his household affairs") and the Duke of Sutherland had failed.[45] He for his part would not make the attempt.

One should not leave the impression that the Duke was cynical about his servants' dishonesty. It was a subject that caused him distress, on moral as well as economic grounds. In this connection he and Haedy devoted voluminous letters to the matter of wax candles. It would seem that candles on being started in the drawing room were usually not burnt out, but were sent to the bedrooms, and the odds and ends then remaining were supposed to go to the wax chandler.[46] But, as the Duke and Haedy knew, candles (or half burnt ones) never got that far. The servants stole them, and such a theft—small as it was—might lead to a deterioration of moral conduct: "in as far as they are perfectly acquainted—the Housekeeper and housemaids especially—with what is going on, and think not unnaturally that if one act of pilfering is connived at another might be." The Duke felt it his duty "to check temptation to his servants as far as he can";[47] although in fact what was done about the wax candles remains a mystery.

Apart from the regulation and reduction of ordinary household expenditure, the Duke sought to reduce what he called his extraordinary expenditure. He resolved early to limit the menagerie: to give up the Corsican deer and to keep no more

[43] *Ibid.*, Haedy to 7th Duke, March 10, 1843.
[44] *Ibid.*
[45] *Ibid.*, 7th Duke to Haedy, March 18, 1845.
[46] *Ibid.*, Haedy to 7th Duke, Jan. 6, 1841.
[47] *Ibid.*, 7th Duke to Haedy, Jan. 7, 1841.

than a dozen swans.[48] He ordered reductions in the gardens and in the forcing houses: "the Pines and the Grapes should be disposed of," he wrote to Haedy, "except the few I may want at Oakley." [49] He also informed Haedy that no further additions need be made to the library: "As for Books, I am not likely to purchase any, as there would be no room for them, even if I were disposed to do so." [50] Bookbinding would therefore end, and he suggested dispensing with the services of a librarian whose salary was £200 a year. It becomes clear how at Woburn the age of aristocratic connoisseurship came to an end.

Expenditure on elections was also curtailed, for moral as well as for prudential reasons. The Duke maintained his electoral interest, and at a General Election might intervene in as many as five constituencies.[51] If the evidence relating to the General Election of 1841 is typical, he was inclined to employ what he once called his "starvation system": [52] that is, he granted limited sums on condition that they be not used for corrupt purposes. "There is no money I regret so much," he once declared, "as money spent [on electoral bribery] because it not only does no good, but inflicts a positive injury upon the community." [53] So far as it can be learned, his expenditure in the General Election of 1841 was between £3,000–£4,000 —a relatively modest sum in the light of the ducal income and of what a nobleman still might spend on a General Election.[54] What was achieved by the Duke's reforms and economies?

[48] *Ibid.*, 7th Duke to Haedy, Dec. 19, 1839.
[49] *Ibid.*, 7th Duke to Haedy, Dec. 21, 1839. Oakley was a small house on the Woburn estate.
[50] *Ibid.*
[51] Add. MSS, 47,223, folio 31, 7th Duke to Lord Broughton, Aug. 6, 1847: "My own personal triumphs have been very great—I undertook for 5 seats—3 Counties and 2 Boroughs—and I have succeeded in all."
[52] *Letters to Lord G. W. Russell*, I, 188.
[53] Bedford MSS, 7th Duke to Haedy, Jan. 17, 1841.
[54] *Letters to Lord G. W. Russell*, I, 341: "To please John I gave £1,000 to Howick and Ben Stanley for their elections and the same to the friends of Ellice to fight Derbyshire and Leicestershire." To these sums one should add the financial provision for Lord John Russell: interest on £10,000.

For the year 1839, of which his father was responsible for at least ten months' expenditure, total household costs amounted to £34,936. This sum covered the expense of four houses and their grounds: Endsleigh in Devon, Oakley in Bedfordshire, the London house in Belgrave Square, and Woburn—of which the last accounted for at least 80 per cent. Total household expenditure covered strictly household costs such as food, fuel, furniture, and servants, together with such items as taxes, game, gardens, park, stables, charities, pensions, and what was called "voluntary payments," which comprised donations to agricultural and bible societies, the local Whig organization, and the Bedford races. Strictly household costs amounted to £20,010.[55]

Total household expenditure declined in 1840 from the sixth Duke's £34,936 to his son's £24,488. The chief saving appeared under strictly household costs, gardens, and voluntary payments—the first having been reduced from £20,010 to £9,545, the second from £3,371 to £2,364, and the third from £2,298 to £1,210.[56] Expenditure on the park, however, increased, as the Duke, undertaking a program of general improvements, drained it and erected new fences. The Duke was in part pleased with what he saw in this year's report of his affairs, declaring to his brother that "I am able to tell not only the amount of every branch of expenditure, but the increase or decrease." [57] It was less pleasing, however, that he had not reduced his expenditure as much as he had wished: indeed, as he pointed out, the expenditure of £24,488 did not include pocket money, personal expenditure, purchase of horses, or occasional charities. He therefore feared that in fact it would be difficult to keep his total expenditure within £30,000.[58] It is not clear what the Duke meant by personal expenditure: possibly gifts to his family and friends, traveling expenses, clothes, etc.

[55] Bedford MSS, Annual Reports, 1841; see also Appendix III.
[56] *Ibid.*
[57] *Letters to Lord G. W. Russell*, 1, 324–25.
[58] *Ibid.*

Without including such things, the Duke's total household expenditure rose in the following year to £27,693. This increase came largely under the heads of strict household expenditure, park, and pensions, the first rising from £9,545 to £11,607, the second from £1,595 to £1,958, and the last from £1,119 to £1,544. The records are such for this year that it is possible to calculate what the annual expenditure on a great house like Woburn would be under a Duke given to prudence and economy, but mindful of the position of his family. Household bills for food, fuel, and furniture amounted to £6,207. Servants' wages amounted to £2,138. Stable bills amounted to £2,110. And taxes, game, gardens, park, charities, and pensions probably amounted to another £6,000—£7,000 at least.[59] Woburn managed economically would appear to have cost something like £16,000–£17,000 a year.[60] Greville, who was at Woburn in 1841 and again in 1842, found life there very pleasant: "a house abounding in every sort of luxury and comfort and with inexhaustible resources for every taste . . . everything that wealth and refined taste can supply."[61] If the Duke brought "order [and] economy" to Woburn, these did not dispel its customary "grandeur, comfort and general content."[62]

Although the Duke may have achieved less than he hoped for, he gave little sign of relaxing his vigilance as an economical manager. A devoted house steward could not have been more careful. The Duke complained, for example, about the consumption of food and meat at Woburn for the year 1843. "It appears to me," he wrote to Haedy, "that there has

---

[59] Bedford MSS, Annual Reports, 1841; see also Appendix IV.
[60] See Thompson, "The End of a Great Estate," *Ec. Hist. Rev.*, Aug., 1955, for figures of household expenditure in other landed families; Dr. Thompson does not, unfortunately, specify the several items of household expenditure.
[61] *The Greville Memoirs*, IV, 417.
[62] *Ibid.*, V, 39. Two decades earlier Greville had written: "The house, place, establishment and manner of living are the most magnificent I have seen. There is no place which gives so splendid an example of a Great English Lord as this." (*Memoirs*, I, 86).

been an improper consumption of ale especially when the family were not here. You will see that under the head of Post Boys there has been irregular consumption. I have always understood that ale is not allowed in families where Servants are on board wages." [63] The consumption of meat was also excessive: "The Servants certainly eat a great deal of Meat, and I believe press strangers because they think it hospitable and for the credit of the House to do so—Lord William's foreign servant told Mr. Hastings Russell last year that they had given him a surfeit in that way and that it was now well for his health that he was returning to Germany." [64] And why, he wanted to know, had the consumption of coffee and sugar increased so much? [65]

The Duke was no less vigilant about the prices he was charged. His coal merchant in 1842 had charged him thirty shillings a ton, and in 1843 offered him a reduction of sixpence a ton. The Duke found, however, "that other great Coal merchants have served families for 27 shillings per ton with the best Coals sent in September—the same people now charge twenty-eight shillings per ton or will contract for that price, and twenty-six shillings for the 'seconds' which they say burn quicker, but make quite as good a fire." [66] He also brought it to Haedy's attention that the blacksmith at Woburn charged one shilling and four pence each for a coach horse's shoes, but the blacksmith at Oakley did an equally good job for only one shilling.[67]

## III

"I am surprised to see," the Duke wrote to his brother, "how very strongly both the Adams [his father's auditors] con-

[63] Bedford MSS, 7th Duke to Haedy, Sept. 15, 1844.
[64] *Ibid.*, 7th Duke to Haedy, April 3, 1844.
[65] *Ibid.*, 7th Duke to Haedy, March 23, 1844.
[66] *Ibid.*, 7th Duke to Haedy, March 8, 1843.
[67] *Ibid.*, 7th Duke to Haedy, Jan. 23, 1842.

tinued, for more than thirty years, to remonstrate with my father (and in pretty strong terms too) on his annual excess of expenditure over income and his consequent increasing debt. It is very creditable to them." [68] Haedy, of course, had no need for such remonstrances. From the start, he and the Duke saw eye to eye not only on the Duke's keeping within his income but also on the urgent need to reduce the indebtedness bequeathed to him by his father.

In 1839 the Duke's indebtedness amounted to £551,940. Of this sum, £482,970 comprised mortgages (many of which were family charges), £40,520 bonds, and £28,230 legacies bequeathed by his father. The Duke's creditors, apart from members of his family, included Arthur and Henry Craven (£60,000 at 4% interest), F. P. Delmé Radcliffe (£22,000 at 4½%), the Sun Fire Office (£40,000 at 4%), and the bankers Child and Co. (£55,000 at 4%) and Barclays (£22,000 at 4%). It is impossible to account for the history of the debt apart from the family charges. The longest standing of these charges was that of the Duke's uncle, Lord William Russell (1767–1840); most of them had come upon the estate by reason of the sixth Duke's large family, the product of two marriages. Previous Dukes of Bedford had not been prolific, and the Russell estates in the eighteenth century had been burdened with portions for but three daughters and one younger son, that son being Lord William.

Of the mortgage debt of £482,970, family charges amounted to £283,910. Of this sum, £88,910 is accounted for by the portion of Lord William (£45,000 at 5%) and that of his son, John, (£43,910 at 5%). It is difficult to explain why Lord William's son should have been so generously provided for, except that he married the Baroness de Clifford and there was a title to be considered. As to the remaining family charges, all are to be accounted for by the portions of the sixth Duke's children: £47,000 to Lord G. W. Russell, £40,000 to Lord John Russell, and £12,000 to each of nine children of the

[68] *Letters to Lord G. W. Russell,* I, 357.

second marriage, all portions paying a rate of interest of 5 per cent. At least £17,650 of the bond debt was incurred for members of the Duke's family, and £21,000 of the legacies can be similarly accounted for.[69]

Interest payments on the ducal indebtedness amounted in 1840 to £26,553, of which £14,195 represented the annual cost of family portions. This last was quite apart from the cost of annuities, largely but not entirely paid to members of the Duke's family. The Dowager Duchess received a jointure of £5,000; the Duke's eldest son, Lord Tavistock, received £1,500; the Duke's wife, her pin money of £700; the Duke's many brothers and sisters an average of £300 each; his uncle Lord William and Lord William's children the same; to say nothing of a long train of family dependents and friends who were also provided for. Altogether the cost of annuities was something like £16,000. If the total household expenditure is put at £30,000 (the sum which the Duke thought was a minimum), and if the net income of the Russell estates (net after estate upkeep) is put at £100,000, it is clear that after all payments the Duke still had a surplus of something like £27,000–£28,000 annually. This may be what he had in mind when he wrote to his brother, "I expect to have about one third of the whole rental, or income after paying interest of debt etc. If I was to squander that portion I should have the estate bankrupt, and the next Duke of Bedford might in vain attempt to repair the extravagance of former generations." [70]

If the Duke's financial condition is compared with that of other great landowners at the time, it does not appear grave. It may be compared, for example, with that of Earl Spencer. The Duke and Spencer were close friends, and when the Duke wrote to him about his financial perplexities Spencer replied as follows: "I fear you find yourself somewhat in a similar position to that in which I was (but I hope and trust not near so bad) viz., that your real income bears a small proportion to

[69] See Appendix V.
[70] *Letters to Lord G. W. Russell*, I, 308–11.

your rent roll. This, even if your real income is sufficient, which mine by no means was, is a disagreeable and dangerous position to be in, for a very small percentage fall in rent, a rise in interest would bring a man so situated to a complete standstill." [71] Spencer had in fact been brought to a standstill when he succeeded to Althorp in 1834; but his financial predicament was much graver than the Duke's. Interest and annuities on the Althorp estate accounted for about 79 per cent of Spencer's net income,[72] as compared to 42 per cent for the Duke. Indeed, as the Duke confessed to Haedy, "my case is certainly not near so bad as his." [73]

Nonetheless it would appear that the Duke—and Haedy— were alarmed. The Duke, as it has already been noted, spoke of himself as one of those landowners "who have succeeded to great debts and family charges." Haedy also spoke of the estates being "heavily burdened": "It will take more years than the Duke can be expected to live of prudent and restricted expenditure to bring down the Incumbrances to something like a moderate amount." [74] The Duke, however, was addressing himself to a brother, and Haedy to the Dowager Duchess; and both may have concluded that it was convenient to make extravagant claims to poverty, the better to fend off members of the family. Yet even between themselves, the Duke and Haedy, if using less dramatic language, gave voice to fears. What they feared was not a fall of income so much as a sudden stringency in the money market (there was a threat of war with France in 1839–40) which might bring about a disastrous rise in the rate of interest and would prompt "strangers" to call in their loans.[75]

There was some discussion between Haedy and the Duke in the months immediately after the sixth Duke's death about ob-

[71] Bedford MSS, 7th Duke to Haedy, Dec. 5, 1839.
[72] Althorp MSS, Box 13, 3rd Earl's Papers, Paper entitled "Private Income Account" in 3rd Earl's hand, probably dated Jan., 1835.
[73] Bedford MSS, 7th Duke to Haedy, Dec. 5, 1839.
[74] Ibid., Haedy to Dowager Duchess of Bedford, March 10, 1840.
[75] Ibid., Annual Reports, 1844.

taining a lower rate of interest on some of the mortgages. In his country-house visiting the Duke had heard of landowners who borrowed large sums at a lower rate of interest from the Bank of England and from insurance companies: the Duke of Rutland, he had heard, had borrowed £300,000 from the Bank of England at 3½ per cent and £100,000 from the Equitable Assurance at 3 per cent.[76] In the end, however, the Duke and Haedy agreed that a consolidation of the debts, even for the purpose of reducing the interest payments, was not a prudent course: if the Bank called for its money it would be in a time of great pressure, and the money would be hard to come by elsewhere.[77] Motivated by this fear, the Duke and Haedy soon resolved on the more drastic course of paying off the encumbrances.

At first some thought was given to paying them off by the sale of land. This was the course which Earl Spencer had taken—a course which in the long run proved most unprofitable for his family as the land he sold became extremely valuable suburban property. It is possible that if left to his own devices the Duke might have followed Spencer's example and sold some part of his London estate. But fortunately Haedy advised him well: to sell only land that had little possibility of long-term capital appreciation, such as some of his outlying country estates.[78] He also reminded the Duke that in the 1820's the Adams had decided against selling land on the ground that "to sell to a sufficient extent materially to lessen the Incumbrances might reduce the family from the first to one of the second class of Proprietors in the public estimation." [79] No argument could have been better calculated to turn the Duke's mind altogether away from selling land and fixing it on paying off the encumbrances out of income.

---

[76] Ibid., 7th Duke to Haedy, Dec. 31, 1839. The Equitable did not lend at 3 per cent.
[77] Ibid., Haedy to 7th Duke, Dec. 26, 1839.
[78] Ibid., Haedy to 7th Duke, Dec. 6, 1839.
[79] Ibid.

It would seem that a family dispute over his father's will suggested to the Duke the desirability of first paying off the younger children's portions, depending (as Haedy put it) on "what course Lord Wriothesley and his brothers and sisters take with respect to the codicil." [80] But family harmony prevailed, and the Duke took to paying off the strangers' mortgages rather than inflicting retribution on his brothers and sisters; for they might not have obtained five per cent on their portions as readily somewhere else. It proved quicker work than either he or Haedy had ever contemplated, or for that matter than the surplus of 1840 might indicate. By 1844 Haedy was able to announce triumphantly that "for the first time for a very long period Your Grace's estates become free from Mortgages to Strangers, leaving them subject only to Family charges and to Miss Ansell's Bond debt . . . The accomplishment of this most important object, namely the freeing of the Estates from Mortgages to Strangers, and from the danger from them of foreclosure, to which, in times of great pecuniary difficulty, they were exposed, was long ardently desired, but, till recently, deemed almost hopeless." [81]

The reduction of debt went steadily ahead, so that by the mid-1850's even the family portions were paid off and the Russell estates were entirely freed of debt. Careful management and living under his income did for the Duke of Bedford what sales of land or enhanced incomes did for other landowners.[82] Haedy and the Duke were now in the pleasant position of having to think afresh of how to apply the surplus income. Further capital investment in permanent improvements seemed the preferable course. It was also suggested that a fund

[80] *Ibid.*, Haedy to 7th Duke, Dec. 4, 1839.
[81] *Ibid.*, Annual Reports, 1844.
[82] In F. M. L. Thompson, "English Great Estates in the 19th Century (1790–1914)," in *Contributions to First International Conference of Economic History* (Paris, 1960), p. 390, there is mention of a theory of "debt-driven developers." If Dr. Thompson attributes this theory to me, I should like to disavow it. Not all encumbered landowners, as he points out, took to developing their mines or town holdings.

be set apart to assist the Duke's successor on his coming into the estate when he might find himself temporarily in want of ready cash, and thus spare him "the necessity of borrowing by which a dangerous habit might be created." [83]

This chronic alarm about borrowing and debt needs some scrutiny. The Duke was, of course, given to alarm, but landowners less anxious by nature commonly enough expressed themselves as he did on the subject of indebtedness. They were not, as a rule, given to precise measurements of debt, and it is therefore not surprising to find the Duke's financial condition described by contemporaries as "frightfully encumbered." [84] Neither the Duke nor most of his fellow landowners, however, can have meant by such words that they were on the verge of bankruptcy or that they were forced to contemplate the sale of the greater part of their estates. It was not this extremity that they had in mind so much as the prospect of declining wealth. Here their fright was not senseless. They were after all on the defensive. Not too long ago landowners had been unchallenged both politically and economically, and now in the 1830's they were confronted by the challenge of public opinion and by rich men of a new sort. It was not enough to be rich, one needed to be richer than other rich men.[85] Something of this sort may have been in their minds, and may be sensed in the Duke's declaration that "while we live under a Monarchy, and have an aristocracy, it should be at least an independent, if not a powerful, aristocracy." [86]

[83] Bedford MSS, Annual Reports, 1858.

[84] The story is to be found in Sir D. Le Marchant, *Lord Althorp* (London, 1876), p. 258.

[85] John Stuart Mill once said that in the nineteenth century men desired "not to be rich but to be richer than other men"; see J. S. Mill, "Posthumous Essay on Social Freedom," *Oxford and Cambridge Review*, June, 1907, quoted in R. M. Titmuss, *Essays on 'The Welfare State'* (London, 1958), p. 108.

[86] *Letters to Lord G. W. Russell*, I, 311.

# IV

The business of scrutinizing household expenditure and reducing indebtedness claimed much of the Duke's attention. He gave himself to these perhaps more readily than to other departments of estate business. The management and development of his property—its farms and woodlands, mines, and urban houses—may have claimed less of his attention, although like many of his generation of landowners he was an enthusiastic agriculturist. The estate which provided him with the greater part of his income—the London estate—threw up little business that was to the Duke's taste. This estate comprised 119 acres in the center of London—perhaps the most valuable land in the world. Of an average annual net remittance from all his estates for the years 1832–38, amounting to £104,760, the average net return from the London property amounted to £71,858, roughly 72 per cent.[87] The property fell into three parts: Bloomsbury and St. Pancras, returning in 1838 a net rental of £34,500; Covent Garden, £24,100; and St. Martins, £8,700.[88] These sums comprised several kinds of rent: ground rents, rack rents from houses and buildings, and tolls and rents in Covent Garden Market.

As Haedy once observed, "all the large Estates in London have come into existence, through letting land for building, and keeping the ground rents till the expiration of the building Leases." [89] On the Russell estate in 1839 the most recently built-up areas (in and around Bedford, Woburn, Bloomsbury, and Tavistock squares) were still on building leases which would not begin to expire until the 'seventies.[90] There were of

[87] Bedford MSS, Annual Reports, 1841; see also Appendix VI.
[88] By the 1850's there was a fourth part built on, in Bedford New Town, as it was called.
[89] Bedford MSS, Haedy to 7th Duke, June 19, 1841.
[90] These leases were roughly ninety-nine year leases. They would begin to expire on the Bedford Square area (begun about 1773) first.

course much older sections on the estate, such as Covent Garden, where building leases had expired. When that happened, the building became the property of the landowner who sometimes levied a fine before renewing the lease. Haedy abolished the practice of taking fines, preferring instead to renew at an improved rent—usually on a shorter lease conditional on the tenant's making the necessary repairs.[91] On the oldest parts of the estate, buildings beyond repair had been demolished and new ones put up in their place, so that the course of things was brought full circle, with a repairing lease giving way to a building lease and rack rents giving way to ground rents. The entire process was thus described:

> the old parts of the Estate sink into ground rents, thro' the houses upon them requiring to be rebuilt, the new parts will rise by the falling in of the building Leases, from ground-rents to house-rents, and this process will always be going on as the new parts of the Estate become old and the old parts new.[92]

On the London estate, since the landlord bore a limited responsibility for repairs and building, the burdens of estate administration were naturally less than those on an agricultural estate. The chief tasks of administration were looking to the observance of covenants which were designed to prevent the deterioration of the estate and managing Covent Garden Market. With the growth of London the market had come to hold a dominant position, being "the principal Sale place for London and the standard for quotations throughout the country." [93] By 1830 the sixth Duke had constructed permanent market buildings. A staff of about a dozen men managed the market— letting stalls, collecting tolls on produce sold, and keeping the peace. In 1840 the net return from Covent Garden Market was £5,711.

As the correspondence between Haedy and the Duke tends

[91] Bedford MSS, Haedy to 7th Duke, May 5, 1840.
[92] *Ibid.*, Annual Reports, 1851.
[93] *Ibid.*, London Reports, vol. 2.

to suggest, the details of administration on the London estate were pretty much left to Haedy. It was a rare occasion when the Duke reported a country-house conversation to Haedy in which mention was made of some aspect of managing urban property. The few instances of the Duke's discussing such matters with Haedy rather tend to underline his indifference. It has already been noted that the Duke raised the question whether it was not advantageous to sell ground rents which provoked the blunt reply, "exceedingly disadvantageous, even to the extent of being ruinous to do so." [94] One would conclude that the main development on the London estate during the seventh Duke's regime—namely the laying out of Bedford New Town—was largely inspired and supervised by Haedy.

The Duke's indifference to the mining ventures on his estates was no less plain. The chief of these, Devon Great Consols, was situated on the Devon estate, near Tavistock and close to the river Tamar. It sprang up in the 1840's, and as if to prove that the Russells had the touch of Midas, became the richest copper and arsenic mine in the British Isles and one of the largest in the world. The Duke let the mine, but he built docks and tramways to assist in the mining operations.[95] Again, his correspondence with Haedy rarely touched on these matters. It almost seemed as if the Duke accepted this unforeseen wealth with some reluctance; Greville noted that the Duke feared that his Devon mines would encroach on the farming of the neighborhood.[96] Later, when ironstone was found on his Midland estates, the Duke refused to allow it to be mined because it would disfigure the countryside.[97]

Agriculture, however, was another matter. The business of

[94] *Ibid.*, Haedy to 7th Duke, June 19, 1841.
[95] B.P.P., *Second Report of Royal Commission on Mining Royalties* (1890–1, XLI) Minutes of Evidence, no. 9530; *Report from Select Committee (H. of C.) on Rating of Mines* (1856, XVI), pp. 29–31.
[96] *The Greville Memoirs*, VI, 90. The Duke wrote to Haedy (Bedford MSS, April 13, 1845) that he had heard that "all classes at, and near Tavistock are mad about mines . . . neither Tradesmen nor Farmers think half so much of their own affairs as of these mining speculations."
[97] Bedford MSS, Annual Reports, 1858.

the Woburn home farm, of the estate farms and woodlands in Bedfordshire, the West Country, and East Anglia, was congenial to him. It seemed as natural as his Whiggism. His view of the world and society was a countryman's view. It is likely that Manchester and Sheffield seemed remote, strange, and unnatural to him; that he never set foot in them, let alone thought much about them. Was it merely a momentary oversight that once when reviewing the classes of English society he mentioned only the aristocracy, gentry, farmers, and laborers? [98] Within the rural world, however, the Duke had his favorites: the upper and the lower classes, the landowners and the laborers. The farmers he disliked; for they were wanting in enlightenment, and showed "a grudging and grinding spirit towards those below them." [99] The Duke's conception of himself as an aristocratic landowner, paternal yet scientific, was offended.

Not unnaturally the country estates provided much business to the Duke's taste. He was often found deep in technical discussion with Haedy—usually about the cost of some agricultural operation. For example, on the Woburn estate, where the woodlands were extensive and remunerative, the question of how to fell timber most economically presented itself. The Duke objected to the frequent use of the axe: "the seller [meaning himself] loses *much* more than a foot, if the Tree is not felled as close as possible which can only be done with a saw." [100] Haedy explained that the workmen preferred the axe to the saw, "as they have to work harder and earn less money, when they use the latter than when they work the former." [101] At the same time he assured the Duke that the saw was being introduced throughout the estate.

The Duke also looked into the cost of sawing and preparing timber in the Woburn workyard. It appeared to him that a

[98] *Ibid.*, 7th Duke to Haedy, Nov. 18, 1845.
[99] *Ibid.*, 7th Duke to Haedy, Nov. 11, 1845.
[100] *Ibid.*, 7th Duke to Haedy, April 20, 1841.
[101] *Ibid.*, Haedy to 7th Duke, April 22, 1841.

saving might be effected by installing steam-driven machinery.
In 1846 this was done at a cost of £12,800, with an estimated
annual saving of £1,500.[102] It was said that "with such Machinery the Duke as a Builder for himself has all the appliances
and is quite on a par to do work with the most eminent Builders in London or any other large town."[103] On a visit to Woburn in 1849 Sir Robert Peel reported, "[I] am full of wonder
at the extent of the Establishment—one portion of it—that in
which materials for buildings are prepared is more like a Dock
Yard than a domestic office."[104]

The cost of building on the Woburn estate—building farm
houses and cottages—was also a subject which the Duke showed
himself capable of taking up with gusto. Very soon after his
coming into the estate he and Haedy were busily discussing it.
Costs had been brought sharply to his attention by a summary
of estate accounts prepared by Haedy for the years 1823–38:
"the expenses appear to have been enormous," the Duke exclaimed, "and for a longer period than I had imagined."[105]
He proposed to reduce building costs by having such work
done by contractors rather than by his agents and workmen
on the ground that the latter were too idle and their labor
correspondingly expensive. Haedy argued to the contrary: that
the cost of materials was double the cost of labor, and that
contractors skimped on material which led in time to excessive
repair bills.[106] The Duke eventually yielded to Haedy—although not without hiring a surveyor and a surveyor's clerk
to supervise the Woburn workmen and uttering vague threats
of trying out his ideas at Oakley.[107]

This discussion between Haedy and the Duke ended on a
curious if revealing note. After dutifully exploring a subject

---

[102] *Ibid.*, Annual Reports, 1846.
[103] *Ibid.*, Annual Reports, 1864.
[104] Netherby MSS (on microfilm), reel 17, Sir R. Peel to Sir J. Graham, Nov. 27, 1849.
[105] Bedford MSS, 7th Duke to Haedy, Jan. 5, 1840.
[106] *Ibid.*, Haedy to 7th Duke, April 30, 1840.
[107] *Ibid.*, 7th Duke to Haedy, April 29, 1840.

which the Duke had himself broached, and pressing home his
argument for a contrary policy but still a policy of economy,
Haedy was met with the rebuke that "a Gentleman ought not
to expect to make or to save by building what a Tradesman can
realise." [108] Haedy must have asked himself whether the Duke's
lectures on economy were to be taken literally. He could not
have helped being taken aback, since the Duke was at him so
often about savings and profits.

For example, the Duke was much concerned about the profitability of the Woburn home farm. The Duke had warned
Haedy from the start that he was not of the old school of wasteful landowners whose farming was an extravagant hobby.
"Every money expended," he declared, "which is not expected
to produce a return is not money well laid out either by Tenant
or Gentleman Farmer." [109] His farm bailiff, therefore, instead
of losing money "ought not only to have paid rent, but to have
produced me 5 per cent interest on my capital." [110] Such was
the return obtained by Lord Albemarle in Norfolk, by Lord
Hardwicke in Cambridgeshire, as these noblemen had themselves informed him. It would distress him, the Duke concluded, to have it known "to my Tenants that I have lost by
farming as it w$^d$ convey a reflection either on my Bailiff
or myself or furnish argument to them that Farming is an unprofitable business." [111]

Yet in fact the Duke's farming, either as cultivator or as
landlord, was less profitable than such statements might suggest. There is no sign that the home farm was ever put on that
footing which the Duke sought.[112] And it is plain enough
that his major investment in farming, namely the provision of

[108] *Ibid.*, 7th Duke to Haedy, May 27, 1840.
[109] *Ibid.*, 7th Duke to Haedy, Nov. 20, 1840.
[110] *Ibid.*, 7th Duke to Haedy, April 3, 1842.
[111] *Ibid.*
[112] In 1848 the Woburn agent reported that the home farm was still
not paying interest on the Duke's capital (Bedford MSS, Annual Reports, 1848).

landlord's capital for permanent improvements like building and draining, failed to bring the sort of return for which he yearned.

From the start the Duke and Haedy were impressed with the necessity for extensive improvements on the various estates. The West Country estate in particular was in a backward condition. The holdings were too small to be efficiently farmed; the lease for lives made for tenants' laxity in repairs (at any rate so the Duke and Haedy believed); and the tenants themselves needed elementary instruction.[113] On the Bedfordshire estate the farm buildings had fallen into disrepair owing to the use of poor building materials under the fifth Duke as well as to failure to enforce covenants. The Bedfordshire estate was also in need of draining. And if the Fen estate had already been massively drained, literally snatched from the waters, this was but the preliminary to providing the dry land with the necessary buildings.[114]

Not surprisingly these tasks were taken up vigorously. The Duke came of that generation of landowners which witnessed in the 1830's and '40's the advent of agricultural techniques consonant with the best agricultural knowledge. The draining pipe, artificial manures, cheap building materials, together with the railways—all these spelt a revival of agriculture after that postwar depression which reached its depths in the mid–1830's. Caught up in this revival, landowners showed a combination of enthusiasm and technical knowledge possibly unrivaled by any earlier generation.

In this the Duke shared. He was a devoted improver, "in the habit [he once said] of reading most of the best modern publications on rural subjects." [115] His country-house visits rarely failed to provide a fruitful exchange of opinion or a valuable piece of information. Lord Salisbury put him on to a

---

[113] Bedford MSS, Haedy to 7th Duke, Sept. 16, 1842.
[114] *Ibid.*, Annual Reports, 1851.
[115] *Ibid.*, 7th Duke to Haedy, July 2, 1844.

cheap method of manufacturing draining tiles, cheaper at any rate than the Marquis of Tweeddale's.[116] The Duke of Richmond brought to his notice the new farm buildings on Sir William Heathcote's estate and Sir William's use of steam-driven saws.[117] The Duke seems to have acquired a good deal of useful knowledge, and there were times when he found himself in advance of his agents, as when he and Benson (the West Country agent) disagreed about "the treatment of Beasts in winter." [118] It would seem that the Duke needed no urging from his agents to become an improver.[119]

In consequence the Duke's expenditure on permanent improvements—especially on new farm buildings and draining —was large. On the Bedfordshire estates, for example, the aggregate sum expended on permanent improvements for the nineteen years between 1816 and 1835 amounted to £31,231. For the nineteen years between 1836 and 1855, however, the sum amounted to £194,652, or six times as much. On the Devonshire estate the cost of permanent improvements sprang from £60 in 1843 to £3,804 in 1844, and to an annual average of £7,400 for the next decade. On the Thorney estate from 1816 to 1835 there was no expenditure on permanent improvements; between 1836 and 1855 there was an expenditure of £46,478. In 1850 the Duke himself protested against the magnitude of his outlay.[120] Presumably it was proved to his satisfaction that the outlay was justified, for its size increased rather than diminished during the 'fifties.[121]

---

[116] *Ibid.*, 7th Duke to Haedy, Jan. 21, 1841.
[117] *Ibid.*, 7th Duke to Haedy, Aug. 1, 1844.
[118] *Ibid.*, 7th Duke to Haedy, July 2, 1844.
[119] According to Dr. Thompson: "It was common for agents to urge and owners to agree that the way to meet agricultural distress was to undertake improvements"; see Thompson, "English Great Estates . . . ," *Contributions*, p. 394.
[120] Bedford MSS, Annual Reports, 1851.
[121] For my figures I have relied mainly on the published accounts in Duke of Bedford, *A Great Agricultural Estate*, pp. 218–47. These accounts do not agree precisely year by year with the manuscript accounts in the Bedford Office, London, although the aggregate amounts over

If this expenditure—a very large part of which was laid out on new farm buildings—is set beside the rise in gross rental received, it is obvious that the Duke's return was considerably less than he had hoped for from his home farm. On the Bedfordshire estate between 1842 and 1861, gross rents received rose from £34,117 to £41,822, outlay on permanent improvements amounted to £275,799, and the Duke's return was thus 2.4 per cent.[122] On the Devonshire estate during the same years, rents rose from £15,191 to something like £18,500, improvement outlay amounted to about £140,000, and the Duke's return was about 2.3 per cent.[123] On the Thorney estate the return was more heartening: rents rose from £25,993 to £35,273, improvement outlay was £108,456, and the Duke's return was 8 per cent; but this included land recently brought into cultivation. Modest as these figures show profits to have been they still overstate them, for they make no allowance for depreciation.

It would seem, however, that the Duke's return on his agricultural investment was not unusual in the age of high farming, at any rate not unusual among the great improving landowners. It has been said of the fourth Duke of Northumberland's improvements on his Alnwick estate that "if all increase in rent was taken to be a return on [his] non-drainage improvement outlay, then £500,000 invested in [his] estate in this period [1847–65] yielded about 2½%."[124] In Wiltshire on the estates of the Marquis of Bath and of Lord Pembroke, as in

---

periods of years are roughly similar. The published accounts refer only to the Bedfordshire and Thorney estates, and for information about the Devonshire estate I have relied mainly on the manuscript accounts. Appendix VII is derived from the published accounts.

[122] The year, 1842, was a good starting point, since the purchase of the Ampthill estate was by then effected.

[123] The Devonshire figures were in part obtained from B.P.P., *Royal Commission on Agricultural Depression*, 1896, Particulars of Expenditures and Outgoings on Certain Estates in Great Britain; and the amounts for improvement outlay were assessed arbitrarily for three years: 1858, 1860, and 1861.

[124] Thompson, "English Great Estates . . . ," *Contributions*, p. 394.

Cumberland on Sir James Graham's estate, returns were also modest.[125] It has been suggested that this was in fact a general state of affairs among the great landowners—"that much of the landowner's investment in high farming never was an economic proposition." [126]

From time to time the Duke showed uneasiness at the high level of capital outlay on his estates.[127] He was plainly disappointed at not getting 5 per cent or more on his outlay—the more so, as he seems to have believed that it was common for other landowners to do much better than he did. The "most common practice with landlords," he once observed to Haedy, "is to charge 7 and ½ % on all new buildings and draining which is done entirely by them." [128] Nevertheless, in face of doubts and anxieties, he persisted in spending lavishly on agricultural improvements.

Is there a paradox here? On the one hand, a closefisted Duke anxiously scrutinizing his household accounts and admonishing his agents on their duty to economize; on the other, an openhanded Duke generously subsidizing his tenants' farming. It may be unwise to look for too much consistency in anyone's pattern of expenditure, still the Duke's may not be inexplicable. What appears a paradox on the surface may largely vanish on closer examination.

Either parsimonious or extravagant, the Duke was at bottom faithful to the traditional role of the Russell family. If he spent

[125] F. M. L. Thompson, "Agriculture since 1870" in E. Crittall, ed., *A History of Wiltshire* (London, 1959), vol. 4; D. Spring, "A Great Agricultural Estate: Netherby under Sir James Graham, 1820–45," *Agricultural History*, April, 1955.

[126] Thompson, "English Great Estates . . . ," *Contributions*, p. 394; J. H. Clapham, *The Economic History of Modern Britain* (Cambridge, 1926), 3 vols., II, 278.

[127] Bedford MSS, Annual Reports, 1851.

[128] *Ibid.*, 7th Duke to Haedy, Dec 15, 1843. This was not, of course, common practice; what was often done was to charge 5 per cent on draining. Thompson, "English Great Estates . . . ," *Contributions*, p. 394, makes this point; see also B.P.P., *Report of Select Committee (H. of L.) on the Improvement of Land* (1873, XVI), *passim;* and chapter five below.

less on politics, the Russells still remained in the highest ranks of the political nation. And if he spent more than his father on agricultural improvements, he did so in large part because the Russells were still to be found in the vanguard of agricultural progress. Among those landed families who took it as their duty "to exercise a stewardship of the national patrimony in the fertility of the soil," [129] they had long been prominent. The seventh Duke may not have had his Woburn sheepshearings, but he had the beginnings of an experimental station conducted by Gilbert and Lawes.[130] And he continued to exercise the landowner's traditional economic function of encouraging and assisting his tenants in their cultivation; by the mid-nineteenth century such encouragement and assistance cost more than it ever had before.

What, in short, helps to make the Duke's economic behavior explicable was his conception of the social leadership provided by a great landed family. In May, 1858, Lord Burlington who had just succeeded to the vast Cavendish estates sought advice from the Duke on their proper management. He was in the habit of doing so, for he considered the Duke "a first-rate man of business." [131] The Duke's concluding words of advice bear repeating. "The duties and responsibilities of such an estate as yours or mine are very great—we must discharge them as best we can, and make a good amount to look back upon at the close of life—I am pleased to see you paying so much attention to yours—it will afford a fund of satisfaction to others as well as to yourself—and conduce to the well being of those who live upon them." [132]

There was something more than cant here. The idea of trusteeship—of maintaining his estate for the benefit of its

[129] J. D. Chambers, *The Workshop of the World* (London, 1961), p. 81.
[130] Clark, "Agriculture and the House of Russell," *Journ. of R. Agric. Soc.*, 1891.
[131] Chatsworth MSS, MSS Diary of 7th Duke of Devonshire, June 3, 1845.
[132] *Ibid.*, 7th Duke of Bedford to 7th Duke of Devonshire, May 15, 1858.

future owners and its present and future occupiers—struck a responsive chord in the Duke. From the start of his regime he endeavored to hand on to posterity a greater fortune than had come to him; as he wrote to Haedy in 1842, "if you and I have a few years longer, we shall have done a great deal not only towards regenerating the Estate, but also to improve and reform the management in every department." [133] At the same time he was not singleminded in accumulating wealth for posterity. Conflicting considerations of compassion and personal attachment came to him more readily than to his agents—as when a tenant proved delinquent and the Duke hesitated to remove him on the ground of his being long resident on the estate, or when laborers were victimized by farmers and the Duke came to their aid.

These conflicting considerations showed themselves clearly in the Duke's policy on the letting and building of cottages. As a rule he tried to avoid letting cottages with farms, preferring to keep the control of them in his own hands. When he found in 1840 that the cottages on his Dorset farms were out of his control, he gave orders that the farmers be regulated in the cottage rents they took, and that the cottages be inspected periodically for overcrowding.[134] The Duke had many cottages built on his estates—288 on the Devonshire estate and 374 on the Bedfordshire estate—and let them at uneconomic rents.[135] If some people could persuade themselves that a landowner's outlay on draining and farm buildings was economic, no one could do so with respect to a landowner's expenditure on cottages.[136] As one of the Duke's agents put it, cottage building "satisfies an obligation appertaining to the possession of large Estates, and tends to secure the goodwill of the peasantry, and it sets an example to other landlords the following of which could not fail to be greatly beneficial." [137]

[133] Bedford MSS, 7th Duke to Haedy, March 21, 1842.
[134] Bedford MSS, 7th Duke to Haedy, April 18, 1840.
[135] *Ibid.*, Annual Reports, 1862.
[136] B.P.P., *Rep. of S.C. on Improvement of Land*, p. iv.
[137] Bedford MSS, Annual Reports, 1849.

In such ways the Duke sought to give coherence to the landed society over which he presided. It was a society in which inequality and poverty were conspicuous; in which tenants and laborers were in some sense dependants, the former being generously provided with the means to farm, the latter being saved from the worst pangs of pauperism. The Duke as a man of business thus accommodated himself to a society so constructed.

## V

John Stuart Mill would probably have denied that the Duke was typical of the great landowners in nineteenth-century England. It is impossible, of course, to be statistical and therefore certain about such matters. The most that one can do is to make a tentative judgment, relying on one's sense of the situation—that is, the sum of one's own observations and those of others. There is much evidence to suggest that, by the mid-nineteenth century, aristocracy in England had undergone something of a change in social type, a change not unlike that which had taken place in the course of two generations of the Russell family.[138] Administrative and agricultural affairs probably took more of a landowner's time than they had ever before. As a far more reliable observer of Victorian England than John Stuart Mill put it, perhaps too confidently, "the country gentleman of the nineteenth century is an administrator and a scientific man." [139]

If by science is meant the science of agriculture, this description fitted the Duke well enough. As an administrator and an agriculturist, moreover, his achievements won respect:

[138] The evidence is to be found in my paper read to the Victorian Studies conference at Bloomington, Indiana, March, 1962, entitled "Aristocracy, Social Structure and Religion in the Early Victorian Period." It is to be published in *Victorian Studies*, March, 1963.
[139] G. M. Young, *Last Essays* (London, 1950), pp. 149–50.

Greville's for example; [140] or that of fellow noblemen who came to him for advice about estate management; or that of Prince Albert who pressed him to take over the management of the Duchy of Lancaster's estates.[141] One should not, however, forget Bagehot's words: that "an aristocracy is necessarily inferior in business to the classes nearer business." [142] If this in a sense is unjust to the landowner who takes the responsibility for decisions, it should still remind us that the Duke's administrative success was in some degree dependant on the ability of his agents. Of these, the next chapter will deal with the lawyers.

[140] *The Greville Memoirs*, VI, 409.
[141] *Ibid.*, V, 358.
[142] W. Bagehot, *The English Constitution* (The World's Classics ed.), p. 107.

# CHAPTER III

# THE LAWYER

ARISTOCRATIC ACTIVITY—whether concerned with the management of landed estates or with governmental affairs—grew apace between the middle of the eighteenth century and the middle of the nineteenth. As to the management of the landed estate, it is clear that some families vastly increased the size of their possessions through marriage, inheritance, and purchase; and that many landed families were touched by the increasingly scientific aspect of agriculture, with its new enclosures and new methods of cultivation. As to government, it grew in volume and diversity, both in the localities and at Westminster. A justice of the peace and a Member of Parliament had more to know and more to do in 1830 than in 1760.[1]

Aristocratic affairs thus grew more burdensome. The ability of landowners to carry such burdens may well have diminished, if it had not been for the emergence of the modern professional spirit which invigorated old professions and created new ones.

## I

Professor T. H. Marshall has pointed out that in early times the professions were gentlemanly occupations, in the sense that

[1] On the changing position of the Member of Parliament, see R. Pares, *King George III and the Politicians* (Oxford, 1953), p. 204.

they were leisurely pursuits free from excessive labor.[2] So thought at a later time Sir Walter Elliot in Jane Austen's *Persuasion*. That gentleman was of the opinion that the naval profession was a deplorable one, in fact not a profession at all: not only did it elevate people in society but "it cuts up a man's youth and vigour most horribly." Mrs. Clay's reply to Sir Walter was most illuminating: "is not it the same," she asked, "with many other professions, perhaps most others? . . . even in the quieter professions, there is a toil and a labour of the mind, if not of the body, which seldom leaves a man's looks to the natural effect of time." [3] Mrs. Clay was a better observer of society than Sir Walter; professional types of an older time were giving way to types better suited to the strenuous life of nineteenth-century England.

The extent to which the new professional life was immersed in laborious activity was one of its characteristic features. It was taken for granted—by Lord Eldon, for example—that young men underwent "privations" in order "to get forward in professions." [4] But having undergone privations and labors, they no longer ran the risk of being thought wanting in gentility; instead their labors might confer gentility. Devotion to the discipline of a professional calling had come to be looked upon as labor of a special sort. As Lionel Trilling has put it, "in nineteenth-century England the ideal of professional commitment inherits a large part of the moral prestige of the ideal of the gentleman." [5]

This transformation in English professional life had significant consequences for English society. In the long run it would lead to the destruction of the old order: an aristocratic society resting on hereditary privilege and personal ties had little in common with the impersonal ideals of professional excellence

[2] T. H. Marshall, *Citizenship and Social Class and other essays* (Cambridge, 1950), p. 128.

[3] J. Austen, *Persuasion*, chap. 3.

[4] H. Twiss, *The Public and Private Life of Lord Chancellor Eldon* (Philadelphia, 1844), 2 vols., II, 82.

[5] L. Trilling, *The Opposing Self* (New York, 1955), pp. 214–16.

and effort. But in the short run, before English society was thoroughly suffused with the professional ethos, the old order in some ways stood to benefit from the new professionalism.

It may be said to have benefited in two ways. First, it found in the new professionalism—as in the old—articulate defenders of aristocracy, generating not social antagonism but social co-operation. A recent study of the attorney in the eighteenth century puts forward this thesis convincingly. Dr. Robson contends that the professions by the end of the eighteenth century "had gained much, and stood to gain much more, so that for the moment their influence was exerted to strengthen society, not to weaken it." [6] This the government may have understood in 1792 when it made use of attorneys throughout the country to report examples of seditious literature.[7]

The second way in which aristocracy benefited was by finding assistance in the execution of its business. The clergy of the Church of England, for example, aided substantially in the business of the localities. They worked harder after 1770 than before—as Miss McClatchey's study of the Oxfordshire clergy suggests [8]—and they worked at things useful to landowners. It has been noted that the eighteenth century saw a remarkable growth in the work of the justice of the peace. A sizable portion of the entire Commission of the Peace was clerical; in some counties at the end of the eighteenth century, such as Cambridgeshire, the working justices were almost all clergymen.[9] It was not altogether an accident that the chief manual on the justice of the peace was written by a Cumberland clergyman, the Rev. Richard Burns.

Equally important for the business of the localities was the

[6] R. Robson, *The Attorney in Eighteenth-Century England* (Cambridge, 1959), p. 153.

[7] A. Mitchell, "The Association Movement of 1792–93," *The Historical Journal*, no. 1, 1961.

[8] D. McClatchey, *Oxfordshire Clergy 1777–1869: A Study of the Established Church and of the role of its Clergy in local society* (Oxford, 1960).

[9] Order Books, Cambridgeshire Quarter Sessions.

assistance rendered by the lawyers—both barristers and solicitors. Property in land in the eighteenth century increasingly generated legal business; the century has been called "the great age of conveyancing." [10] Rural enclosure, the exploitation of mineral lands, and the increased use of strict family settlement prompted landowners to resort more frequently to men trained in the law. Not unnaturally they were tempted to make their lawyers their estate agents, their "man of business" as they often called them.

## II

The man of business was usually a solicitor, but he was sometimes a barrister. If the latter, he was likely to be at the head of a great estate. The solicitor served on the large or small estate, and might be either the chief agent or a subordinate. Most often perhaps the coveted positions went to a lawyer in London; but provincial lawyers, usually country solicitors, did much landed business, and sometimes on the great estates.

How large a proportion of landed estates had lawyers associated in one way or another with their day-to-day administration it is impossible to say. It has recently been stated that the proportion was small, since the eighteenth century witnessed the emergence of the specialized estate agent, who presumably ousted the lawyer-agent.[11] While it is true that the eighteenth century witnessed the emergence of this agent, it is no less true that he took a long time in establishing himself on the majority of English landed estates.

Even though one must rely on fragmentary and unstatistical evidence, it would seem safe enough to conclude that the lawyer-agent, was found on the majority of landed estates in

[10] E. Hughes, "The Professions in the Eighteenth Century," *Durham University Journal*, March, 1952.
[11] Hughes, "The Eighteenth Century Estate Agent," in *Essays in British and Irish History*.

the early nineteenth century. In the first place, examples are readily come by. It would be idle to list them here; perhaps enough of them are cited throughout this work. In the second place, handbooks on estate administration from the beginning of the eighteenth century to the latter part of the nineteenth agree that lawyers are commonly found administering estates. Finally it would seem reasonable that landowners recruited many of their agents from the ranks of the lawyers, for the legal profession provided an adequate number of the qualifications necessary for administering landed estates.

This last, however, was both frequently and emphatically denied. The authors of handbooks on estate administration almost invariably deplored the employment of solicitors as agents on such grounds as that they neglected their estate business for other kinds of business, and that they knew little about agriculture.[12] Landowners and statesmen like Lord Shelburne in the eighteenth century and Sir Robert Peel in the nineteenth found solicitors wanting in integrity. "The scourge of all that is honest or good," Shelburne once declared of them; "no man has a lower opinion than I have" of the motives of country attorneys, Peel once confessed.[13]

What does one make of such criticism? Plainly it is far too sweeping. Unfortunately it is impossible to know in detail how well or how badly many lawyers performed their tasks as estate agents; therefore whatever general statements one ventures about them should be tentative and qualified. But on balance a case might be made that lawyers employed in estate management proved useful rather than harmful to landowners.

[12] For example, in the nineteenth century: G. A. Dean, *The Land Steward* (London, 1851), p. 237; D. G. F. Macdonald, *Estate Management* (London, 1868), p. 18; J. L. Morton, *The Resources of Estates* (London, 1858), p. 94. But there were exceptions, such as J. Lawrence, *The Modern Land Steward* (London, 1801), pp. 45–46.

[13] Lord E. Fitzmaurice, *Life of William, Earl of Shelburne* (London, 1912), 2 vols., II, 360; Netherby MSS, reel 4, Sir R. Peel to Sir J. Graham, Jan. 31, 1835. Peel was here referring to the motives which underlay the hostility of country attorneys to himself.

To begin with Lord Shelburne's complaint that solicitors lacked integrity. It is true that there was in the early nineteenth century a solicitors' underworld fully deserving an unsavoury reputation. Dickens immortalized it in the persons of Dodson and Fogg. Sir George Stephen, himself once a solicitor, freely admitted to its existence: there are solicitors "whose manners would exclude them from our servants' hall, and whose characters would compel us to count our spoons, if by any accident they gained admission there. It is but too true that we have among us a large body of adventurers, who have little education, less principle, and neither capital nor connexion." Such men, Sir George continued, fed upon the unfortunate and the criminal, "the inferior tradesman trembling on the verge of bankruptcy . . . the ruined spendthrift . . . thieves and pickpockets." [14]

As Stephen explained, however, this business was fortunately but a part—the "inferior" part—of the business of the solicitor's profession. Writing in 1839 he looked back on the past fifty years as a time that witnessed a remarkable growth of new and more respectable kinds of business. Merchants, landowners, and public companies—all had come increasingly to need the solicitor's services; the varied business of the nation touched more and more on points of law. The business of the solicitor was thus purified and elevated—to use Stephen's words—and this in turn led to the recruitment of "many young men from that rank of life, who, less than half a century ago, would have spurned the calling as derogatory to their birth." [15] Stephen thus went beyond what men had begun to say of the solicitor's profession at the end of the eighteenth century, when (as Dr. Robson has pointed out) they were beginning to make a distinction between an elite of respectable solicitors and the less reputable majority.[16] Forty years later, according to Stephen,

[14] Sir G. Stephen, *Adventures of an Attorney in Search of Practice* (Philadelphia, 1839), 2 vols., II, 9–10.

[15] *Ibid.*, II, 7.

[16] Robson, *The Attorney*, p. 151.

respectability was the mark not of a minority of the profession but of the majority.

By the mid-century, if not earlier, public opinion seems to have agreed with Stephen. The signs were various. Knighthoods were being offered to solicitors, Stephen himself being among the first to be so honored.[17] Novelists also testified to the solicitor's respectability. Surtees, who had been articled to a solicitor, found "the blacksheep of the profession . . . so small a proportion compared to the white." [18] Trollope, whose novels were thickly populated with solicitors, declared in *The Eustace Diamonds*, "There is no form of belief stronger than that which the ordinary English gentleman has in the discretion and honesty of his own family lawyer." [19] In *Doctor Thorne* (published in 1858) Trollope has Mortimer Gazebee, the London solicitor, embark on what was still a bold and unconventional enterprise, the wooing of an aristocratic lady.[20] In real life, at almost the same time, Lady Charlotte Guest—by then Lady Charlotte Schreiber—was contemplating the marriage of her daughter to Richard Du Cane, the family solicitor. "I did not feel at all sure," she observed, "whether her brothers and sisters and her other friends would have been pleased with the union, on account of his profession"; and when the Earl of Carlisle—who also employed Du Cane—first saw the young people together, Lady Charlotte thought that his Lordship raised his eyebrows. Nonetheless the marriage took place.[21]

Perhaps the weightiest commendations of the solicitor appeared in the *Saturday Review* and *The Times*. The 1850's witnessed some resounding scandals involving solicitors, the most notorious probably being the case of Henry and Cheslyn

[17] Stephen was knighted on Queen Victoria's accession; see article in *D.N.B.*

[18] R. S. Surtees, *Plain or Ringlets*, chap. 25.

[19] A. Trollope, *The Eustace Diamonds*, chap. 10.

[20] A. Trollope, *Doctor Thorne*, chap. 38.

[21] Earl of Bessborough, ed., *Lady Charlotte Schreiber: Extracts from her Journal 1853–91* (London, 1952), pp. 103–4.

Hall of New Boswell Court, Lincoln's Inn. They were said to "have abstracted the money of their credulous clients . . . pretended to effect mortgages which they did not effect . . . sold out stock which they had no authority to sell out . . . rendered false accounts, cooked and spiced in a manner which would have satisfied the critical palate of Mr. George Hudson himself." [22] This offence, however, only prompted an energetic endorsement of solicitors as a profession. The *Saturday Review*, which was given to measuring its words, spoke out strongly.[23]

> The solicitors of the higher order are men of conspicuous intelligence, honour, and cultivation; the body to which they belong absorbs a much larger part than the Bar does of the money paid by the country for legal assistance & advice; and their fitness for employment is guaranteed by a *bona fide* examination, the absence of which is steadily degrading the Bar. Their designation as the 'lower' branch of the legal profession would be a mere conventionalism, if it were not that there are certain walks of practice which lead an attorney deeper into the dirt than a barrister can easily go.

*The Times* echoed the *Saturday Review:* "it has always been with us a matter of surprise that where such unbounded confidence is placed in the probity, the accuracy and the diligence of a class of men, there are so few defaulters to their trust." [24]

A further and more chronic complaint than the solicitor's lack of integrity was his technical inadequacy as a land agent. This is a more difficult matter to deal with. It is clear, however, that on certain levels of estate administration the solicitor's performance was in fact adequate. Where his functions were managerial, as on large estates where he acted as auditor or supervisory agent and had available the expert advice of resident land agents who did the specialized out-of-door work, the solicitor (and the barrister-auditor as well) was likely to demonstrate his usefulness.

[22] *The Times*, Jan. 30, 1858.
[23] *Saturday Review*, Dec. 5, 1857.
[24] *The Times*, Jan. 30, 1858.

Walter Bagehot who was (among other things) a serious student of what he called the "art of business" would not have found this surprising. "Success depends," he once wrote about business, "on a due mixture of special and non special minds." He offered the example of the London joint-stock bank which was managed "by a board of persons mostly *not* trained to the business, supplemented by, and annexed to, a body of specially trained officers, who have been bred to banking all their lives." [25] The great success of these banks, according to Bagehot, was the result in large part of their having non-special minds at the top of the administrative structure, thereby diffusing throughout its length and breadth "a greater and more flexible knowledge" than would otherwise have been possible. It might be argued that the solicitor and the barrister—both of whom had non-special minds in that they were not bred to farming —often did for the great estate what Bagehot's directors did for the joint-stock bank. At any rate, most of the auditors described in detail later in this chapter served their employers well.

But there were exceptions. A notorious one was that of the Robsons, London solicitors, who acquired something of a reputation for presiding at the dissolution of landed families.[26] They were solicitors to the Grenvilles (the first and second Dukes of Buckingham), and in charge of their estates. In the voluminous Stowe MSS there is no indication that the Robsons ever proposed a reform of the administration of the estates although few great estates were managed in so slovenly a fashion.[27] But such lack of ingenuity and enterprise was anomalous, certainly on the large estates.

At a lower level—that of the country solicitor who was in charge of several small estates and who received only such assistance as was furnished by bailiffs—there may well have been more reason for complaint. Early in the eighteenth century Edward Laurence, author of *The Duty and Office of a*

[25] Bagehot, *The English Constitution*, p. 174.
[26] Sackville MSS, Lord West to his mother, Nov. 10, 1852.
[27] Stowe MSS, T. Grenville to Lord Chandos, May 3, 1828.

*Land Steward*, wrote of country attorneys who do "nothing else but attend the Court-keeping and collecting of Rents; by which means the Tenants have taken the advantage of doing what they would with their Farms, quickly lessening the Value of the Estates by Over-Ploughing etc." [28] In 1868 William Sturge, a well-known land agent and surveyor, declared, "By far the greater part, probably, of the landed property of England is under the management of Solicitors who are usually little more than receivers." [29] It would be surprising if there was not some truth in these complaints, if solicitors were not sometimes perfunctory, if they were not sometimes seriously deficient in their knowledge of farming.

More evidence about the work of solicitor-agents on this level would be helpful. We know, however, that some owners of small and middling estates much valued their solicitor's services. The Lincolnshire squire, Sir Robert Heron, had little but praise for his Newark solicitor and agent, W. E. Tallents.[30] Another Lincolnshire landowner, Lord Monson, in declaring his gratitude for his solicitor's services—the London solicitor, Gem—specified the usefulness of his agricultural knowledge. As Lord Monson observed to his son on one of Gem's inspections of the estate, "Gem has been busy and of great service—he has walked about all over the estate—explored the drains, seen how they were working." [31]

Was Gem's farming knowledge unusual among solicitors? We are probably predisposed to think it was. This predisposition may be a consequence of the stubborn belief that agriculture and commerce were very different pursuits in nineteenth-century England, that the countryside and the town were sharply divided, that they were at once hostile and antithetical societies. Since solicitors were often townsmen, we

[28] E. Laurence, *The Duty and Office of a Land Steward* (London, 1731), p. 8.
[29] W. Sturge, *The Education of the Surveyor*, address to the Institution of Chartered Surveyors, 1868.
[30] Sir R. Heron, *Notes* (London, 1851), p. 234.
[31] Monson MSS, Lord Monson to eldest son, Feb. 28, 1848.

are prone to conclude that they had little to do with the countryside and, having little to do with it, knew little about it. Some such notion may be at work in shaping our views on solicitors as estate agents and farmers; if it is, our views might well do with some re-examination.

It is obvious, of course, that the two Englands—that of the countryside and that of the towns—were in some respects distinct and separate. But it would be seriously misleading to envisage them as in all respects different and therefore as deeply divided. There was much in the business of agriculture which was akin to the business of manufacture. Being a great industry, moreover, agriculture supported a varied society, consisting not only of farmers, laborers, and landowners but of members of the professional and semi-professional classes as well: surveyors, land agents, bankers, lawyers, etc. These last might well move freely in both town and countryside, being in this respect amphibious like the aristocracy.

Presumably the technical aspects of farming offered a less formidable obstacle than they might to-day. Fashionable journals like the *Quarterly* and the *Edinburgh Review* published serious articles on deep draining and soil chemistry.[32] As the *Quarterly* reviewer declared in 1849, "In England everybody farms. Prince Albert farms, the Lord Chancellor and the Attorney-General farm; the Duke farms; Admiral Sir Charles Napier farms; Sir Benjamin Brodie farms; the Speaker farms; the ex-Premier farms." [33] The list could easily have been lengthened with less distinguished names: such as John Arthur Roebuck, the Radical barrister, who was a breeder of pigs; [34] or, if drawn up earlier, with such names as George Webb Hall, the Bristol solicitor, who was a leading breeder of Merino sheep.

Webb Hall offers a revealing example of the solicitor im-

[32] *The Edinburgh Review*, Jan., 1845, article entitled "Progress of Scientific Agriculture."

[33] *The Quarterly Review*, Dec., 1849, article entitled "Agriculture—Drainage."

[34] R. E. Leader, ed., *Life and Letters of John Arthur Roebuck* (London, 1897), p. 236.

mersed in the affairs of town and countryside.[35] He seems to have had two careers. The first was in Bristol, and of the sort which Dr. Robson has held up as typical of the respectable solicitor of the day. At an early age he was appointed Chief Clerk to the Court of Requests in the city. Later he became solicitor to the Corporation of Bristol, a post which he held for a quarter of a century. In addition he was agent of the Bristol Dock Company, and was instrumental in securing the passage of parliamentary acts for the improvement of the port and harbor; as one obituary put it, "few were better qualified to surmount those numerous obstacles which are frequently opposed to the progress of such bills." [36]

Webb Hall's second career was that of a large-scale farmer who specialized in woolgrowing and agrarian politics. In 1798 or 1799 he leased Leigh Court, an estate not far from Bristol; and two years later he took a second farm near Uxbridge, Somerset. Towards the end of the war he took still another farm, Sneed Park in Gloucestershire, where he spent his last years. He was said to occupy at one time nearly 2,300 acres, and to have invested by 1814 £20,000 in agricultural improvements. Through connections in the Spanish wool trade Webb Hall began to purchase Merino sheep for his farms, and by importing directly from Spain through the port of Bristol he was able to collect a large flock in a short time. On his Uxbridge farm alone it was said that he had 3,000 Merinos, thereby making him probably "the largest Merino flockmaster in the kingdom."

The vicissitudes of Merino wool in particular, and the decline of agricultural prices in general, took Webb Hall into agrarian politics. When he began his career in politics is not known, but by 1815 as a critic of the Corn Law he was writing letters under the pen name of "Alpha" to the *Farmers' Journal*. Soon he gathered about him some of the leading woolgrowers like

---

[35] See D. Spring and T. L. Crosby, "George Webb Hall and the Agricultural Association," *The Journal of British Studies*, Nov., 1962, from which this account of Hall is drawn.

[36] *Bristol Journal*, Feb. 23, 1824.

the Ellmans, father and son, organizing in 1817 what was probably the first local protectionist society in England, and two years later what was certainly the first national farmers' movement, the Loyal and Constitutional Association of Agriculturists. Its particular plan of increasing protection proved impracticable, and the Association virtually vanished by the time of Webb Hall's death in 1824. But he and his Association had set a precedent for later farmers' organizations, and had helped to prompt a protracted national debate on the merits of agricultural protection.

When H. H. Smith, agent of the Marquis of Lansdowne, wrote his manual on estate management in 1898 he noted the decline in the number of solicitors employed as land agents which (in his opinion) set in after 1870. Smith ascribed this decline to two things: the marked growth in estate business, and the founding of the Institution of Surveyors in 1868 which became a sort of training school for professional land agents and greatly increased their supply.[37] These developments would suggest that before 1870, the needs of estate management being what they were and the supply of agents being what it was, the solicitor as agent served a useful purpose, even though the performance of his tasks may not always have satisfied the highest of professional standards, even though not every solicitor became like John Hawkins of Hitchin a very proficient farmer.[38] It was E. P. Squarey, a land agent and not a lawyer, who testified to the Richmond Commission when asked what he thought of lawyers as agents, "There are very many lawyers who are good judges of land, who are good judges of their business . . . I have known many lawyer agents who do their work remarkably well, and do it to the satisfaction of their clients and to their tenants as well."[39]

---

[37] H. H. Smith, *The Principles of Landed Estate Management* (London, 1898), pp. 299–301; see also A. M. Carr-Saunders and P. A. Wilson, *The Professions* (Oxford, 1933), p. 199.

[38] R. L. Hines, *Hitchin Worthies* (London, 1932), pp. 201–9.

[39] B.P.P., *Report of Royal Commission on the Depressed Condition of the Agricultural Interests* (1881, XV), p. 144.

Apart from their integrity and a reasonable acquaintance with agriculture, many solicitors commended themselves to landowners on other grounds. Knowledge of the law of real property was plainly one of these. It was a subject whose mysteries were vast and forbidding and on which landowners were exceedingly dependent, especially in connection with that private constitution for a landed family known as strict family settlement. Still another was the central place in local society held by many solicitors. In Richard Jefferies' *Hodge and His Masters* there is a vivid account of this place. To the solicitor's office, he wrote, "the entire round of country life comes," and in its japanned deed boxes lie the "written counterparts" of the surrounding hills and fields.[40] A man so situated was likely to be useful in the conduct of elections, and the landowner was often involved in politics as much as in agriculture. All these things may help to explain the persistence of the solicitor in the hierarchy of estate management until so late in the nineteenth century.

# III

It might profit us at this point to scrutinize the life and work of a single solicitor, agent to a great estate: Christopher Haedy, chief agent to the Dukes of Bedford from 1838 to 1859. Of his birth, social origins, and education, very little is known. Periodicals dealing with the law and the legal profession—like the *Solicitors' Journal* and the *Law Times*—failed to mention him in the year of his death, although they published obituaries of lawyers in less responsible positions. It is known, however, that he was employed in the Bloomsbury office under the sixth Duke and his auditor, William Adam, and that the latter recommended Haedy as his successor. For two decades after 1839 Haedy formed an effective partnership with the seventh Duke—one notable in the long history of the Russell estates.

---

[40] R. Jefferies, *Hodge and His Masters* (London, 1937), p. 194.

The details of this partnership are far more accessible than the details of Haedy's biography. Indeed it would almost seem that Haedy had no life apart from the varied concerns of an agent-in-chief. He held two offices simultaneously: that of auditor for all the estates and that of agent for the Bloomsbury estate. The office of auditor might mean many things, as the remainder of this chapter will indicate. At all times, of course, it entailed an auditing of estate accounts; but in addition to this, Haedy took charge of the day-to-day administration of the Russell estates. He served no other master than the Duke of Bedford, and his remuneration was probably £1,800 a year and a London house.[41]

There is little doubt that he was well worth his large salary. Like many of his contemporaries he was a highly energetic and industrious man. He kept up a voluminous correspondence with the agents of the country estates, even with the bailiff of the Woburn home farm, and his correspondence with the Duke was also large. On the Bloomsbury estate, by his own account, "there is scarcely a day in which they [the tenants] do not occupy several hours, and I make a point of personally hearing all complaints and . . . hearing all they have to say."[42] Elsewhere on the Russell estates, he made periodic inspections: "where large work is under way, or being proposed or completed."[43] On one such visit to Woburn he was invited to dine with the Duke and his family. Haedy characteristically excused himself:

> To make the most of my time when I am at Woburn I make use of the morning for out of door work and the Evening for pen and ink work. I find it necessary to make somewhat copious memorandums of my proceedings for further reference, and that and answering my letters make the loss of more than one or two Evenings inconvenient.[44]

[41] After Haedy's death the office of auditor was separated from that of the London agent, the salary of the first becoming £1,000 and of the second, £800 and a house.
[42] Bedford MSS, Haedy to 7th Duke, July 5, 1841.
[43] Ibid., Haedy to 7th Duke, Aug. 3, 1840.
[44] Ibid., Haedy to 7th Duke, Oct. 12, 1841.

Haedy's labors revealed an impressive grasp of detail. Nothing seems to have been too trivial for him. He made all the arrangements for the sixth Duke's funeral, down to deciding what servants were to wear mourning and what tenant farmers were to be invited.[45] When Victoria and Albert visited Woburn in the summer of 1841, it was Haedy who determined the order of procession, and hired London detectives to keep an eye out for London thieves.[46] When he and the Duke undertook their investigations into the consumption of wax candles, it was Haedy who made minute comparisons between candles recommended to him at two shillings one pence a pound and those purchased for the Duke's houses at three shillings a pound: "By way of trial," he wrote to the Duke, "I have bought a pound of each. I cannot detect any difference in their appearance except that those supplied to your Grace have patent wicks . . . I am now trying them to see whether there is any difference in the material of which they are made." [47]

His knowledge of persons and of their duties on the estate was minute. There was the fat porter at Woburn who was given to falling asleep; the chief clerk in the Tavistock office who held up business; and Elizabeth Wire, the Woburn laundry maid, who was worn out by her labors. He knew with nicety what domestic servants could be expected to do—even apparently in the lower reaches of that elaborate world. A still-room maid, he explained to the Duke, was the housekeeper's maid; she assisted the housekeeper, and when Woburn was occupied made the toast and the tea for the family and visitors, and made gruel for poor lying-in women. The confectioner, he added, made preserves and pickles. And the laundry maids would under no circumstances assist the housemaids or vice versa.[48]

Detail, however, did not bemuse Haedy. His conduct of

[45] *Ibid.*, Haedy to 7th Duke, Oct. 31, 1839.
[46] *Ibid.*, Haedy to 7th Duke, July 9, 1841.
[47] *Ibid.*, Haedy to 7th Duke, March 8, 1843.
[48] *Ibid.*, Haedy to 7th Duke, Nov. 13, 1839.

estate policy showed that flexibility which Bagehot found in
the management of joint-stock banks by non-special directors.
He was quick, for example, to sense the disadvantages of a
landowners' vendetta against the railways, and in 1840 advised
the Duke to support the building of railways in the West
Country.[49] His mind moved with ease from one department
of estate affairs to another, from railways and mining in the
West Country to building in Bloomsbury or to draining in the
Fens. London solicitor though he was, Haedy was also enough
the countryman to discuss rural business knowledgeably with
the Duke and his agents.

He was at the same time—much to the Duke's good fortune
—fully aware of the relative values of urban and rural land,
of how much more profitable urban land was to its owner than
rural. Once when discussing the high cost of improvement on
a Devon farm, Haedy observed:

> This is a strong instance to show how small must be the value of
> land, viewed as raw material to be manufactured into farms at
> such great cost, and how much more nearly the right to it of its
> possessors must approach to a manufacturer's right to the goods
> he has fabricated than is generally supposed. It exhibits too the
> striking difference in respect to the cost of farming them, of a
> landed Estate and an Estate in London, the former being made
> in a great degree by the outlay of the Landlord's capital and the
> latter at the cost of the Tenants, expended nevertheless advanta-
> geously to themselves.[50]

Not surprisingly Haedy's management of the London estate
was such as to ensure the Russells' prosperity. It has been seen
in the previous chapter that without Haedy's intervention the
Duke might well have sold some part of the London property
to pay off encumbrances. Haedy was also responsible for abol-
ishing the taking of fines on the London estate—a practice
which on many estates led to the consumption of capital as

[49] *Ibid.*, Haedy to 7th Duke, July 21, 1840.
[50] *Ibid.*, Annual Reports, 1849.

income.[51] And finally it was Haedy who saw through to its completion the last important addition to the London estate—Bedford New Town. He was responsible for its quick completion and for its being laid out in squares and wide streets—both of which objects were obtained by advancing money to the builders. Somewhere on those valuable London acres—if on nothing more than a street sign—it would have been appropriate to inscribe Haedy's name.[52]

When Haedy retired at Christmas 1858 and handed over the auditorship to his successor (T. T. Wing, a London solicitor), he made his final report to the Duke of Bedford. He began by listing all the principal transactions which had been recently completed—the new lease of the Great Devon Consolidated Mines, the new railway in the West Country, and the new street from St. Martin's Lane through Rose Street to Bedford Street. He went on to assure the Duke that payments for all the next year's transactions that could be foreseen were provided for. In a farewell note he added:

> Your Grace's Estates having been relieved from the heavy pressure of the Incumbrances to which they were subject, and being under the care of Agents under whose management they are sure to prosper and with all of whom I have had every reason to be satisfied . . . I retire from the Auditorship with the pleasing consciousness that your Grace's Estates and affairs are in a condition as prosperous as can well be desired.[53]

Complacent as this last statement may sound, it was probably not seriously inaccurate as a summing-up of Haedy's career.

What informed that career? Some notion of what moved Haedy may be got from George Eliot's *Middlemarch* where she explains what "business" meant to Caleb Garth—a character modeled on her land-agent father, Robert Evans. Business for Garth was a word to be uttered with "peculiar reverence";

[51] *Ibid.*, Haedy to 7th Duke, May 5, 1840.
[52] *Ibid.*, Annual Reports, 1851.
[53] *Ibid.*, Annual Reports, 1858.

it signified the "myriad-headed, myriad-handed labour by which the social body is fed, clothed and housed"; and Garth's divinities therefore were "good practical schemes, accurate work, and the faithful completion of undertakings: his prince of darkness was a slack workman." His imagination responded to schemes for "better land drainage, solid building, correct measuring, and judicious boring (for coal)." [54] By business he "never meant money transactions but the skilful application of labor." [55] Not as indifferent as Garth to the financial side of business, Haedy worshipped the same divinities; like him he combined "a reverential soul with a strong practical intelligence." [56] In this combination both Garth and Haedy displayed something that was characteristic of nineteenth-century professional life, among the established as among the near professions.

For Haedy there was but one world—that of business. So far as one can see, he was completely absorbed by it. Garth recognized the existence of other worlds; but Haedy barely mentioned them in his correspondence with the Duke. A reading of his letters, mainly written in the years 1839–46, gives no indication of the high political excitement of these years. The Duke sometimes discussed such political questions as Corn-Law repeal, but Haedy merely listened and went on with what presumably was to him of greater consequence— some current piece of business on the estate.

According to Haedy the conduct of business was never so businesslike as in his own day. He was inclined to speak with a trace of condescension of the "old school": men of business who lacked his own degree of enthusiasm for rational organization—for dispatch, system, and centralization. He got rid of the chief clerk in the Tavistock office whose accounts were "more in arrear than was desirable or consistent with the quicker manner in which Business is now generally con-

[54] G. Eliot, *Middlemarch*, chap. 24.
[55] *Ibid.*, chap. 56.
[56] *Ibid.*, chap. 24.

ducted." [57] Gradually he imposed on the Russell estates a more centralized direction of affairs. Quite early he put auditing on a quarterly basis; he made accounting more particular on the side of payments; and he set on foot a system of estimating outgoings in advance. Not until the end of his regime did he establish so thoroughgoing a system of centralization that gross receipts were sent to London; previously the agents had remitted only the net receipts, net after payments for estate upkeep. Probably this reform would have come sooner if Haedy had not been confronted by such formidable and trusted subordinates as Tycho Wing, the agent on the Fen estate, who was known as King of the Fens.[58]

For Haedy as for Garth a "slack workman" was the "prince of darkness." Haedy was therefore indignant—more so than the Duke—at the thought of the corrupt but longstanding custom among domestic servants of taking tips from tradesmen who supplied the Duke's household: "the vicious principle," as he called it, "of allowing a Servant to receive presents from those whom he is to look after, and whose weights quantities and prices and the quality of whose Articles, he is to check." [59] With the same distaste he criticized the Duke's forester at Woburn:

> he may not have activity enough to enter upon a new system, especially one at variance with what appears to have been the principle on which he seems to have acted, namely, that the men under him should earn as good wages and at as little Labour as possible. Not that I suppose he has ever proposed to himself this, as his plan of proceeding. But he is a man of a quiet, easy temper and he has lived in times when much error prevailed on the subject of the employment of Labourers.[60]

Accordingly Haedy looked upon the tenant farmers much as he did upon anyone else—as men who were to be assessed

[57] Bedford MSS, Annual Reports, 1851.
[58] Portland MSS, Lord George Bentinck to 4th Duke of Portland, March 23, 1845.
[59] Bedford MSS, Haedy to 7th Duke, March 10, 1843.
[60] *Ibid.*, Haedy to 7th Duke, April 26, 1841.

by their skill and industry in their particular line of business. Of all the farmers on the Russell estates, the Devon farmers were most often the object of his strictures. Not only was the layout of their farms and farm buildings miserably inadequate —for which they were only in some degree responsible—but they were ignorant of the best farming practices. "A large portion [of them] require teaching," he informed the Duke, "Mr. Benson does all he can to teach them. Making manure, growing green Crops, and keeping Cattle in the winter, all points they were wholly defective in." [61] Haedy himself drew up a form of agreement which might help Benson to drive his lessons home: "it will serve to point out to the Tenants what they are to do and what they are to avoid doing." [62]

Not surprisingly, when an opportunity arose of ridding the estate of a slovenly tenant, Haedy was inclined to take it. He would take it even though the tenant had been on the estate for a long time. The Tophams, for example, were a tenant family long associated with the Woburn estate whom the Woburn agent wanted to get rid of. They appealed to the Duke, justifying the renewal of their lease on the ground that an uncle would provide the necessary farming capital. The Duke promised them a reconsideration of their case. "It is one of those distressing cases," he wrote to Haedy, "in which feeling or compassion are pulling one way, against feeling and duty to the Farm on the other . . . Of course, I had rather keep the son of an old Tenant, if I can do so consistently with my duty to that part of the Estate." [63] Haedy, however, did not waver. Getting rid of a bad tenant, he told the Duke, "is a salutary warning to other tenants." [64] The Tophams left Woburn.

Aged tenants of long standing on the estate were sometimes granted a pension—probably if they had no prospects of family

[61] *Ibid.*, Haedy to 7th Duke, Sept. 16, 1842.
[62] *Ibid.*, Haedy to 7th Duke, Sept. 14, 1840.
[63] *Ibid.*, 7th Duke to Haedy, Feb. 21, 1841.
[64] *Ibid.*, Haedy to 7th Duke, Feb. 25, 1841.

assistance. It would appear that Haedy acquiesced in this policy, although he seems to have been motivated largely by the idea that such philanthropy was justified by its prudence. When aged tenants on the Thorney estate were removed and pensioned off, Haedy observed to the Duke, "Some allowance of this kind is always well made when it brings about the beneficial results of exchanging a bad Tenant for a good one." [65]

If Haedy disliked a slack tenant, he disliked equally a slack landowner; if he expected tenants to do well by the land and the estate, he expected landowners to do the same. As was noted earlier, he and the Duke were much concerned about the cost of building. But as Haedy himself once admitted, the Duke paid more for his farm buildings than most landowners did; the buildings were constructed in a more durable fashion, and they were fitted out more generously.[66] In all probability Haedy waited on his country agents to advise him on how the farms were to be rebuilt, but he plainly agreed with them that the building was to be done well, that dukes should maintain high standards.

Taking such a view of the duties of landlord and tenant, it followed that Haedy desired to see the relations of the Duke with his tenants put on a more systematic and businesslike footing in respect of buildings, repairs, and leases. Haedy's object was to shift the responsibility for repairs to the tenants' shoulders—"which [as he told the Duke] cannot be done till the buildings are either rebuilt or put into a state to justify calling upon the Tenants to keep them in repair." [67] Once the buildings were put in such a state, the Duke's responsibility would extend no further than conducting a semi-annual inspection of the buildings and warning tenants of what needed doing. If they ignored the warning, the Duke would undertake the repairs, and the tenant would be charged interest.

Tenants' leases were to be adjusted in the same spirit. The

[65] *Ibid.*, Haedy to 7th Duke, Nov. 8, 1839.
[66] *Ibid.*, Annual Reports, 1853.
[67] *Ibid.*, Haedy to 7th Duke, April 15, 1840.

Dukes of Bedford—"acting under the advice and following the practice of their great Friend Mr. Coke of Holkham" [68]—had been long concerned to grant leases and assure their tenants fixity of tenure. In 1822, when old leases were running out, new leases had been granted for fourteen years. But the stress of agricultural depression had rendered them embarrassing by 1830: "The Duke was at that time continually teased by complaints and applications for abatement of rent, which were met in one way or another; probably not one agreement made in 1822 was carried out so far as payment of the rent then agreed upon." [69] In 1836, therefore, the term of years had been reduced to seven, and it being a time of severe depression, rents had been fixed at a low level. But times had suddenly improved and "the Tenants had a lucky turn in their favour." [70] Such was the background for the innovations which Haedy set about in 1843.

What he—and the Duke as well—sought for at this time was to avoid the experience of the previous two decades: "to give the Tenants certainty of tenure," but to avoid "the inconsistency of the Landlord being held bound for the whole period of the term while the Tenants played fast and loose and always sought for an abatement of rent on every adverse occasion, no matter how trifling that was." [71] The plan which they adopted provided long leases of varying lengths—twelve, sixteen, or twenty years—subject to quadrennial revision of rentals according to the price of corn, and shorter leases of seven or eight years with fixed rents. Tenants were encouraged to choose the long lease. This plan, among other things associated with Woburn, won the commendation of James Caird in his famous survey of English agriculture. [72]

In all this Haedy plainly assumed that a businesslike Duke and his businesslike auditor should resist unreasonable demands

---

[68] *Ibid.*, Annual Reports, 1862.
[69] *Ibid.*
[70] *Ibid.*
[71] *Ibid.*
[72] J. Caird, *English Agriculture in 1850–1* (London, 1852), p. 436.

and insist on businesslike transactions. Yet on occasion one is led to wonder how consistently businesslike Haedy was. When Ampthill—Lord Holland's estate adjoining Woburn—was up for sale, Haedy sneered at London bankers like Samuel Loyd and Baron Rothschild for contemplating its purchase "on the principle of receiving a given percentage on every hundred pounds of purchase money." [73] When Haedy himself made a higher offer—on the ground that Ampthill's rents were low and its timber valuable—he prefaced the offer "by saying that I was not going to make such an offer as a man from the Stock Exchange might make but one which one nobleman might make to another." [74] It may well be that this was little more than a touch of snobbery which Haedy felt befitting—or perhaps required of—the chief agent to the House of Russell.

Haedy's attitude to the low rate of return on the Duke's investment in agriculture gives one rather more reason to wonder. It seems that he never protested about it. Perhaps he had early concluded that the return on the country estates was of little moment given the immense value and profitability of the urban estate; that Bloomsbury, in short, could quite easily subsidize Woburn's farming. Also he may well have agreed with the Duke that low agricultural profits were justified by perpetuating the distinctive society of the countryside; that it was an obligation of the Duke of Bedford to bring the best farmers to his estate by providing them with the most up-to-date equipment. So far as is known Haedy never recorded such opinions—perhaps because he took them so much for granted.


## IV


It was noted earlier in this chapter that the chief agent to a great estate was sometimes a barrister. For example, the wicked

[73] Bedford MSS, Haedy to 7th Duke, May 25, 1841.
[74] *Ibid.*, Haedy to 7th Duke, May 21, 1841.

Marquis of Hertford was served by John Wilson Croker; the pious Lady Olivia Sparrow by Alexander Haldane. The Lambtons employed Henry Stephenson, the Spencers John Shaw-Lefevre, the Cavendishes James Abercrombie, the Russells George and William Adam, the Fitzwilliams Francis and Daniel Maude, the Somersets Serjeant Ludlow, the Granvilles Loftus Lowndes, and the Leveson-Gowers, Howards, and Wards— James Loch.

That sharp-tongued nobleman, Lord Shelburne, in denouncing lawyers had denounced the barrister–auditor as well as the solicitor: "of all the follies," he once wrote, "the greatest is that, which formerly was practised and is still continued in some great families, that of having some considerable lawyer or some eminent man of business at a considerable salary to audit your accounts." [75] But this ill repute seems to have gone no further than Lord Shelburne. When John Lockhart was looking about for a profession in 1826, Sir Walter Scott recommended the Bar to him: "there are so many things which a man of talents and character may do in that line without being an actual pleader. . . . Auditorships etc. are often casting up." [76] That they were, had something to do with the social status of barristers: as Tocqueville put it, "they constituted, as it were, the younger branch of the English aristocracy." [77] Moreover, barristers often received the sort of technical training that solicitors received. Complaints were uttered in the mid-nineteenth century that barristers were "grievously deficient as jurists . . . mere legal mechanics"; [78] but this may have been an advantage rather than a disadvantage so far as their managerial function was concerned.

As the four case studies that follow reveal, the managerial

[75] Fitzmaurice, *Life of Shelburne*, II, 347.
[76] H. J. C. Grierson, ed., *The Letters of Sir Walter Scott* (London, 1932–37), 12 vols., IX, 434–35.
[77] A. de Tocqueville, *Democracy in America* (transl. Henry Reeve), 2 vols., I, 282.
[78] Sir W. Holdsworth, *A History of English Law* (London, 1903–52), 13 vols., XII, 88–9, footnote 2.

function of the barrister–auditor varied considerably. Of the four—Daniel Maude, Henry Stephenson, Alexander Haldane, and James Loch—the last came closest to Haedy's detailed, day-to-day administration of a landed estate. Haldane's auditorship was scarcely an auditorship at all—in large part because of the peculiar personality of his employer. Stephenson's auditorship was perhaps typical of what most barristers did who served as estate agents.

Daniel Maude, who came of a long established Yorkshire family, succeeded his father, Francis Maude, in the office of auditor to the Earls Fitzwilliam.[79] He was called to the Bar in 1829 when aged twenty-eight, having graduated from Cambridge four years earlier, and thereafter having been a Fellow of Caius.[80] During the 1830's he was on the Northern Circuit, and was appointed stipendiary magistrate in Manchester by Lord John Russell; he was in the public eye during the Chartist riots in Manchester in August, 1842.[81] About that time he took over his father's work on the Fitzwilliam estates, although he remained on the Manchester bench until 1860. There is no evidence that he was employed by a landed family other than the Fitzwilliams; and it would seem that soon after the fifth Earl's death in 1858 he left their employ and migrated to the South where he became stipendiary magistrate in Greenwich, dying there in 1874.[82]

Of the several barrister–auditors examined here Maude had the least to do with the day-to-day administration of his employer's estates. Each of the Fitzwilliam estates had its own agent, responsible for (among other things) the keeping of accounts. The Yorkshire and Irish accounts were sent to Wentworth Woodhouse for auditing and the Milton accounts to

[79] J. Foster, *Pedigrees of the County Families of Yorkshire* (London, 1874), 3 vols.

[80] J. and J. A. Venn, *Alumni Cantabrigienses* (Cambridge, 1922–53), 10 vols., Part II, vol. 4, p. 365.

[81] G. Kitson Clark, "Hunger and Politics in 1842," *The Journal of Modern History*, Dec., 1953.

[82] Venn, *Alumni Cantabrigienses*.

Milton House. Once a year Maude visited these places to serve (as he once put it) as "a check on your Lordship's behalf against the steward." [83] This annual auditing, however, did not bring forth a comprehensive report by Maude, as it did on some other estates; Haedy, for example, drew up a very detailed annual report. Nor did Maude's auditing provide a single balance sheet for the entire estate. As noted earlier, it was left to Earl Fitzwilliam himself to draw up a sketchy balance sheet.[84] Presumably this was the way the Earl wanted things done.

Maude was, however, drawn into affairs, for the Earl sought his advice on minor as well as major matters. He thus gave his opinion on the painting of estate buildings, and on how best to keep the peace in the Wentworth Woodhouse estate office. He also gave his opinion on the reliability of the manager of the Earl's iron works, on the legal arrangements for the sale of the Derwent Navigation, and on the advisability of buying Foxley, an estate owned by the Earl's friend, Sir Robert Price. In short he acted as the Earl's principal adviser in the administration of his estates, and there came a time when he began to offer advice without its being solicited.

It was the subject of expenditure—particularly that incurred by the collieries on the Wentworth Woodhouse estate—that drew his critical attention. Wentworth Woodhouse was in some respects a curiously administered estate. Its agent in the 1830's and '40's was a Barnsley solicitor, William Newman, who collected the rents, kept the accounts, and did the legal business. The chief enterprise on the estate was that of the collieries, in which large investments had been made in the first half of the nineteenth century, and from which by the 1850's came a large part of the gross income.[85] But important as the collieries were, Newman was not responsible for their operation. Instead

[83] Milton MSS, Maude to Earl Fitzwilliam, Oct. 30, 1847.
[84] These are to be found in the Milton MSS.
[85] Spring, "Earl Fitzwilliam and the Corn Laws," *Am. Hist. Rev.*, Jan. 1954; see also J. T. Ward, "The Earls Fitzwilliam and the Wentworth Woodhouse Estate in the Nineteenth Century," *Yorkshire Bulletin of Economic and Social Research*, March, 1960.

they were in the charge of Joshua and Benjamin Biram, father and son, who were at one and the same time house stewards in Wentworth Woodhouse and colliery engineers in the estate mines. The collieries had begun as a department of the household administration, like the home farm, and so they had remained. Until the fifth Earl's death, the colliery accounts were kept in the household account books, together with statements on the purchase of tea and calico; and the Birams managed the domestic servants while they pondered the problems of ventilating the mines.

The largest item of expenditure on the Wentworth Woodhouse estate was in the colliery department. In all probability it soon caught Maude's eye; there is evidence that he doubted Biram's judgment at least as early as 1849.[86] Three years later, perhaps sooner, Maude flatly accused Biram of extravagance; he was conscientious enough, Maude admitted, but was given too much freedom.[87] What Maude came close to saying was that the Earl was the real culprit. In 1855 he came to the point. "I have long thought," he wrote to the Earl, "that your affairs required a more vigorous treatment than you have been disposed to give them." His example of laxity in estate management was Newman's lack of authority over Biram. Newman had agreed with Maude that certain items of Biram's expenditure were extravagant. "My obvious question to him was, why had he sanctioned them? The answer was that he had no control over them." Maude feared that "this want of proper check" was universal on the Fitzwilliam estates: "each departmental head does what seems to him good in his own eyes. The result must be extravagance."[88]

This was bold enough, but Maude went even further. He proposed that the Earl follow the example of his son, Lord Milton, and bring in someone to look closely into expenditure—as Lord Milton had done when he took over the management of

[86] Milton MSS, Maude to Earl Fitzwilliam, July 3, 1849.
[87] *Ibid.*, Maude to Earl Fitzwilliam, Nov. 26, 1852.
[88] *Ibid.*, Maude to Earl Fitzwilliam, Dec. 20, 1855.

the Irish estate. More intrepidly still, he pointed an accusing finger at the Earl's personal expenditure: what need had he for a menagerie considering the shortness of his visits to Wentworth Woodhouse? Apparently the Earl did not welcome his auditor's unsolicited advice; for in his next letter Maude hastened to explain that he was chiefly concerned with Biram's expenditure, not the Earl's, and he dropped the subject of a general overhaul of estate outgoings.[89] Presumably he never ventured such criticism again. Being the Earl's junior both in age and in years of experience on the Fitzwilliam estates, Maude may have found it especially difficult to act as the Earl's tutor. Whatever the reasons for its being so, his auditorship was of limited scope, the most limited of the four examples considered here.

Henry Stephenson (1789?–1858), auditor to the Earls of Durham, had a mysterious and colorful background. Some thought he was the illegitimate son of a Duke, although they differed as to whether his father was the Duke of Norfolk or the Duke of York.[90] He became a Chancery barrister—not a very good one, it was alleged [91]—and man of business to the Duke of Sussex. In the 1830's he entered the civil service as Commissioner of Excise, and later became a Commissioner of Internal Revenue which position he held from 1849 to his death.[92] He moved freely in Whig aristocratic society, eventually winning the hand of Lady Mary Keppel, daughter of the Earl of Albemarle, thereby becoming brother-in-law to Coke of Norfolk—much, it was said, to Coke's chagrin.[93] In 1826 he had become the Earl of Durham's auditor, thus be-

[89] Ibid., Maude to Earl Fitzwilliam, Dec. 26, 1855.
[90] Le Marchant describes him as "the natural son of the late Duke of Norfolk"; see A. Aspinall, ed., Three Early Nineteenth Century Diaries (London, 1952), p. 14. Sir Herbert Maxwell describes him as the "natural son of [the] Duke of York"; see Sir H. Maxwell, ed., The Creevey Papers (London, 1903), 2 vols., II, 366.
[91] Aspinall, Early Nineteenth Century Diaries, p. 14.
[92] F. Boase, Modern English Biography, article on Stephenson.
[93] The Creevey Papers, II, 97.

ginning a long career in the service of the Lambton family which ran simultaneously with his career in the civil service.[94]

From the very start of his employment in the Lambton family, Stephenson did the kind of work which Maude had never done for the Fitzwilliams. He was brought in at a time of serious financial embarrassment, expressly to inquire closely into the Lambton affairs. He was nothing if not thorough: estate administration, the collieries, the Earl's personal finances, all were minutely surveyed. The collieries, being the source of the largest part of the Lambtons' income, received special attention; operating costs were analyzed, and proposals made as to their reduction. As for the Earl's personal expenditure, Stephenson unlike Maude took the bull by the horns. He prescribed retrenchment: therefore the Earl should live abroad, and spend no more than £8,000 a year; building at Lambton Castle must be suspended, and the domestic staff reduced.[95]

This was the kind of thing which Stephenson put into his annual reports—of which, unfortunately, only two survive (for the years 1834 and 1835), together with a special report for 1849 occasioned by the second Earl's coming of age. Stephenson himself described his reports as concerned with "every material transaction, stating the annual expenditure on items— the profits of the collieries—of the Estate—every variation of debt—by increase or decrease—and also general and material remarks touching the condition of affairs." These reports, he added, "form I hope and believe a tolerably correct annual history of all essential particulars and transactions." They were not as voluminous as Haedy's reports, but their usefulness was beyond question.

For about a quarter of a century Stephenson audited the Lambton accounts and drew up his annual reports. The day-to-day business was left to a resident agent, Henry Morton;

---

[94] The material on Stephenson used here is to be found at greater length in D. Spring, "Agents to the Earls of Durham in the Nineteenth Century," *Durham University Journal*, June, 1962.

[95] Lambton MSS, Stephenson to Lord Durham, May 4, 1827.

Stephenson himself resided in London, coming North only for special need. In London there was occasional legal business, such as the vexing matter of the Chancery suit instituted by the Earl's aunt which was fought to the House of Lords.[96] There was also some political business: finding suitably Whiggish candidates for the parliamentary seats of county Durham; and more important, keeping government in mind of the needs of coal owners whenever legislation was considered touching on their affairs, that is legislation which dealt with railways, coal duties, or church leases.[97] Stephenson seems to have done more of this than Maude ever did.

Stephenson's retirement from the auditorship in 1853 remains in some obscurity. One might guess that advancing age alone accounted for it. But there is evidence to suggest that increasing strain between Morton, the resident agent, and himself also played a part. Stephenson had brought Morton along, possibly at the very start bringing him to the Earl's attention, instructing him in the best mode of keeping accounts, and commending him to the Earl as having "every disposition and great capabilities to do full justice to your affairs." [98] As the years went on, Morton's pupilage ended; he began to differ with Stephenson on the vital subject of colliery management. The falling coal prices of the 1840's had made Stephenson a pessimist about the future prosperity of the coal trade, and reluctant to expand colliery concerns; Morton remained an optimist, and his views—which turned out to be the correct ones—prevailed, for the Earl came to his support. In a sense, perhaps, Stephenson had reformed the Lambton administration so well that it was able to dispense with him. For some time after his retirement, it would seem, his place went unfilled.

To find Alexander Haldane (1800–1882) in this gallery of barrister–auditors is a trifle startling. For it was Haldane whom

---

[96] *The Law Reports,* House of Lords, vol. 6, Durham *v.* Wharton.
[97] See D. Spring, "The Earls of Durham and the Great Northern Coal Field," *The Canadian Historical Review,* Sept., 1952.
[98] Lambton MSS, Stephenson to Lord Durham, April 12, 1833.

the Provost of King's once described as "that odious Scots bigot . . . who edited the Evangelical rag, the *Record*." [99] In the 1820's, like many an enterprising Scot before him, Haldane came up to London from Edinburgh University to qualify as a barrister at the English Bar. Being the nephew of Robert and James Haldane (and their eventual biographer) he moved in evangelical circles, among men like Edward Irving, Joseph Wolff, and Henry Drummond. The last—banker, Member of Parliament, and religious eccentric—convened annual conferences from 1826 to 1830 at his Surrey country house, Albury, where biblical prophecy was the chief topic. Presumably Haldane found Drummond too extravagant and breaking with him founded the *Record*. It would seem that he was never its editor, although he wrote a great deal for it and was one of its proprietors. In later life Haldane and his wife—in their London house—"were among the first to set the example of the Drawing-room meetings for religious and benevolent objects." [100]

Through his circle of religious acquaintance Haldane eventually found employment as auditor to Lady Olivia Sparrow. That formidable lady was one of the *grandes dames* of Evangelicalism, an intimate of Wilberforce and Hannah More. She was well enough acquainted with Haldane in 1847 to speak favorably of him as a good lawyer and "nephew to the writer on Romans." [101] The next year Lady Olivia's daughter, the Duchess of Manchester, died—thus setting on foot a long and bitter litigation between Lady Olivia and her son-in-law. Early in 1849 she sought Haldane's professional advice about her daughter's will, and in the next year he became her auditor.

---

[99] N. G. Annan, *Leslie Stephen: His Thought and Character in Relation to His Time* (London, 1951), p. 122.

[100] This biographical information is to be found in a sketch of Haldane's life originally published in the *Record*, and later added to the ninth edition of A. Haldane, *The Lives of Robert Haldane of Airthrey and his brother James Alexander Haldane* (Edinburgh, n.d.).

[101] Kimbolton MSS, Lady O. Sparrow to Duchess of Manchester, July, 1847.

He described himself as "a Chamber counsellor and the greatest part of the business relates to wills conveyances marriage settlements, etc. It also comprehends the office of auditorship, that is the oversight and management of property." [102] Lady Sparrow's estates in Huntingdonshire and Essex—the main estate being in the former county—returned a gross rental of something like £11,000 in 1850; [103] and Haldane assured her that "several moderately large Estates" employed barristers as auditors and that doing so would save her thousands. With characteristic unctuousness he added: "My prayers on *your* behalf must ascend with my gratitude to the Giver of all good, accompanied with the earnest desire to render any little knowledge or talent I possess useful to *you* and *yours*." [104]

Haldane's auditorship lasted about eight years. Before his time the auditorship was in the hands of a London solicitor who examined the accounts annually, and reported generally on the resident agent's work. The latter was caught pocketing some part of the rents, and Haldane reluctantly took over his duties, including those of receiver.[105] Partly because Lady Olivia deeply resented the failure of the litigation with her son-in-law, for which she blamed Haldane, and partly because of the unusual nature of the auditorship, Haldane eventually fell out with Lady Olivia, being for a time threatened with a suit in Chancery alleging misapplication of rents.

The peculiarities of his auditorship were bound to make for trouble. In the first place, Haldane did without a resident agent. By all accounts the farming on the Sparrow estates was backward, and Haldane confessed to being ill-informed about agriculture. He therefore requested that a Mr. Beadel be hired to act as a kind of consulting land agent, to inform him about agricultural affairs "on which as a barrister I professed my in-

[102] *Ibid.*, In Chancery: Lady O. Sparrow *v.* Haldane: Bill of Complaint and Answers.
[103] *Ibid.*, Rental of Lady O. Sparrow's Estates, 1850.
[104] *Ibid.*, Haldane to Lady O. Sparrow, n.d., probably 1851.
[105] *Ibid.*, In Chancery: Lady O. Sparrow *v.* Haldane.

ability adequately to advise." [106] This arrangement did not prove satisfactory. Although Beadel attended the audit dinners and gave technical advice to the tenants, and although something was done to improve the most dilapidated farms, the absence of a resident agent on so large an estate was felt.

In the second place, it was illogical to combine the offices of receiver and auditor. It meant in effect that the estate went without a genuine audit of its accounts, relying instead upon a mock audit by Lady Olivia to whom Haldane's clerk explained whatever she wanted to know.[107] All went pleasantly enough until Lady Olivia's suspicious nature was aroused by rumors circulating in Huntingdon that she was in Haldane's power.[108] She then became convinced—apparently without ground—that Haldane had used £7,000 of her money without her knowledge, and had falsified the wood and manorial receipts.[109]

Haldane denied everything; Lady Olivia, he said, was the victim of a "delusive panic." [110] A bill of complaint was filed in Chancery, to which Haldane made a lengthy reply. He was removed at the end of 1858, and the old system of resident land agent and London solicitor-auditor was restored. Some months later Lady Olivia's friends and family persuaded her to drop the charges. Haldane had the last word:

> Poor Lady Olivia! I feel much for her, and as was observed by one who knows her well that she should be so near to the eternal world and still so occupied with "business, business, business." Happy should I be to learn that she was beginning to fix her thoughts more directly upon the things of Heaven.[111]

Of the four barrister–auditors described here, James Loch was the only one to achieve the distinction of being noticed by *The Dictionary of National Biography*. Haldane perhaps

[106] *Ibid.*
[107] *Ibid.*
[108] *Ibid.*, Haldane to Lord Ossulston, Sept. 16, 1858.
[109] *Ibid.*, In Chancery: Lady O. Sparrow *v.* Haldane.
[110] *Ibid.*, Haldane to Lord Ossulston, Sept. 16, 1858.
[111] *Ibid.*, Haldane to Rev. E. Selwyn, March 12, 1859.

should have been similarly distinguished, although not for his auditorship but for his career in religious journalism. Loch, however, was the king of auditors in the first half of the nineteenth century, and nothing else need have justified his inclusion. He came in the course of time to serve the Duke of Sutherland, the Earl of Ellesmere (Lord Francis Egerton), the Howards of Castle Howard, and other great families. The name of Loch seems to have been a kind of household word in the highest circles of aristocracy. When the Dowager Duchess of Bedford sought advice, she consulted James Loch: "she could not possibly have a better or more able adviser," she was told, her informant being Christopher Haedy.[112] Lord Wharncliffe's eldest son urged him to bring Loch to Wortley to look into the family finances: "a few minutes conversation with him would be worth guineas of manuscripts." [113] Ralph Sneyd referred to him as "Loch the infallible." [114] When Parliament wished the benefit of expert knowledge on the working of entail and family settlement, it brought James Loch before its Select Committee.[115]

Of Scottish origin like Haldane, Loch came of quite another Scottish milieu: not the evangelical–prophetic milieu of Carlyle and Irving but the rationalist milieu of the *Edinburgh* reviewers. A contemporary and intimate of Brougham and Horner, he attended the University and the Speculative Society, and wrote for the *Review* in its early numbers. In that of July, 1804, he was responsible for the article on the Rev. W. Tennant's *Indian Recreations: Consisting chiefly of Strictures on the Domestic and Rural Economy of the Mohammedans and Hindoos.*[116] This was a subject nicely suited to a Scottish in-

---

[112] Bedford MSS, Haedy to 7th Duke, May 1, 1840.
[113] Wharncliffe MSS, Wh. M. 434, Eldest son to Lord Wharncliffe, Sept. 11, 1829.
[114] Sneyd MSS, R. Sneyd to Earl of Clare, Sept. 9, 1846.
[115] B.P.P., *Report from the Select Committee on the Bill for altering the law concerning Entails in Scotland* (1828, VII).
[116] R. H. M. Buddle Atkinson and G. A. Jackson, *Brougham and His Early Friends: Letters to James Loch 1798-1809* (London, 1908), 3 vols., II, 129–30; III, 278–79.

tellectual of Loch's sort, a pleasant opportunity to dwell on the material backwardness of Indian agriculture, the moral turpitude of the Hindu, and the defective economics of the East India Company's monopoly. The last was deemed unwise on Loch's part, although it followed naturally enough, as he pointed out, from Adam Smith's teachings. But Brougham warned him that the "politics" of his article were "decidedly wrong"—by which he seems to have meant that Charles Grant, a director of the East India Company and a leading member of the Clapham Sect, did not like them. Possibly Brougham knew more of the great world than Loch did and had already found it a leading principle of life that impecunious young lawyers ought not to offend influential people. He advised Loch not to divulge the authorship of the article.[117]

Loch did not take the high road to London as soon as Brougham and Horner did. Until he was called to the English Bar as a conveyancing barrister in 1806, he remained in Scotland, improving the Blair Athol estate which belonged to his uncle, William Adam. In 1808 Adam brought to his notice a post with Lord Grenville, a sort of secretaryship responsible for communicating with the press: "it is," Adam wrote, "in respectability from the very great confidence it produces with persons of the Highest Consideration not ineligible." [118] This was an entree to public life not unlike that which Brougham had found with Lord Holland and the Whigs. For reasons that are unknown Loch chose to avoid a career so much in the public eye. Shortly afterwards—perhaps again with the aid of his uncle who was auditor to the Dukes of Bedford—he became auditor to Lord Stafford (later the Duke of Sutherland).

In 1820 Loch published a report on the first decade or so of his management; it was entitled *An Account of the Improvements on the Estates of the Marquess of Stafford*. Generally speaking, the report made two points worthy of notice here—

---

[117] *Ibid.*, II, 143–45.
[118] *Ibid.*, II, 295.

both of which underlay the practical policies of those who administered landed estates in the nineteenth century, especially the agents. The first point was the wisdom and necessity of improvements—that is, of those several expedients publicized by such agricultural reporters as Arthur Young and William Marshall to heighten the productivity of landed estates. Loch wrote of their necessity rather like a modern economist propounding the gospel of development to backward nations; Lord Stafford's Scottish estate was a little like darkest Africa. Outmoded tenures were an institutional obstacle to progress; housing and sanitation were primitive; famine was periodic; and poverty and indolence were chronic.

The second point made was that a policy of agricultural improvement was a matter not only of profit for a landowner but of duty as well. But which in fact was more important, or how great were the demands of duty if profits should fall, neither Loch nor the land agents who shared his opinions made clear. This is a subject which will be pursued in the next chapter; here it may suffice merely to quote Loch:

> To better their condition however; to raise them from such a state of continual poverty and occasional want; to supply them with the means, and to create in them the habits of industry, was, and is the bounden duty of every such property. And it was not less their duty to do so, because the same arrangement, which was calculated to produce this salutary effect, was at the same time the best suited to increase the value of their property, and to add to the general wealth of the community. The greater the means, and the more extensive the influence of the proprietors, the more were they called on for this exertion, as well for the sake of their own people, as an example to others. None felt the full extent of this obligation more than the proprietors of the estate of Sutherland. But such an attempt was one not to be undertaken without much consideration; and when fully determined on, it was not a matter to be easily accomplished.[119]

[119] J. Loch, *An Account of the Improvements on the Estates of the Marquess of Stafford* (London, 1820), pp. 59–60.

Such detailed considerations as Loch took in managing Lord Stafford's estates before 1820 do not emerge in his report sufficiently to assess his capacities as a supervisory agent. The Ellesmere MSS do, however, provide materials by which an assessment may be made. In them there are a number of letters for the years 1837–46, mostly written by Loch to Lord Francis Egerton, later first Earl of Ellesmere, which throw some light on his conduct of business. Lord Francis had inherited a highly diversified estate, comprising canals, mines, and farms. In its administration, which Loch oversaw, the farms constituted a separate department, as did the canals and mines, each with its own agent.

There is much that reminds one of Haedy in Loch's conduct of affairs—much that they shared in common with the chief agents on other great estates. There was the same grasp of detail, the same desire for businesslike subordinates, the same flexibility and soundness of judgment. The journal of his tour of the Worsley farms in 1843 clearly reveals Loch's attention to detail: he is seen estimating repairs on Thomas Smith's farm, "one of the most industrious tenants on the estate"; catching out another tenant, William Smith, who "I fear . . . is a little of a speculative turn, his steam churning machine was not in order"; and visiting Sarah Sneaden in her new house, who "says she has no money to purchase grates." [120] Canal affairs were looked into with equal minuteness: when superfluous workmen needed turning away, each case was closely examined; when costs were scrutinized, economies were found in the purchase of oats for the canal horses, obtaining them on contract "on the same principle that the Army is supplied." [121]

Loch chose his subordinate agents with care. When he chose a "deputy superintendent" for the management of the canal, he looked out for the best available man, finding him in the employment of Lord Dudley, and offering him an attractive

[120] Ellesmere MSS, Loch to Lord F. Egerton, Aug. 15, 1843.
[121] *Ibid.*, Loch to Lord F. Egerton, Nov. 10, 1837.

salary. Lord Dudley had paid him £1,000 a year, with house, coals, and traveling expenses; Loch offered him £1,200 and the same perquisites "which of course includes the horses he uses for business." [122] Loch was aware that the Secretary of the Liverpool and Manchester Railway, Henry Booth, received £1,000 a year without perquisites. He was plainly in the market for the best man he could get.

For Loch as for Haedy the old school of business needed remodeling. On entering Lord Egerton's service Loch decided to reform the system of accounting as soon as it was possible, although seeing no harm in its continuance for a while "as it is clear that they [presumably the subordinates on the estate] are all very much alarmed and on the alert." [123] He proposed that the administration be divided into distinct departments; that the profit and loss of every unit, down to the last coal pit, be clearly accounted for; and that agents be allowed to keep in their hands only such moneys as were remitted to them for authorized expenditures.[124]

The soundness of Loch's judgment in affairs was perhaps best demonstrated in his management of the canal. Chief among the profitable enterprises on the estate, it earned large clear profits year in and year out, sometimes as high as £80,000; [125] Loch had reason to describe it, as he once did, "as a subject of infinite importance to Lord Stafford and his family." [126] But in 1830, with the coming of the railways, and the Liverpool and Manchester Railway in particular, the canal was faced, according to widespread belief, with the threat of being overwhelmed by competition. Loch, however, never shared this belief. "It is still," he assured Huskisson, "a matter for serious investigation and of doubtful result whether they [the railways] will carry heavy and bulky goods, cheaper than canals,

---

[122] *Ibid.*, Loch to Lord F. Egerton, Jan. 30, 1837.
[123] *Ibid.*, Loch to Lord F. Egerton, April 2, 1837.
[124] *Ibid.*, G. S. Smith to Loch, Sept. 20, 1837.
[125] *Ibid.*, Estate Accounts. This was the profit for 1824.
[126] Add. MSS, 38,758, folio 76, Loch to Huskisson, Dec. 25, 1829.

and especially unless speed is to form an item in the calculations." [127]

By 1845 the Earl of Ellesmere had joined the ranks of the pessimists, and was complaining to Barry, the architect, "that I own the last canal or nearly which can be said to exist in England, and I do not suppose anybody in Manchester would give me three years purchase for the article." [128] Loch, however, had in the intervening years only slightly changed his ground. "Long canals," he assured the Earl, "if not too circuitous, having no local trade, will cease or become Railways. Short canals such as the Bridgewater with a very large local trade will continue to flourish. It has now a vast trade." [129] And in fact, in 1857, when the Earl died and Loch himself was dead, the canal still earned £40,000 clear.[130] Several decades later when it was sold, it fetched a great deal more than three years' purchase.[131] Keeping it in a profitable state was probably no easy matter. There were endless negotiations fending off competing railways and canals, and Loch must have had his anxious moments. He told the story—possibly a revealing one—of how during negotiations with the Old Quay Company he had "dreamt for three nights successively and three times every night that I have got into the barge on the Canal and have been forcibly taken and put on board a passage boat on the old Quay." [132]

Like Haedy's, Loch's world of business extended to agricultural affairs—but he was probably a better farmer, more experienced, less conventional than Haedy. He seems to have relied less than Haedy on the advice of his subordinate agents. Indeed, in some important matters the initiative came wholly

---

[127] *Ibid.*

[128] Ellesmere MSS, Lord F. Egerton to Barry, Oct. 20, 1845.

[129] *Ibid.*, Loch to Lord F. Egerton, June 10, 1844.

[130] Earl of Ellesmere's Succession Duty Account, 1857.

[131] The Earl of Ellesmere's canals were eventually purchased by the Midland Railway for £1,100,000; see B.P.P., *Report of Royal Commission on Depressed Condition of Agricultural Interests* (1882, XV), p. 63.

[132] Ellesmere MSS, Loch to Lord F. Egerton, Jan. 8, 1844.

from Loch. It was on his instigation alone, for example, that the system of corn rents—by which rents were regulated according to the price of corn—was early established on the Ellesmere estate.[133] On the subject of draining—which so concerned and sometimes bemused farmers and landowners in the 1840's—Loch also spoke with confidence. He drew diagrams for the land agent of what needed doing; and his observations on the controversy between shallow and deep drainers were refreshingly eclectic. He agreed with Josiah Parkes about the proper depth to drain, but would have nothing to do with Parkes's dogmatizing on the one-inch pipe.[134]

Loch as man of business had the habit of authority—even with his employer. It is hard to conceive of Haedy's supervising the Duke of Bedford's personal expenditure as closely as Loch did Lord Francis Egerton's. He warned about extravagance in church building, the Egertons being zealous church builders. When Lord Francis threatened to overspend generally, Loch brought him up short, although adding the comforting assurance that "your Lordship may depend on my apprizing you at the earliest possible period when I shall be able to report that I see your affairs quite safe up to the end of the year, and when you may again increase your outlay." [135] It may be that the Duke of Bedford was less the spender than Lord Francis and therefore offered Haedy less provocation. But even if Haedy had been provoked to offer such advice he would scarcely have dared compliment the Duke—as Loch complimented Lord Francis—on "the straightforward manly and sound manner in which you express yourself in regard to the temporary derangement of the financial measures contemplated." [136]

---

[133] Ibid., Loch to J. Haynes, Aug. 2, 1841.
[134] Ibid., Loch to P. Rasbotham, Jan. 19, 1846. For Josiah Parkes's ideas on draining, see his evidence in B.P.P., Report of Select Committee (H. of L.) to enable Possessors of Entailed Estates to charge . . . for the Purpose of Draining (1845, XII), p. 11.
[135] Ibid., Loch to Lord F. Egerton, April 5, 1844.
[136] Ibid., Loch to Lord F. Egerton, April 9, 1844.

But Loch was, after all, the king of auditors. And besides he was a Member of Parliament and a cultivated man. He was the friend of Huskisson, Peel, and Brougham. He was a director of the English Historical Society, and sprinkled his letters to Lord Francis with erudite bits of etymological lore.[137] In cultivation he was his employer's equal; in business, his master and tutor. Such men demonstrated the power of professional excellence, and in time would cast doubt by their mere existence on the purported excellences of a hereditary aristocracy.

It may well be that after Loch's death in 1855 the race of barrister–auditor, never a very numerous one, dwindled away. The growth in social status of the solicitor may have been a factor at work. Some great families like the Fitzwilliams had looked upon the solicitor as a tradesman, fit to move in circles no higher than those found in the steward's room, and therefore unfit to serve as agent-in-chief of a great estate; but by the second half of the nineteenth century, as was noted earlier, it was becoming increasingly difficult to entertain this social prejudice. More important, both the barrister-auditor and the solicitor may have suffered at the hands of a new competitor, the professional land agent. Henry Morton's victory over Henry Stephenson on the estate of the Earls of Durham may have had more than local significance.

---

[137] *Ibid.*, Loch to Lord F. Egerton, Feb. 5, 1846.

# CHAPTER IV

# THE LAND AGENT

THE AGGLOMERATION OF ESTATES, the revolution in agriculture, the growth in mineral output—all contributed in some degree to the emergence during the eighteenth century of specialized activity in the management of land. Professor Hughes has noted that the word "agent" itself—used in connection with the management of landed estates—gained currency in the eighteenth century.[1] Possibly the substitution of "agent" for "steward" was a sign of the land agent's growing self-consciousness, of his attempt to make an occupation into a profession.[2] Some agents' handbooks plainly struck a note of professional self-consciousness at the end of the eighteenth century.[3]

Owing mainly to the accidents of research, this chapter will be concerned chiefly with land agents resident on large estates. Such agents specialized in the close, day-to-day supervision of a farming tenantry: receiving rents, selecting tenants, negotiating agreements and leases, maintaining and improving the

[1] Hughes, "The Eighteenth Century Estate Agent," in *Essays in British and Irish History*.

[2] Dr. Robson suggests that "linguistic affectations" may also have had their social significance in the rise of the attorney; see Robson, *The Attorney*, p. 152.

[3] N. Kent, *Hints to Gentlemen of Landed Property* (London, 1799), p. 245.

permanent equipment of the estate, spurring tenants to greater enterprise, participating in local government, even invigilating parochial morality.

This chapter will say little about agents in general business— for example, such London firms as the Cluttons, employed by the Ecclesiastical Commissioners, or Pickering and Smith, similarly employed, or such provincial firms as that of Thomas Smith Woolley of Newark or William Sturge of Bristol.[4] This neglect may have some warrant. Agents like the Cluttons often administered corporate estates [5]—and this book is chiefly concerned with private estates. Although it would be useful for an exhaustive account of estate administration to know more about such agents in general business as were connected with small private estates, it may be doubted that they were very different in outlook from the resident agents on the great estates.

# I

What was the social background and education of nineteenth-century land agents? Professor Hughes cites some examples of land agents in Hanoverian England who were cadets of landed families, or in some way related to such families, like Henry Ellison, nephew to Colonel George Liddell of Ravensworth, who became the Liddell agent in 1726. Even more impressive examples can be found a century or so later: Frederick Grey, son of Earl Grey of the Reform Bill, a naval Captain who managed the family estates in Northumberland from 1846 to 1852; [6] Algernon Egerton, second son of the Earl of Ellesmere,

---

[4] There is some mention of these agents in A. Clapham, *A Short History of the Surveyor's Profession* (London, 1949).

[5] This was implied by the Estate Committee of the Ecclesiastical Commissioners in its report on land agents and estate administration in 1862; see B.P.P., *Report of the Select Committee on the Ecclesiastical Commission* (1862, VIII), pp. 423–24.

[6] G. Lyster, ed., *A Family Chronicle* (London, 1908), p. 235.

who served on the family estates after 1855;[7] and Henry Noel, son of Lord Gainsborough, who was agent at Exton Park in 1851.[8]

But these examples probably do not signify much. In 1816 Lord Dudley expressed a preference for agents of high social standing—such as were to be found in Ireland.[9] But Dudley was an eccentric, and even he admitted that "this is an opinion that don't seem to prevail among the great lords of the soil; and they are, for the most part, better pleased to go on in the old way with their indigenous stewards and attornies." [10] It is not likely that Dudley's opinion prevailed at any time in the nineteenth century: that aristocratic families ever became an important source for the recruitment of land agents, or that land agency ever became a vocation mainly of the upper middle classes.

If land agents were not Lord Dudley's sort of gentleman, they were often—as Surtees once called them—"gentlemen of the second class": [11] that is, respectable men drawn largely from the provincial middle classes. Some with the highest reputation came from Scotland, part of that impressive migration of talent which marked Anglo-Scottish history. Francis Blaikie, agent to Coke of Norfolk, was a Scot; so were Andrew Thompson, agent to Ralph Sneyd, John Yule, agent to Sir James Graham, and John Matthew whom Caird recommended to Sir Robert Peel.[12] Blaikie's social origins are unknown.[13] But

[7] B. Falk, *The Bridgewater Millions* (London, 1942), chap. 9.

[8] Add. MSS, 36,472, folio 66, Sophia Hobhouse to Lord Broughton, 1851 (?). And there was Henry Petre who was agent to his brother, Lord Petre; see L. Petre, *The Life of the Hon. Henry W. Petre* (Privately printed, 1907).

[9] S. M. Hussey, *Reminiscences of an Irish Land Agent* (London, 1904), p. 41, quoted in Hughes, "The Eighteenth Century Estate Agent," in *Essays in British and Irish History.*

[10] Bishop of Llandaff, *Letters of the Earl of Dudley* (London, 1840), pp. 141–42.

[11] R. S. Surtees, *Ask Mama*, chap. XI.

[12] Add. MSS, 40,602, folios 269 ff., Caird to Sir R. Peel, Nov. 29, 1849.

[13] At any rate there is no mention of them in A. M. W. Stirling, *Coke of Norfolk and His Friends* (London, 1908), 2 vols.; or in A. M. W.

in all probability they were the same as Thompson's and Yule's and Matthews'—a Scottish farming family.

The social origins of English land agents were probably much the same. They tended to be sons of tenant farmers and yeomen; of land agents, builders, and surveyors; and of mining engineers. In a word they were sons of practical men, often familiar from youth with the varied business of land management. Henry Morton, agent to the Earls of Durham, came from substantial farming stock in the Northumberland border country.[14] Grey of Dilston, agent to the Greenwich Hospital estates in the North Country, came from a Northumbrian yeoman family.[15] The Dixons were for four generations agents of the Charlton family at Hesleyside in Northumberland.[16] For an even longer time the Wings were agents to the Dukes of Bedford on their Fen estate.[17] Robert Evans, George Eliot's father and agent to the Newdegate family in Warwickshire, was the son of a builder.[18] Hugh Taylor, Commissioner to the Duke of Northumberland, was the son of the Duke's mineral agent who was also a farmer.[19] William Sturge, the Bristol land agent, was the son and grandson of land agents.[20]

In 1896 the Royal Commission on the Land of Wales and Monmouthshire set down what it took to be the proper training of a land agent.

---

Stirling, *The Letter-Bag of Lady Elizabeth Spencer-Stanhope* (London, 1913), 2 vols.

[14] See Spring, "The Earls of Durham and the Great Northern Coal Field," *Can. Hist. Rev.*, Sept., 1952.

[15] J. E. Butler, *Memoir of John Grey of Dilston* (Edinburgh, 1869), *passim.*

[16] L. E. O. Charlton, ed., *The Recollections of a Northumbrian Lady 1815–1866* (London, 1949), pp. 126–27.

[17] See article in *D.N.B.* on an earlier Tycho Wing (1696–1750) which refers to the later Tycho (1794–1851) and to John Wing (1752–1812), both agents to the Dukes of Bedford.

[18] J. W. Cross, ed., *George Eliot's Life* (New York, n.d.), 3 vols., I, 2.

[19] Welford, *Men of Mark*, III, 494–97.

[20] E. Sturge, *Reminiscences of My Life* (Privately printed, 1928), pp. 71–78.

We think that such [an] agent should be one who in addition to a sound preliminary, general, and scientific education has received a special theoretical training in agriculture and land surveying, and in the sciences (such as mathematics, chemistry etc.) upon which the practise of these arts depends, as well as practical experience in an estate office and on a farm. To put the matter in another way, we think a young man, intending to become a land agent should, in addition to acquiring the average degree of culture and knowledge of a university man, attend courses of study at an agricultural college or a college giving technical instruction in the practical arts, and then pass some time gaining practical and actual experience in an office or on a farm. In short, we would have him prepare himself professionally in a manner analogous to that in which the physician qualifies himself to practice the art of medicine, or a solicitor that of the law.[21]

Of the land agents who figure prominently in this chapter—men who usually had passed their prime by the 1870's—none underwent much of this training. What is known of their formal education suggests that it was relatively slight. Henry Morton went to the famous High School in Edinburgh, a fellow pupil of Brougham and Jeffrey, but failed to go on with them to the University.[22] Grey of Dilston went to Dr. Tate's school in Yorkshire, and spent two further years being privately taught in the home of a Cumberland clergyman.[23] In all probability this kind of schooling was typical; land agents were products not of Oxford or Cambridge nor for that matter of London colleges or Scottish universities.

As to a theoretical training in agriculture, it was simply not available anywhere in England; at any rate not until the founding of the Royal Agricultural College at Cirencester in 1845.

[21] B.P.P., *Second Report of Royal Commission on Land in Wales and Monmouthshire* (1896, XXXIV), p. 258.
[22] Spring, "Agents to the Earls of Durham . . . ," *Durham Univ. Journ.*, June, 1962.
[23] Butler, *John Grey of Dilston*, p. 12.

This school was originally intended as a school for the sons of farmers, and might well have provided from its beginning a professional training for land agents.[24] But it seems that financial difficulties forced up fees to such an extent that farmers' sons found the College too expensive. It was thus largely used, as it was said in 1881, "for the sons of gentlemen." [25] Although some of its graduates became land agents—like S. D. Dodgson, agent to the Earl of Lonsdale, and Nevile Day, agent to the Earl of Westmorland—these were probably not typical products of the Royal Agricultural College.[26]

It would seem then that nineteenth-century land agents picked up their knowledge, both theoretical and practical, without the aid of much formal instruction. What theoretical knowledge they acquired—self-confessedly slight, since they took pride in their being practical men—came to them from books, journals, conversations, and from the meetings of local and national agricultural societies. Their practical knowledge was the product of a life bred to the soil—"from my cradle," as John Yule once observed to Sir James Graham.[27] Some agents, like William Sturge, were articled to surveyors—Sturge himself entering his father's Bristol office at the age of sixteen.[28] Some went as pupils to an established agent, like John Beasley, the Spencers' agent at Althorp, who trained young men as he trained his sons: [29] probably in much the way Caleb Garth instructed his nephew, Fred Vincey. And some took to land agency as a side line to their own farming. This emphasis on the

[24] *Mark Lane Express,* July 3, 1843, for an account of the projected agricultural college.

[25] B.P.P., *Rep. of R.C. on the Depressed Condition of the Agricultural Interests* (1881, XVII), p. 820.

[26] C. Bathurst and E. Kinch, eds., *Register of the Staff and Students of the Royal Agricultural College* (Cirencester, 1897), *passim.*

[27] Netherby MSS, Yule to Sir J. Graham, July 4, 1843.

[28] Sturge, *Reminiscences,* pp. 71–78.

[29] Beasley was also agent to Lord Overstone. His farming was commended in Caird, *English Agriculture,* pp. 421–34. Landowners from all parts of England sought out their agents from among his pupils.

practical was probably not misplaced, given the nature of much of the agent's work.[30]

It would be misleading to suggest that all land agents were of the type here described. There was reason for the remark made by Miss Aldclyffe in Thomas Hardy's *Desperate Remedies*: "a steward's is an indefinite, fast and loose profession, it seems to me." [31] Some men made their way into it, or offered to enter it, with little or no experience of farming and estate business, often for the very good reason of having nothing else to do. In the 1890's the complaint was still heard that too many ex-soldiers and sailors took to land agency.[32] Miss Mitford was quite sure that her father would make a reasonably good agent, although he had been trained as a doctor.[33] Robert Oastler, agent to the Thornhills at Fixby in Yorkshire, was until the age of fifty-three a cloth merchant. His better-known son, Richard, the humanitarian reformer, who succeeded him at Fixby, first sought his livelihood as a commission agent in the cloth trade after having gained some experience of an architect's office.[34]

Still it is not likely that the great estates often employed such men—or even that such men frequently offered themselves for employment on the great estates. For what it is worth, there is the example of Cornwall Legh, owner of a moderately sized estate in Cheshire, who lost his agent in a fatal accident in 1859, with the result that a number of men made application to fill the vacancy. All but one of them had had some farming experience. Most of them had sought some sort of practical experience as agent: one had been a pupil under H. W. Keary, the Earl of Leicester's agent on his Holkham estate in Norfolk;

[30] Carr-Saunders and Wilson, *The Professions*, pp. 376–79.
[31] T. Hardy, *Desperate Remedies*, chap. 7.
[32] Smith, *Principles of Estate Management*, p. 298.
[33] A. G. L. Estrange, *The Life of Mary Russell Mitford* (London, 1870), 3 vols., III, 163–64.
[34] C. H. Driver, *Tory Radical: The Life of Richard Oastler* (New York, 1946), pp. 18–20.

another had gone to the Royal Agricultural College, thence to the estate office of T. S. Wooley and to a farmer on the Lincolnshire wolds to see "the best agriculture in England." [35]

Qualified men managed to obtain the positions even under landowners so little acquainted with farming and estate business as Ralph Sneyd. In 1848 he was known to be looking for an agent, and Sir Francis Lawley mentioned this fact to his friend, Charles Arbuthnot, the Tory politician and intimate of the Duke of Wellington. Arbuthnot happened to own a small estate at Woodford in Northamptonshire, small enough to require no more than the services of a farm bailiff. For fifteen to twenty years he had employed as bailiff two brothers, Scots named Thompson, first one and then the other. The first eventually left to become agent to the Duke of Beaufort. The second, Andrew, was Arbuthnot's choice as agent to Ralph Sneyd. Andrew had recently married, and his brother-in-law objected to his remaining a bailiff. Arbuthnot also thought that Andrew was "more fit to be agent to some one of great landed property than to remain with me." [36] Fortunately there was a third Thompson brother ready to take Andrew's place at Woodford—which he did, rendering the same satisfaction as his brothers had before him.[37]

Andrew Thompson proved a happy find for Sneyd. He was but twenty-six years of age and had already come to the notice of Josiah Parkes, the drainage engineer, and by him had been recommended as an Assistant Commissioner under the Public Money Drainage Act.[38] The Duke of Northumberland had also heard of Andrew Thompson's abilities, in particular of his system of accounting, and had requested an example of it. Arbuthnot found him "one of the most intelligent men, in respect to all agricultural concerns, that I ever knew." No one,

[35] Cornwall Legh MSS, T. S. Wooley to Countess Macclesfield, Dec. 29, 1859.

[36] Sneyd MSS, C. Arbuthnot to R. Sneyd, June 23, 1848.

[37] Add. MSS, 40,602, folios 68–69, C. Arbuthnot to Sir R. Peel, Aug. 22, 1849; folios 325 ff., C. Arbuthnot to Sir R. Peel, Dec. 7, 1849.

[38] There is an account of this Act in the next chapter.

he concluded, "would be so likely to introduce a good system into a badly farmed district." [39]

# II

Of all his functions that of introducing a good system of farming was what the land agent took as chief. And to do so, as most agents were aware, needed certain qualities of mind and spirit.

According to Beasley, an efficient agent needed to be "an active man." [40] Few things are more conspicuous than the incessant industry of the leading land agents in the nineteenth century—of which Grey of Dilston's labors provide an example. The Greenwich Hospital estates to which he came in the 1830's were widely scattered, so that he had to travel almost to Carlisle in the west, to Berwick-on-Tweed in the north, and to Newcastle in the east. "When I went there," he said in his old age,

> I was almost killed in the first year and a half; for I rode over every farm and every field, and I made a report every night when I came home of its value and its capabilities, whether you could employ water power instead of horse power, and so on. This was a thing that every one could not have done, but I had been brought up in the country, and seven or eight hours in the saddle was no great matter to me.[41]

Agents like Grey of Dilston seemed to go on endlessly, with little rest from their labors. John Beasley himself died in his seventy-third year, but not until the age of sixty did he miss the holding of a rental audit on the Spencer estates.[42] Three

---

[39] Sneyd MSS, C. Arbuthnot to R. Sneyd, June 23, 1848.

[40] J. Beasley, *The Duties and Privileges of the Landowners, Occupiers and Cultivators of the Soil* (London, 1860).

[41] B.P.P., *Report of the Commissioners appointed to inquire into Greenwich Hospital* (1860, XXX), p. 120.

[42] Althorp MSS, L. Beasley to Earl Spencer, Jan. 14, 1861.

years later he reported to the Earl that a hard summer's work left him "disposed to run away, if only for a few days, but something always springs up to make it inconvenient." [43] A son, who followed the family profession as his father's assistant, complained of a want of work, to which the father replied, "I cannot help this, that is, I must do all that I can, so long as I am able to do it." [44] At the very end, on his death bed, he was uneasy lest his son forget the date of the Brington Rent Days.[45]

Versatility, no less than activity, was held a desirable quality in an agent. The good agent, Beasley declared, should "be enough of a builder to know how a building can be well and economically done"; "enough of an engineer to design and direct ordinary engineering works; he should understand draining works and be something of a chemist and a geologist." [46] This sort of versatility was not uncommon among the leading land agents. Grey of Dilston, for example, came to an estate on which lead, iron ore, and coal were mined, and although unfamiliar with mining business he set out to learn it, himself valuing the whole estate "instead of having it done for him, that he might be independent of everyone." [47] Henry Morton took over responsibility for the management of the Lambton collieries in 1827, having up to that time apparently been in charge of the Lambtons' agricultural concerns. George Eliot remarked that her father, Robert Evans, had without special training acquired a "large knowledge of building, of mines, of plantations, of various branches of valuation and measurement,—of all that is essential to the management of large estates." [48] Plainly in these matters professionalism was not yet the enemy of versatility.

However varied and numerous an agent's skills, fundamental to them all was his skill in farming, and what hung on that, his

[43] *Ibid.*, Beasley to Earl Spencer, Oct. 6, 1864.
[44] *Ibid.*, Beasley to Earl Spencer, March 6, 1865.
[45] *Ibid.*, Joseph Beasley (the son) to Earl Spencer, Jan. 19, 1874.
[46] Beasley, *Duties and Privileges.*
[47] Butler, *John Grey of Dilston*, pp. 156–57.
[48] Cross, *George Eliot's Life*, I, 23.

skill in the management of his tenantry. As Beasley put it, "farming is the grammar of an agent's education." [49] The land agent of the nineteenth century—at any rate of the era of high farming—paid more attention to his tenants' farming than his predecessors had, being less content (as Surtees, the novelist, observed of agents in county Durham) with "receiving what they could, and drinking the landlord's health twice a year," and more inclined to "urge their tenants to activity." [50] F. F. Fox, the agent on the Melbourne estate, reported to his employer in 1850, "a constant effort requires to be made to induce the farmers to keep up and improve their cultivation." [51]

If we are to believe Caleb Garth, the effort brought its own reward. As he put it, "it's a fine thing to come to a man when he's seen into the nature of business: to have a chance of getting a bit of the country into good fettle, as they say, and putting men in the right way with their farming, and getting a bit of good contriving and solid building done." [52]

To improve was also a duty, as was noted in the previous chapter. Sometime in the eighteenth century, perhaps earlier, land agent's manuals began to view agricultural improvements as an obligation of both tenants and landowners. Writing at the end of the century William Marshall declared: "A tenanted estate differs widely from other species of property. . . . It has a dignity, and a set of duties, attached to it, which are peculiar to itself." [53] A recent work on the sociology of the professions has suggested that in the process by which an occupation becomes a profession those engaged in that occupation "claim a *mandate* to define what is proper conduct of others toward the matters concerned with their work." [54]

[49] Beasley, *Duties and Privileges*.
[50] R. S. Surtees and E. D. Cuming, *Robert Smith Surtees (Creator of Jorrocks), 1803–64* (Edinburgh and London, 1924), p. 158.
[51] Panshanger MSS, Fox to Lord Melbourne, Sept. 4, 1850.
[52] Eliot, *Middlemarch*, chap. 40.
[53] W. Marshall, *On the Landed Property of England, An Elementary and Practical Treatise; containing the Purchase, the Improvement, and the Management of Landed Estates* (London, 1804), p. 335.
[54] E. C. Hughes, *Men and their Work* (Glencoe, Illinois, 1958), p. 78.

Something like this may very well have happened among land agents by the end of the eighteenth century, as the mood of professionalism began to overtake their occupation. By the 1860's Beasley might even state with a flourish: "That man who owns or occupies an acre of land, and does not make it produce all it is capable of producing is an enemy to his country." [55]

More soberly put, this was the message of high farming—of which James Caird was a noted popularizer. Its object was to increase productivity in order (it was hoped) to withstand a fall in agricultural prices. It emphasized several things. There was a general emphasis on effecting capital improvements, the most important of which were draining and new farm buildings, and on employing scientific discoveries such as artificial fertilizers, new feeding stuffs, and improved implements. There was a particular emphasis on the integration and intensification of mixed farming, that is, of the system which makes complementary use of crops and livestock. Drained fields and liberal application of manure and artificial fertilizer led to increased crops, some part of which (along with new feeding stuffs) was fed to fatten livestock. Better housing for livestock and more efficient means of preserving manure led to greater fertility in the field, and thus the circle of mixed farming was expanded. This stepping-up of productivity inevitably involved land agents in a closer supervision of their farming tenantry.

It began with the selection of tenants before they came onto the estate, and persisted throughout the occupation of their farms. The problems of selection confronting agents of the great estates in the nineteenth century were not unlike those described by a historian of eighteenth-century farming.[56] Landowners and agents in the nineteenth century as in the eighteenth preferred large to small farms, since the large units made for savings in buildings and management. Large farms meant large tenants: that is, men of large capital, of skill and

[55] Beasley, *Duties and Privileges.*
[56] G. E. Mingay, "The Size of Farms in the Eighteenth Century," *The Economic History Review,* April, 1962.

industry and good character. But such farmers were never plentiful, and it was important that their credentials be carefully scrutinized. Not unnaturally agents preferred to find them through personal knowledge. One of Grey of Dilston's first innovations on the Greenwich Hospital estate was to abolish the system of tender previously employed in the letting of estate farms.[57] John Yule avoided advertising his vacant farms if he could help it; he preferred local men whom he knew—and who in turn knew the farming of the locality.[58]

On one occasion Yule was left with no choice. This happened in 1842, at a time when many farms, including the largest ones on the Netherby estate, were up for re-letting. For almost two decades Yule had followed a policy of extensive improvements, a policy which had involved Sir James Graham in large expenditure.[59] Yule hoped in 1842 to gain some interest on that expenditure in the shape of increased rents. The largest farmers on the estate, however, balked at his proposal; they were frightened, he thought, by the drift of Sir Robert Peel's legislation. Yule was nettled and found the fact hard to conceal. "From the first," he wrote to Sir James, "I foresaw great difficulty in managing a few of your first class Farmers, but I little expected the arrogance and vexation I have experienced." [60] But accustomed to having his way with the farmers under him, he proceeded to take steps against them.

In March he recommended that the "four best farms" on the estate be advertised in such local newspapers as the Carlisle *Patriot* and the Dumfries *Northern Advertiser*. Sir James, however, advised that they postpone advertisement until later in the year, possibly in the hope that his old tenants would yield. Accordingly Yule waited until the beginning of July when he

[57] B.P.P., *Rep. into Greenwich Hospital*, p. 118.
[58] Netherby MSS, Yule to Sir J. Graham, April 29, 1842. Neither on the Duke of Bedford's estates nor on the several estates managed by John Beasley were farms advertised or let by tender; see Caird, *English Agriculture*, pp. 432, 435.
[59] Spring, "A Great Agricultural Estate . . . ," *Agric. Hist.*, April, 1955.
[60] Netherby MSS, Yule to Sir J. Graham, March 29, 1842.

reported to Sir James, "I believe by this evening our four best farms are advertised over all Scotland and the north of England." [61] For all his perseverance, one suspects that Yule's heart was not in it. A fortnight later he made the doleful announcement that a Lincolnshire farmer had shown some interest in Netherby—but "I fear his ideas are quite incompatible with matters here." [62] It may be—although there is no sure evidence on the matter—that Yule was bluffing his tenants, that he thought he might intimidate them by advertising their farms. And in fact he may have done just that. In August the tenants relented and Yule sighed with relief.[63]

Side by side with the problems of finding and keeping the right tenant, there was the problem of getting rid of the wrong one. This may have presented less difficulty by the mid-nineteenth century than earlier. If Surtees was correct in his observation that "the old-fashioned agents" would "always rather excite their principals to compassion than urge the tenants to activity," [64] there would seem to be less compassion in the hearts of a later generation of agents. Henry Morton, for example, spoke harshly of farmers in county Durham: "a very stupid set . . . and excessively timid"; [65] he was quite prepared to believe that incendiarism in the North was the work of farmers trying to defraud the insurance company.[66] There was, of course, less reason for compassion after the lifting of the agricultural depression of the 1830's and the invention of draining techniques and appliances which rendered the condition of even the most unfortunate farmers—the small ones on the cold clays—capable of amelioration.

In 1836 Morton resolved that "three or four Tenants must be removed from time to time" [67]—a policy that proved overly ambitious during a period of agricultural depression. Later, in

[61] *Ibid.*, Yule to Sir J. Graham, July 1, 1842.
[62] *Ibid.*, Yule to Sir J. Graham, July 7, 1842.
[63] *Ibid.*, Yule to Sir J. Graham, Aug. 22, 1842.
[64] Surtees and Cuming, *Robert Smith Surtees*, p. 158.
[65] Lambton MSS, Morton to Lord Durham, Dec. 9, 1830.
[66] *Ibid.*, Morton to Lord Durham, Feb. 28, 1834.
[67] *Ibid.*, Morton to Lord Durham, May 22, 1836.

a more prosperous time when "Farms can readily be let," [68] Morton informed the Earl of Durham that "I intend to weed the farmers every year." [69] In 1857 he removed six of them from the estate.[70] There is no way of knowing the precise effects throughout English rural society of this policy which many land agents probably adopted. But Sir Charles Wood's prediction—that "small unskillful farmers will share the fate of the handloom weavers"—may well have had some truth in it.[71]

The policy of weeding the tenantry ran headlong into a principle which agents had in varying degree respected—that of continuity, "the system of succession from father to son," [72] as one of them put it. William Marshall had likened the tenantry to plants, rooted in the soil.[73] Agents of a later generation, anxious under the spur of Corn-Law repeal to find "the kind of men best adapted to meet any changes," [74] were apt to be sceptical of the beneficial results of the principle of continuity. F. F. Fox was "convinced that nothing has injured both landlords and tenants more than a confidence on the part of the latter that be their character and conduct or that of their children what it may, or whatever may be the circumstances in which they are left, they will still be continued in the tenancy." [75] Henry Morton confessed that to violate the principle of continuity was "unpopular and unpleasant"; but not to do so when circumstances warranted it ended only "in greater disappointment and evil . . . [tenants'] moral feelings [becoming] blunted as to render a change of conduct impossible almost." [76]

[68] *Ibid.*, Morton to Lord Durham, Nov. 8, 1854.
[69] *Ibid.*, Morton to Lord Durham, Dec. 16, 1857.
[70] *Ibid.*
[71] Add. MSS, 40,602, folio 13, Sir C. Wood to Sir R. Peel, July, 1849.
[72] Panshanger MSS, Fox to Lord Melbourne, Dec. 1847.
[73] Marshall, *On the Landed Property of England*, p. 334.
[74] Panshanger MSS, Fox to Lord Melbourne, Dec. 1847.
[75] *Ibid.*, Fox to Lord Melbourne, Dec. 3, 1852. David Low, professor of agriculture in the University of Edinburgh, was less critical of continuity; see his *On Landed Property and the Economy of Estates* (London, 1856), p. 19.
[76] Lambton MSS, Morton to Lord Durham, Jan. 14, 1856.

There were, however, emollients which agents applied when tenant families of long standing were removed. In the previous chapter, note was taken of the pensions granted to aged tenants on the Duke of Bedford's estates. Pensions and gifts were also given there to sons and daughters whom the agents judged unfit to succeed to a farm, as in the case of the Chettles on the Fen estate, where a shiftless son was given a gift of £100, and an infirm daughter a pension.[77] When Fox insisted on keeping a farm from falling into the hands of a drunken nephew, the heir of his aged uncle, the old man was given a house on the estate rent free and a pension.[78] In 1839 Yule served notice to quit on Robert Ferguson, the tenant of Bush on Lyne, one of the larger farms on the Netherby estate, but gave him the opportunity of taking a smaller farm; since, as Yule put it, "your forefathers and yourself having for many years been farmers under the Netherby family." [79]

Once an agent had his tenants sorted out, the inefficient removed and the promising installed, he could then proceed to impose on them a set of rules, or farming covenants. If Cadle's prize essay for the Royal Agricultural Society provides a representative account of covenants on great estates, their chief object in the 1860's was—as it had been in the eighteenth century [80]—to keep the tenant from violating the minimum decencies of good farming: he must keep up repairs; he must not plant two crops of wheat or more than two white straw crops in succession; he must keep down weeds in the hedges, ditches, and waste lands; and in general, he must "cultivate and manage the said farm and lands in a good and husbandlike manner." [81]

[77] Bedford MSS, Annual Reports, 1861.
[78] Panshanger MSS, Fox to Lord Melbourne, Nov. 27, 1852.
[79] Netherby MSS, Yule to R. Ferguson, July 9, 1839.
[80] H. J. Habakkuk, "Economic Functions of English Landowners in the Seventeenth and Eighteenth Centuries," *Explorations in Entrepreneurial History*, no. 2, 1953–4.
[81] C. Cadle, "The Farming Customs and Covenants of England," *The Journal of the Royal Agricultural Society*, 1868.

Covenants were probably found on all great estates, although one is less certain how firmly they were enforced, especially in the bad years between 1815 and 1840. Certainly Yule brought his tenants quickly to heel, serving notices to quit if necessary. On the Duke of Bedford's estate, however, during the 1830's, there was some laxity. Bennett, the Woburn agent, found that one of his tenants who was required to leave 45 acres of fallow for turnips sowed 15 with peas. Being an injurious crop in that period of rotation, Bennett insisted that the tenant plough it up. The tenant was reluctant at first, but was finally persuaded. Haedy applauded Bennett's firmness: "The feeling that the Duke of Bedford must not do what other landlords were fairly entitled to do had almost become a morbid feeling of which much advantage has heretofore been unfairly taken." It is probable that such laxity was less common after 1840 than before.

It may be, however, that land agents, especially in the 1860's, held to their covenants, and particularly their cropping covenants, too rigidly. As Caird predicted, livestock prices rose while grain prices remained stationary. It therefore became increasingly advisable for tenants to lean more heavily on the livestock side of mixed farming. This involved adjustments in their covenants. It is not clear to what extent the needed flexibility was introduced. Farmers may well have encountered stubborn resistance on the part of some land agents who clung tenaciously to orthodoxy in farming techniques at the expense of economic efficiency.[82]

A secondary object of covenants—to which Cadle also bears witness—was to encourage virtue rather than prohibit vice. This was seen in the covenants that provided compensation for unexhausted improvements, for what was known as tenant right: as when a tenant had drained his farm or part of it in a permanent and satisfactory manner; or had used artificial ma-

[82] See W. Ashworth, *An Economic History of England: 1870–1939* (London, 1960), p. 48, where it is suggested that some tenants may also have been conservative.

nure on his land. Two decades earlier Lord Yarborough's agent had pointed out in the *Journal of the Royal Agricultural Society* that tenant right on Lord Yarborough's Lincolnshire estate relied not on written agreements but on the custom of the country.[83] In 1851 F. F. Fox advised Lord Melbourne to draw up specific requirements with his tenants concerning unexhausted improvements because "the custom of the country [was] gradually, perhaps I ought to say rapidly altering everywhere in favor of the improving tenant farmer." [84] It may be that by Cadle's time many landowners had accepted this advice, and introduced a modest form of tenant right.

Some agents preferred to make their tenants secure by means of the long lease. This was James Caird's preference, and Caird often spoke for the agents on the great estates. He complained of tenant right on several grounds: that it might lead to fraud, even to poor farming.[85] North Country agents like Yule and Grey of Dilston were all for leases: how else to attract tenants of capital? [86] Yule was thunderstruck when he learned that there were no leases on Sir Robert Peel's estate: "a Tenancy from year to year is a complete ban to all improvement." [87] But Beasley, it should be noted, did without leases too—and as Caird himself reported, without diminishing his tenants' enterprise.[88]

High farming demanded not only a close supervision of the tenantry but also an extensive program of permanent improve-

[83] G. M. Williams, "On the Tenant's Right to unexhausted Improvements, according to the Custom of North Lincolnshire," *The Journal of the Royal Agricultural Society*, 1845.

[84] Panshanger MSS, Fox to Lord Melbourne, Nov. 25, 1851. It is to be noted that the Select Committee on Agricultural Customs, of which Philip Pusey was chairman, had recommended tenant right on a voluntary basis; see B.P.P., *Report from the Select Committee on Agricultural Customs* (1847–8, VII).

[85] Caird, *English Agriculture*, pp. 505–7.

[86] See J. Grey of Dilston, "A View of the past and present state of Agriculture in Northumberland," *The Journal of the Royal Agricultural Society*, 1841.

[87] Netherby MSS, Yule to Sir J. Graham, March 17, 1841.

[88] Caird, *English Agriculture*, pp. 432–33.

ments such as we have seen undertaken on the Duke of Bedford's estate. After 1840 one heard less of the sort of advice offered the Duke of Northumberland by his agents in 1836: "the new occupants require so much to be done, in Buildings, Draining and Fences, when they enter, that it is better to yield a small diminution of Rent, and keep an old Tenant on the premises." [89] Instead the talk was all for improvements and putting the tenant, as Fox said in 1847, "on a good footing to meet the times." [90]

Of all farming improvements, "draining is the first or foundation," as Andrew Thompson once put it; the necessary preparation "for other improvements which ought to be made by the landlord or his occupier in the shape of improved cultivation and manures, of improved Buildings, and frequently a fresh arrangement of the fields." [91] Few if any agents disagreed with him. The subject of draining was considered important enough, especially in the 1840's and '50's, for some of them to draw up a brief lecture on its fundamentals for the benefit of their employers. Hugh Taylor, the fourth Duke of Northumberland's Commissioner, composed a succinct memorandum for the Duke in the estate's Business Minutes, explaining the action of subsoil moisture—"this inferior moisture which may be regarded as a reservoir coextensive with the Country." As he went on to explain, it furnished moisture to the upper soil by evaporation and capillary action: "A great degree of cold is thus produced, and as it is during the spring months that the subsoil is wettest, the growth of the plant is injured by this transmission of damp and cold just at the time when it requires most nursing." [92]

Land agents may well have allowed themselves to be carried

[89] Alnwick Castle MSS, D. W. Smith to 3rd Duke of Northumberland, July 30, 1836.
[90] Panshanger MSS, Fox to Lord Melbourne, Dec., 1847.
[91] Sneyd MSS, A. Thompson's reports to the Inclosure Commissioners, vol. 5, March 15, 1865. Surtees, in a mocking mood, had Jorrocks say something of the same kind in *Hillingdon Hall*, chap. XIII.
[92] Alnwick Castle MSS, Business Minutes, Feb. 29, 1848.

away by their enthusiasm for new techniques and appliances, and particularly by their enthusiasm for the ideas of Josiah Parkes, high priest of deep draining. Beginning in 1848, Hugh Taylor employed Parkes to supervise the draining of 7,300 acres of the wettest land on the Percy estates.[93] Some agents like F. F. Fox, although aware that they might be acting hastily, concluded that "we should lose more by waiting to learn what is the very best system that can be adopted (the land and the tenants suffering greatly all the while) than we should gain by adopting the system several years hence."[94] As it turned out, landowners and agents paid a price for their haste. The Earl of Leicester's agent reported to the Select Committee on the Improvement of Land in 1873 that some drainage systems were being dug up because of the inefficiency of Parkes's one-inch pipes;[95] and other witnesses testified to the speculative element in draining.[96] But Fox was still right; the gains probably outweighed the losses, as large areas of farmland produced earlier and cheaper crops.

Agents often had to arouse the enthusiasm of tenants, who were at first sceptical of innovation and reluctant to shoulder the burden of additional rent. What was more, agents had to persuade tenants that the work would best be done—not by themselves, for they were apt to do it poorly[97]—but by a draining agent especially employed for the purpose. On Lord Melbourne's estate Fox at first found it hard to persuade the tenants to drain 1,000 acres of land most in need of it. Once

[93] *Ibid.*, Business Minutes, Nov. 26, 1855.
[94] Panshanger MSS, Fox to Lord Melbourne, Nov. 25, 1850.
[95] B.P.P., *Rep. of S.C. on Improvement of Land*, p. 175.
[96] *Ibid.*, p. iv. See H. N. Nicholson, *The Principles of Field Drainage* (Cambridge, 1942) for a modern study on the subject. Nicholson points out (p. 65) that tile drainage is commonly regarded as a permanent improvement, but "there is room for doubt as to whether permanent improvement . . . can be effected" in really heavy land and the major clay areas.
[97] As a Drainage Commissioner Andrew Thompson often had cause to report on the poor draining set out by the tenants; see Sneyd MSS, Thompson's reports to the Inclosure Commissioners, vol. 8, July 27, 1868.

he brought them round, he hired a draining engineer who set out the drains and was paid five per cent on the outlay.[98]

Writing to Sir Robert Peel in 1850, James Caird observed, "It will be vain to drain the land and fit it for the culture of green crops, if no suitable housing is provided for economically converting these into a marketable form, and for preserving and accumulating manure." [99] This was a commonplace among agents. Along with it went an awareness of a revolution under way in farm architecture: in the size, design, and structural material of farm buildings.[100] As Fox put it, "the whole system of building Farm premises is undergoing a change." [101] It followed that an enterprising tenantry must be provided with more efficient buildings than their ancestors had made do with. Hence Fox's lament to Lord Melbourne, that he found a "great deficiency of cattle accommodation . . . In many cases the main buildings are bad and inconveniently situated and must at a future time be removed." [102]

In 1843 Grey of Dilston, writing in the *Journal of the Royal Agricultural Society*, proclaimed this deficiency in farm buildings a national phenomenon.

No one can have travelled much in the rural districts of England, even in those which are comparatively well cultivated, without being struck, if he have any sense of neatness and order, with the ill-arranged and patch-work appearance of many of the farm buildings, which are often placed, in relation to their different parts, in utter defiance of the economy of labour in the case of cattle; and what is still worse, with little regard to the production and preservation of the manure, the dry parts of

[98] Panshanger MSS, Fox to Lord Melbourne, Nov. 5, 19, 1850. As an informed witness before the Select Committee on Agricultural Customs put it: "The landlords are now becoming wiser than they were; they keep some person they can depend upon to put in the tiles under their own superintendance." (B.P.P., *Rep. of S.C. on Agricultural Customs*, p. 30.)

[99] Add. MSS, 40,603, folio 134. Caird to Sir R. Peel, March 20, 1850.

[100] N. Harvey, *The Farming Kingdom* (London, 1955), pp. 45–46.

[101] Panshanger MSS, Fox to Lord Melbourne, Nov. 13, 1851.

[102] *Ibid.*

which may be seen exposed to the winds, and the liquid part carried off without being applied to any beneficial purpose.[103]

Besides providing tenants with permanent improvements, the more enthusiastic among agents took the further step of instructing them in the most recent developments in the agricultural world. Some introduced their tenants to the subsoil plough, or to oilcake for cattle. Lord Chichester's agent sent a tenant, chosen by his fellows at the estate audit dinner, to the annual meeting of the Royal Agricultural Society; on his return he reported on his experiences at the "Royal" to the next audit dinner.[104] Grey of Dilston set on foot a farmers' club for the purpose of discussing agricultural affairs, and put at its disposal a library on agricultural subjects; he also established farmers' societies on the Greenwich Hospital estates in which farmers competed for prizes.[105]

The farmers' society was employed to nurture enterprise through competition and emulation. Yule's society at Netherby offered a long list of prizes: for "the best managed, manured and cultivated" turnip crop; for the best potato crop; for the best cow of Galloway breed; for the best brood cart mare of the pure Scotch breed; etc. The farms on the estate were classified according to size, and a prize was awarded to the best managed farm of each class.[106] Fox was delighted with the results of his own society: as he wrote to Lord Melbourne, "prizes for the best crops of Swedish turnips etc. were for the first time given, and one was won by a tenant on land at Selston which I could scarcely let at 10 s. per acre two or three years since." [107]

[103] J. Grey of Dilston, "On Farm Buildings," *The Journal of the Royal Agricultural Society*, 1843.

[104] Bedford MSS, 7th Duke to Haedy, Aug. 20, 1844.

[105] Butler, *John Grey of Dilston*, pp. 162–63.

[106] Netherby MSS, announcement of premiums offered by the Netherby Farmers' Society, 1837.

[107] Panshanger MSS, Fox to Lord Melbourne, Oct. 30, 1852.

# III

John Yule once remarked to Sir James Graham, "I have since early youth had the management of numerous sets of Tenantry —some of them ill enough to guide, but as yet I have never failed by just, determined and firm conduct to carry my point." [108] There is a note of paternalism here, suggestive of the attitude which agents like Yule took to the tenants and agricultural laborers on their estates. John Beasley spoke of the "agricultural family," comprising landowner, agent, tenant, and laborer.[109] Being a family, its head, the landowner or his agent, provided a sort of leadership which went beyond purely economic relations into all corners of rural life.

Accordingly the agent took his place in the several spheres of local government. Sometimes he even reached the Commission of the Peace. It was the custom in Derbyshire for the agents of the Dukes of Devonshire and Rutland—the great landowners in that part of the world—to sit on the Derbyshire Bench. In 1853 the Lord Chancellor challenged this practice; eventually he acquiesced in it on the ground of their being few resident landowners in north Derbyshire. He had notified the Duke of Devonshire that the practice was "not quite without precedent, yet very unusual." [110] In fact Grey of Dilston was justice of the peace for two counties; Henry Morton for county Durham—as was James Buddle, the noted colliery engineer who was agent to the Marquis of Londonderry.

It was much more usual, however, for the land agent to take his place on the lower levels of local government, such as the parish vestry and the poor-law union. An agent like F. F. Fox clearly appreciated what a paternal policy might effect there. As he explained to Lord Melbourne, the agent

[108] Netherby MSS, Yule to Sir J. Graham, April 27, 1838.
[109] Beasley, *Duties and Privileges*.
[110] Chatsworth MSS, Lord Chancellor to 6th Duke of Devonshire, April 5, 1853.

ought to see that all Parish affairs are properly conducted, and also the different charities, so as to ensure their being fairly and judiciously applied—above all he ought to see that proper means of education are provided for all, and that efforts are made to induce the poorer families more particularly to take advantage of them—The want of proper training and education in early life has (taking the lowest and most practical point of view) a very powerful and certain tendency to increase the amount of parochial burdens.[111]

Agents like Fox saw themselves as guardians of parochial morality, and they held it their duty to look into the private lives of their tenants and laborers.[112] When the leading tenants on the Netherby estate proposed to form a coursing club, Yule forbade it on the ground that it led to "gambling and idleness." [113] John Beasley kept a close eye on the moral condition of the laborers, periodically looking into the bastardy rate in the Spencer cottages. "Your Lordship has only 26 cottages," he reported in October, 1860, "and in these I found an addition of three illegitimate children since I was over them in June"; [114] he recommended that the local schools be more closely supervised. The Duke of Newcastle's agent at Clumber was somewhat less enthusiastic about his role as guardian of the local morality. He was prepared to remove the most offensive delinquents on the estate—but warned that depopulation might be the result "if all the immoral characters are to be discharged." [115]

In the nonagricultural affairs of the landed estate, the agent's rule might be of a far sterner sort. Much depended, it would seem, on the degree of social inertia of the laboring population. If the laborers became restive, the agent might show a forbidding harshness. So at least did Henry Morton when the miners of county Durham took to striking. Few land agents were so placed as Morton was: in charge of large mineral

[111] Panshanger MSS, Fox to Lord Melbourne, Sept. 4, 1850.
[112] Ibid.
[113] Netherby MSS, Yule to Sir J. Graham, Feb. 25, 1836.
[114] Althorp MSS, Beasley to Earl Spencer, Oct. 23, 1860.
[115] Newcastle MSS, Henning to 5th Duke of Newcastle, Sept. 14, 1860.

concerns, he was the manager of something like 1,200 pitmen and colliery workers. His dealings with them in 1830–31 are revealing, and might profitably be considered at some length.[116]

The winter months of 1830–31 found Morton advising the Earl on how best to keep order in the colliery districts where a strike threatened. His recommendations were few and simple: first, that the great families take the lead, else the gentry would capitulate; second, that the Earl organize a troop of yeomanry among his tenants and dependants to be stationed in the colliery premises; and third, that when force was used chief reliance be put on the regular troops. "When a mob is quelled," he wrote, "by the regulars and even lives lost—tho' the animosity may be as great towards them for the time being—the troops are soon removed to a distance, and those feelings die away—but from the yeomanry being stationary it is long before these feelings are allayed." [117]

When the pitmen went out on strike, Morton promptly made a show of force, and refused to bargain with the men. He requested the Durham justices to post the troops at Sunderland among the colliery villages. Then he proposed to set such men to work as wished to work; to turn out "some of the worst disposed Pitmen" from their houses; [118] and if the strikers took the law into their own hands, to have them arrested. He himself would "go the first day and station myself with 20 or 25 men in the Engine house"; [119] he had taken the precaution of buying some old muskets. On April 26, having received word that the troops had been sent, he was confident that "this plan will bring the matter to a crisis . . . the Union must fall to pieces." "If they do attack me," Morton assured the Earl, "several must be killed which will more rapidly put an end to the matter." [120]

Within little more than a fortnight, Morton's plan succeeded

---

[116] B.P.P., *Report of the Select Committee on the State of the Coal Trade* (1836, XI), p. 84. This story is told at greater length in Spring, "Agents to the Earls of Durham . . . ," *Durham Univ. Journ.,* June, 1962.

[117] Lambton MSS, Morton to Lord Durham, Dec. 6, 1830.

[118] *Ibid.,* Morton to Lord Durham, April 17, 1831.

[119] *Ibid.,* Morton to Lord Durham, April 18, 1831.

[120] *Ibid.,* Morton to Lord Durham, April 26, 1831.

at Lumley pit. On April 28, he had reported "near 50 Men and Boys in the Pit today." [121] A party of miners had marched on Lumley, but surprised to find troops there, they had dispersed; Morton regretted "that we did not come to blows . . . being so admirably prepared to meet them." [122] With something like pride he announced to the Earl that the men disliked him enough to have dug a grave for him. By May 9 he had noted signs of disunion among the strikers; and ten days later he triumphantly reported that the Lumley pitmen had accepted his terms, yielding when they saw their comrades being paid. Morton observed with some bitterness that he would get no thanks from the other coal owners for setting this example at Lumley.[123]

A week earlier he had been pleased to find the coal owners on Tyneside following his example to the extent of "getting military stationed at the Pits and letting as many men as possible to work with protection." [124] But as it turned out the coal owners lacked Morton's resolution. On the Wear, so he reported, Lord Londonderry and his wife had shamefully pleaded with their men to return to work.[125] Then, in the last week of May, the news arrived that the coal owners had capitulated. At the time Morton was busy at Newbottle pit turning out pitmen and their families from their homes: first, six families, and "if that does not produce the desired effect I shall proceed with 20 or 30 more immediately; there is nothing but decided and determined conduct that will bring these Brutes to reason." [126] The owners' capitulation compelled Morton to follow their example and concede the demands of the Newbottle men. In themselves these were not serious, but "the principle is horrible." [127] On one point, however, Morton refused to yield,

[121] *Ibid.*, Morton to Lord Durham, April 28, 1831.
[122] *Ibid.*, Morton to Lord Durham, May 1, 1831.
[123] *Ibid.*, Morton to Lord Durham, May 14, 1831.
[124] *Ibid.*, Morton to Lord Durham, May 6, 1831.
[125] *Ibid.*, Morton to Lord Durham, May 9, 1831.
[126] *Ibid.*, Morton to Lord Durham, May 17, 1831.
[127] *Ibid.*, Morton to Lord Durham, May 24, 1831.

whatever the cost. He would not rehire the pitmen's leaders: "the matter at issue is this, whether they or I shall have the control over the workmen of the colliery." [128]


## IV


In addition to an aggressive labor force, of which the agricultural world had comparatively little experience in the years of high farming, the world of nonagricultural affairs confronted the land agent with other problems of its own. These problems varied much in their complexity.

Since the Earls of Durham mined their coal, Morton's problems were special and formidable. The chief one was to maintain the competitive strength of the Earl's collieries. As long as the unique position of the Northern coal field endured—that is, until the coming of the railways and the accelerated development of the inland coal fields—he sought to preserve a monopoly of the mining and sale of coal among a few large producers, like the Lambton and Vane-Tempest families, who made regular agreements about output in order to regulate the price of coal. This was the so-called "regulation of the vend." It was Morton's constant business to cope with any threat to this monopoly.[129]

Such a threat became formidable in the mid-1830's when the Durham Colliery Company proposed to enter the Northern coal field in strength by purchasing a large operating colliery, the North Hetton. Morton advised that Lord Durham together with Lord Londonderry and others themselves purchase the colliery—which was done. Generally he advised the Lambtons to purchase or lease dormant collieries and unworked mineral land to achieve the same object of keeping the business of mining coal in their own hands as much as possible.

[128] *Ibid.*, Morton to Lord Durham, June 6, 1831.
[129] See Spring, "The Earls of Durham and the Great Northern Coal Field," *Can. Hist. Rev.*, Sept., 1952.

Projects for new railways were likely to conjure up the same threat for Morton. For example, when a railway from Durham to South Shields was proposed in 1830, Morton conceded that it might be beneficial to the public interest, but so far as the Earl of Durham's private interest was concerned, the line would open a great field of coal to the west of Durham "where it lays at no great depth—and wrought at little expense, and every person possessing one hundred acres of coal might easily make a winning, having the facility of a public railway to carry away the coals—the trade would by this means get into too numerous a body that would render it impossible to carry on a regulation." [130]

So long as he could, Morton supported the regulation of the coal trade by the great coal owners of the Tyne and the Wear. When it came to an end during the 1840's, largely by reason of Lord Londonderry's actions,[131] and when the Lambton collieries became subject not only to the full competition of their neighbors but also to that of the inland coal fields, Morton proved his resourcefulness in facing up to the new competitive conditions. The depression in the coal trade during the 'forties did not dismay him as much as it did the Lambtons' auditor, Henry Stephenson. Morton strove to cut costs wherever he could: most spectacularly, by the introduction of screw-propelled iron vessels into the carrying trade from Sunderland to London. His object was to reduce the cost of transport by two shillings per ton. Early in 1853 he was able to report a successful trial of the first vessel, the *Lady Alice Durham*. "We shall," he wrote, "drive the Yorkshire coals out of the London market"—or, less exuberantly, "at least check their increase." [132]

Since the Duke of Northumberland did not mine his coal, his agent, Hugh Taylor, was spared much of Morton's busi-

---

[130] Lambton MSS, Morton to Lord Durham, July 15, 1830.
[131] See D. Large, "The Third Marquess of Londonderry and the End of the Regulation 1844–5," *Durham University Journal*, Dec., 1958.
[132] Lambton MSS, Morton to Lord Durham, April 8, 1853.

ness. Nevertheless Taylor had certain problems connected with mining, in particular that of wayleaves. The Duke owned the manor of Tynemouth which lying along the north bank of the river Tyne controlled the access to that river of many of the Tyne collieries. The operators of these collieries therefore paid the Duke a wayleave, that is an annual rent for the right to move their coal across his land. By 1851 ten collieries paid such rent, the total sum having reached the not inconsiderable amount of £8,560, about ten per cent of the Duke's gross income.[133] It was Hugh Taylor's object to maintain the wayleave income—which by 1850 had become somewhat precarious.

The lessees had become restive, complaining that wayleave rents were such as to put them at a disadvantage when competing with coal carried by public railway lines on which no wayleave charges were laid; they threatened to support the building of such lines and to support projects for docks at ports like Blyth. Taylor was active in meeting these complaints. When the Bedlington colliery lessees approached the Duke for wayleave to the Tyne in 1849, Taylor declared that "this first step towards bringing the produce of the Coal field North of the Blyth across Your Grace's Property, ought evidently to be met with encouragement." He proposed that the usual rent of ten shillings, six pence per ten [134] be reduced to seven shillings on the ground that Bedlington colliery was among the most distant from the Tyne: "the thing to do is to persuade collieries to use the superior facilities afforded by the Tyne . . . [and] to discourage the getting up of Parliamentary Lines." [135]

Hence Taylor's advocacy of the Hayhole Dock which the Tyne Improvement Commissioners were projecting in 1851. This dock was to be built on the Duke's property. As Taylor

[133] Alnwick Castle MSS, Business Minutes, Sept. 20, 1852.

[134] According to the *Shorter Oxford English Dictionary* a ten is a measure of coal, locally varying from 48 to 50 tons, and is the unit of calculation on which the lessor's rent or royalty is based. That royalty is known as the *tentale* rent.

[135] Alnwick Castle MSS, Business Minutes, Aug. 27, 1849.

observed, it would "act as a check upon the construction of similar works elsewhere, and upon the improvement of little ports like Blyth, in the district, the effect of which would be to abstract a portion of Wayleave Revenue." [136] The Commissioners, however, would not build the dock unless there was a guarantee of the colliery vessels' using it for a reasonably long time. Taylor therefore urged that an agreement be made with the lessees to reduce the wayleave rent for all lessees to six shillings, the agreement to last for forty years, the term which the Commissioners had suggested.[137] On some such footing the dock was built, and the Duke's "wayleave interest" was kept intact.

Where the agent had mining tenants to deal with he would probably find that his relations with them were simpler than those with his farming tenants. Admittedly similarities existed. Agents were anxious to lease their mines to tenants of capital, to "men of business." F. F. Fox was critical of Barber and Walker, the colliery lessees of Lord Melbourne's mines in Nottinghamshire, on the ground that they were lacking in "large capital and are not men of business": "They are entirely in the hands of their Agent Mr. Harrison who has always conducted their concerns on the old fashioned principle of small sales and high prices—The consequence has been that your Lordship's Collieries have not probably yielded half the income that might have been expected from their great extent." [138] Fox therefore advised that if Barber and Walker's lease was renewed, the renewal should depend on their being associated with more enterprising men.

There was also in these relations some suggestion of a partnership. In one form or other the mineral owner may have embarked some of his own capital in the mining enterprise. Sometimes a part of the working stock belonged to him. Some-

[136] *Ibid.*, Nov. 3, 1851.
[137] *Ibid.*, Dec. 29, 1851.
[138] Panshanger MSS, Fox to Lord Melbourne, Jan. 22, 1848.

times he came to the tenant's financial aid. In the years 1838–43 when the lessees of the Percy Main Colliery were faced by a heavy flooding of the mine, the Duke of Northumberland first agreed to reduce his royalty, and later contributed £5,000 to the cost of resisting the flood water.[139] In 1833 the Duke and his agent had set on foot a sliding scale of colliery rents by which such rents were adjusted to the market price of coal.[140]

If there was a kind of partnership here, it was one in which the mineral owner and his agent were junior, if not sleeping, partners. Relations between agent and mining tenants thus had less in them of the tutelary and the paternal than the relations between agent and farming tenants. Once the mines were leased to the proper person, as Fox explained to Lord Melbourne, there was not enough to do to require the employment of a full-time mineral agent. So long as one hired "an intelligent, resident collier," [141] someone to keep a knowing eye on the lessees, they could be left "to make the best of [the mines] and to sell as much as they can." This would do, of course, only on estates where colliery concerns were on a smaller scale than those of the Duke of Northumberland.[142]

## V

Not a few agents identified themselves closely with the cherished objects of their employers—with family continuity, family honor, and family influence. Examples of this disposition are not hard to come by. Yule, for example, displayed it on several notable occasions. In the 1820's, when Sir James Graham despaired of bringing Netherby round and was apparently on the verge of selling a large part of it, Yule felt compelled to protest:

[139] Alnwick Castle MSS, Business Minutes, July 24, 1848.
[140] *Ibid.*, Nov. 5, 1849.
[141] Panshanger MSS, Fox to Lord Melbourne, March 4, 1850.
[142] *Ibid.*, Sept. 19, 1850.

plebeian though I am, I cannot bear to see it [Netherby] go
out of the possession of an Honourable old family, who have
always been beloved by their retainers, into the hands of a Hard
hearted grinding speculator without lifting up my humble voice
against such a measure, which if I know anything at all of
Human Nature I think fraught with great mischief in the first
place to a devoted race of men born and bred on the soil, but
with endless regret to their natural Lord, a regret which no
power that the most ample future can give will ever repay.[143]

Twenty years later there was a less dramatic occasion when
Yule had to decide about the wisdom of further borrowing
for the purpose of draining, which would have added signifi-
cantly to an already large debt on the estate. He had no doubt
that draining was a useful improvement, but he feared the
possible consequences for the next generation, and he had
trouble therefore in deciding on the best course to follow.

My long silence in this important matter of draining is caused
by a knowledge of your late Family settlements, and a great
dread of overburthening your successor beyond what he is able
to bear—with his habits, not calculated for a struggle, which
you, when a young man, would easily have encountered and
overcome.[144]

It was not uncommon for agents like Yule—as it was not
uncommon for landowners like Sir James Graham—to en-
deavor to leave an estate in a better financial condition than
they had found it, "in that condition [according to John Beas-
ley] which I think every old Family property ought to be
in." [145] Hence their concern with indebtedness and their evi-
dent desire to reduce it whenever possible. On the Sneyd estate
once colliery income improved in the 'fifties and opportunities
to sell land for building purposes grew more plentiful, Andrew
Thompson announced, "I am now looking forward with great

[143] Netherby MSS, Yule to Sir J. Graham, Nov. 12, 1826, quoted in
Spring, "A Great Agricultural Estate . . . ," *Agric. Hist.*, April, 1955.
[144] *Ibid.*, Yule to Sir J. Graham, March 13, 1847.
[145] Althorp MSS, Beasley to Earl Spencer, April 5, 1852.

confidence to the time when we shall be able to wipe off some
of the debt." [146] Henry Morton echoed this when the Lambton
collieries flourished in the mid-'fifties. And Francis Blaikie in
1828 despaired of achieving that "desirable object"—"the paying off of encumbrances in Mr. Coke's estate"—[147] when loss
of a sizable income from the Dungeness lighthouse threatened.

Since nonagricultural resources were more likely to provide
a surplus that could be applied to debt reduction, they proved
especially attractive to agents. John Lawrence's handbook,
*The Modern Land Steward*, published in 1801, had advised
agents not to overlook such possibilities as the finding of mines
or the letting of land for building, the latter being "one of
the surest methods of raising a great estate." [148] With the coming of the railways, which powerfully stimulated the nonagricultural side of estate business, agents scarcely needed
such advice. Sometimes they looked for nonagricultural resources in what seems highly unlikely places—as when John
Beasley searched for coal on the small Spencer estate in Norfolk.

The attractions of nonagricultural resources were enhanced
by the growing awareness that agricultural profits were not
fat. Early in the century many agents were disposed to make
a case for the profitability of landowner's improvements in
agriculture.[149] But as the years of high farming went by, agents
grew less enthusiastic. The Duke of Bedford's West Country
agent in the 1860's summed up the matter with a pessimism
that may have been heard elsewhere on the great estates:

> If we were solely to be regulated by purely commercial rules,
> that is, only expending money when it will make a profitable

[146] Sneyd MSS, Thompson to R. Sneyd, May 19, 1857.

[147] Holkham MSS, Blaikie to anonymous recipient, June 26, 1828. Coke
of Norfolk owned and operated the Dungeness lighthouse, collecting a
toll from passing ships.

[148] Lawrence, *The Modern Land Steward*, p. 70.

[149] See Kent, *Hints to Gentlemen of Landed Property*, p. 8; Marshall,
*On Landed Property*, p. 304. Marshall, it must be admitted, could be
disconcertingly obscure on this point.

return, I believe very little would be done—for I do not believe that if the cost of buildings and making the fences were calculated and interest charged on the outlay that there is any rent for any Farm on the west side of the parish of Tavistock . . . I have always looked at what the requirements of each farm were, not looking to cost or value first. . . . I have done all I could to provide tenants with the means of doing their work at the least cost—of gradually improving their system of husbandry, and the details of their agricultural operations by teaching them what is being done elsewhere.[150]

Indeed, an agent like Yule, who had begun his improvements so unusually early as the 1820's [151] felt compelled in the 1840's —as a previous quotation has shown—to go cautiously.[152] For there was a large debt on the estate, and there were no non-agricultural resources to speak of; he had drilled for coal but in vain. Thus the burden of ensuring continuity weighed heavily on him.

Where there was a concern for continuity, there was also a concern for the honor and influence of a landed family. Thus Henry Morton took it upon himself to admonish the young Earl of Durham on the duties pertaining to his station in life when that young man showed little inclination to follow in the footsteps of his illustrious father. Or there was the amusing episode in the Coke family when a daughter of the house was about to marry John Spencer Stanhope, scion of the Yorkshire Stanhopes. Francis Blaikie, the Cokes' agent, took a personal interest in the marital negotiations. He was delighted that

[150] Bedford MSS, Annual Reports, 1864.

[151] R. W. Sturgess in his "A Study of Agricultural Change in the Staffordshire Moorlands 1780–1850," *North Staffordshire Journal of Field Studies,* vol. 1, 1961, has written: "Nineteenth century agricultural economic history has been written in terms of arable farming and in particular of eastern England arable farming; it has neglected the western and northern livestock industry and the prosperity of agriculture has been seen in the graph of wheat prices." The example of Netherby points to this neglect. Yule was improving at Netherby when other parts of rural England were depressed.

[152] Spring, "A Great Agricultural Estate . . . ," *Agric. Hist.,* April, 1955.

Miss Coke was to marry a Stanhope, his previous employer having been Lord Chesterfield. Nonetheless, he was taking no risks about the soundness of the prospective son-in-law of the house; and he undertook extensive inquiries among his agent acquaintance in Yorkshire to find if Stanhope "had ever borrowed any money on annuities, whether he was extravagant, in short whether in every possible particular he was a fit person to be entrusted with the happiness of his beloved Miss Coke." He solemnly turned over to her the results of his inquiries, apparently having found them satisfactory.[153]

Not surprisingly, when it was a matter of deploying a family's influence—as happened most obviously in a parliamentary election—the resident land agent was likely to turn electoral agent. Among other things he canvassed the tenants, mustered them at the polls, kept an eye on the local press, and generally acquired much miscellaneous information relevant to electoral strategy and tactics. He might complain about such duties, as Henry Morton did in 1852, finding them "a sad obstacle to business." [154] Nonetheless, even Morton took them most seriously. On his death it was said that "in all the contested elections for the Northern Division [of Durham], and for the town of Sunderland, since he filled the managing place at Lambton, he was actively concerned on behalf of the Whig candidates." [155] His letters bear this out. In 1836, for example, he reported to the Earl of Durham that "in the northern division of [the county] there are a very large number of 40 s. Freeholders who are ready to sell themselves in the event of an election, chiefly Pitmen and labourers," [156] and he inquired whether he should enlist such voters; he was already very busy with the Registration, indeed he and other agents of Lord Durham were the only persons troubling themselves about it

[153] Stirling, *The Letter-Bag of Lady Elizabeth Spencer-Stanhope*, II, 38.
[154] Lambton MSS, Morton to Lord Durham, March 14, 1852.
[155] T. Fordyce, *Local Records or Historical Register of Remarkable Events* (Newcastle-upon-Tyne, 1867), 2 vols., II, 84.
[156] Lambton MSS, Morton to Lord Durham, Oct. 30, 1836.

on the Whig side in the county. The next year he informed the Earl of the difficulty in finding a suitable candidate for the county, and added that he had been in touch with Mr. Stanley of the Treasury to find him such a candidate.[157] On various other occasions, it appears, he wrote the leading articles in the *Durham Chronicle* on political and other subjects. These are but a few examples of Morton's activity as guardian of the Lambtons' family influence.

What was the origin of the land agent's concern with family influence and family continuity? For the most part perhaps it issued from that social conservatism noted in the previous chapter as marking the early history of a profession. This conservatism may have been more marked among land agents, especially among the resident agents, than elsewhere in the new professions. The land agent was comparatively slow in the nineteenth century to establish an independent professional organization,[158] and he long kept a reputation easily recognized in E. M. Forster's Mr. Wilbraham. This Edwardian character was a land agent, who "knew his place and kept others to theirs: all society seemed spread before him like a map. . . . Everything with him was graduated." [159] An agent like Henry Morton usually knew his place. Occasionally he stepped out of it, as he did in the crisis of 1830–31, when he sternly advised Lord Durham and his fellow landowners on their duty to identify themselves with "the respectable middle class of society"— adding, almost threateningly, "perhaps the most influential class of society." [160] But this was a momentary lapse, quickly covered over, and Morton resumed his role of family servant, devoted to the enhancement of the Lambton family fortunes.

What was the remuneration of agents? According to a committee of the Church Commissioners in 1862, if they were paid in the form of a commission, they received from

[157] *Ibid.*, Morton to Lord Durham, July 5, 1837.
[158] The Land Agents' Society was established in 1902.
[159] E. M. Forster, *The Longest Journey*, chap. XI.
[160] Lambton MSS, Morton to Lord Durham, Dec. 8, 9, 1830.

three to five per cent of the gross rental; and if they were paid
in the form of a fixed salary, "it is accompanied with various
allowances for house rent, horses etc. so as to be somewhat
above the lower of these limits." [161] Most if not all agents on
large English estates were paid in the form of a fixed salary with
various allowances (usually a house). Where salaries can be
matched with gross incomes, they are found to be something
like the percentage adduced by the Church Commissioners.
The Duke of Bedford paid his Woburn agent, Thomas Bennett, £760 a year with a house. At the height of their careers,
Blaikie received £650 and John Yule £500. Beasley received
£1,000 as a total salary from the several large landowners
whom he served.

Such remuneration easily made possible the sort of success
in life that land agents usually sought. Their social ambitions
were not exorbitant, usually being satisfied by placing their
sons somewhere in the world of business. John Beasley was
probably unusual in seeking a living in the Church of England
for one of his four sons—and obtaining it with the help of Earl
Spencer; but two of them followed in their father's footsteps.[162]
When Henry Morton's son chose to go up to Oxford to stand
for a scholarship, the father's reaction was probably typical:
"It would have been very much more satisfactory to me, and
infinitely more beneficial to himself had he followed the profession of Mr. Buddle." [163] In spite of Oxford, he managed to
succeed his father as an agent of the Lambton family.

It was a rare agent who achieved something of social distinction, who rose out of the steward's room, so to speak. One
such man was Thomas Sopwith, chief agent to the Beaumont
family, owners of the great lead mines in Northumberland
and Durham. A friend of Buddle and Robert Stephenson, Sopwith began his career articled to a surveyor, and as a young
man he plunged into the new and vastly exciting world of

[161] B.P.P., *Rep. of the S.C. on the Ecclesiastical Commission*, p. 424.
[162] Althorp MSS, *passim*.
[163] Lambton MSS, Morton to Lord Durham, Nov. 16, 1837.

railways and mines in the North Country. Even as a young man he had shown a mind possessed of many interests: natural science, music, architecture. In 1845 he took up the Beaumont agency, "undoubtedly [he said] the first position open to a professional man." [164] By the end of the following decade he had become a Fellow of the Royal Society, a member of the Athenaeum Club, and a Fellow of the Geological Society. In his diary for August 21, 1859, there was this entry: "In the evening I dined with Mr and Lady Margaret Beaumont, the Duc de Richelieu, the Countess of Cork and Sir John Shelley." [165]

To most estate agents such honors and privileges were unknown. Their rewards were in a worldly view of a lesser sort: knowledge of work well done, a position of some authority and comfort, a relationship of trust and confidence with their employers. These were not unmerited. It is true that one hears of dishonest agents: Lord Shaftesbury's Mr. Waters caused a noisy scandal; [166] and the highly reputable Tycho Wing left his affairs in disorder.[167] But by and large the greedy and fraudulent agents of many nineteenth-century novels are misleading. Here George Eliot is probably closer to the truth when she portrays Caleb Garth than is Surtees when he declares: "that whatever becomes of the owner of an estate, the steward invariably thrives." [168]

[164] B. W. Richardson, *Thomas Sopwith* (London, 1891), p. 225.
[165] *Ibid.*, p. 265.
[166] *The Times*, Aug. 15, 1865, leading article.
[167] Bedford MSS, Annual Reports, 1852.
[168] R. S. Surtees, *Hillingdon Hall*, chap. XIV.

# CHAPTER V

# THE STATE

THIS CHAPTER DEALS with the role of the central government, not—as one might expect—in the administration of Crown lands, but in the administration of privately owned estates. In the first half of the nineteenth century a variety of landowner's activities came under the supervision of the state. Although historians have recently become aware that the early nineteenth century saw a large measure of governmental intervention,[1] and have been investigating particular aspects of it, they have so far ignored the story of governmental intervention in agriculture.[2] It is a story which might well be told in some detail; for it throws light both on the role of the state in nineteenth-century economic life and on the administration of English landed estates.

It should be said at the start that no attempt will be made here to tell the entire story of state intervention in nineteenth-century agriculture. Very little will be said, for example, of

[1] Remarked on most forcibly by J. B. Brebner, "Laissez Faire and State Intervention in Nineteenth Century Britain," *The Journal of Economic History*, Supplement VIII, 1948.

[2] This is true of the most comprehensive account of the early Victorian administrative state: D. Roberts, *Victorian Origins of the British Welfare State* (New Haven, 1960). The name of William Blamire, who was the chief member of the Tithe and Inclosure Commissions, does not appear in this work.

the work of the Tithe Commissioners which would need a book in itself. Instead the chapter will confine itself to that aspect of state intervention which was perhaps most characteristic of land management in the years of high farming—that is, the provision of capital and the promotion of agricultural improvements. And even this aspect will not be treated exhaustively. There were many changes in the land law which aimed at facilitating improvements, not all of which will be traced here: for example, there will be no mention of legislation dealing with the lease and sale of settled land, and little mention of the revolutionary Settled Land Act of 1882; these also might require a book. This chapter will be limited to a consideration of how the state financed improvements such as draining and farm buildings, and how it administered them. This work fell to the Board of Inclosure Commissioners, a body which had been established, as its name suggests, for other though allied purposes. The origins, growth, and decline of this public body will therefore be the subject of this chapter.

# I

The Board of Inclosure Commissioners traces its origins back to Lord Worsley's bill of June, 1843, to facilitate inclosure. What Lord Worsley sought was to avoid the high cost of the traditional mode of inclosure by private act of Parliament, a cost amounting to something like £400–£600.[3] The legal business associated with a private act of Parliament accounted for part of the expense; the lengthy proceedings in the localities for the rest. A general act of Parliament would abolish the first; and a board of commissioners—which, according to Lord Worsley, should be the Tithe Commissioners—would reduce the second. Instead of several commissioners at work haphazardly in the locality, a single assistant commissioner, appointed by the Board in London, would firmly

[3] Hansard's *Parliamentary Debates* (hereafter designated *Hansard*), 3rd S., vol. 70, pp. 182–85.

expedite proceedings there. Lord Worsley's critics objected to the bill on the ground that "there was not a single clause in it which, in a distinct manner, declared the rights of the poor, or which gave to them a portion of the waste land of this country."[4] Lord Worsley hoped that the protection of the poor might be left to the discretion of the Inclosure Commissioners.

In July, 1844, Lord Worsley's bill went before a Select Committee on Commons' Inclosure which reported the following month. The report strengthened Lord Worsley's case. It was emphatic about the expense of private acts of Parliament as "a serious impediment" to inclosure. It drew attention to "the present time [being] more favourable than any that has preceded it for a general measure of Inclosure": first, because tithes, having been settled, would no longer act as a deterrent to improvement; second, because of the recent appearance of new techniques of draining and new kinds of artificial manure; and last, because of the reduction in expenditure made possible by the maps and evaluations used by the Tithe Commissioners which might also be used for the purposes of inclosure. The report also noted the work which the Inclosure Commissioners might do in arranging the exchange of lands which were "divided into parcels of such inconvenient form and size as to be incapable of improved and advantageous cultivation." The report, however, did not recommend the Tithe Commissioners as the new Inclosure Commissioners; it merely urged the appointment of "some central body" responsible to Parliament.[5]

The chief Tithe Commissioners—William Blamire and the Rev. Richard Jones—provided the weightiest evidence in support of Lord Worsley's bill. They estimated that eight to ten million acres of land in England and Wales was common or waste land, arriving at this figure from calculations made in the course of the Tithe Commission's work. Both were sure from their own experience that a Board of Inclosure Com-

---

[4] *Ibid.*, p. 185.
[5] B.P.P., *Report of Select Committee on Commons' Inclosure* (1844, V), pp. iii–iv.

missioners would reduce the cost of inclosure: the Rev. Richard Jones declared "that the business of the apportioners under the Tithe Act would have lasted four times as long as it has had, had we not control over it." [6] Both were also sure that a new Board would afford greater protection to the poor: Jones pointed out that "the people who appear against an Inclosure Bill in Parliament are not the poor people." [7]

The upshot of the Committee's report and evidence was a government measure in May, 1845, for a general scheme of inclosure, Lord Worsley having agreed to withdraw his own bill. This new bill, introduced by Lord Lincoln, sought the same objects as the old.[8] However, it found the Inclosure Commission not in the Tithe Commission but in a quite separate body, although one of the Commissioners—William Blamire—was to be both a Tithe Commissioner and an Inclosure Commissioner. According to Lord Lincoln, it had been feared that the work of supervising a general scheme of inclosure would put an insupportable burden on the Tithe Commission which (it was felt) had enough to do for the remaining two years of its allotted period of life. (Nothing seems to have been said about the burden put on Blamire.) It had also been feared that the Tithe Commission was not sufficiently responsible to Parliament.[9] Hence the new body was brought to life, comprising three Commissioners—Lord Lincoln, William Blamire, and George Darby—the last a barrister and Member of Parliament, the first the Commissioner of Woods and Forests.[10] Initially Parliament set a period of five years on its life, and made it responsible to the Home Office.[11]

[6] *Ibid.*, p. 3.

[7] *Ibid.*, p. 13.

[8] *Hansard*, 3rd S., vol. 80, p. 25.

[9] *Ibid.*, p. 26.

[10] During the early years of the Inclosure Commission it was customary to make the Commissioner of Woods and Forests an Inclosure Commissioner.

[11] The Commission's annual reports were addressed to the Home Secretary. In 1865, the Home Secretary, Sir George Grey, declared he had no control over the Commission; see below.

On the day after Lord Lincoln brought forward his bill establishing the Inclosure Commission, he introduced a further measure which began that lengthy process of ever adding to the functions of the Inclosure Commissioners. He proposed to make them responsible for "more effectually draining waste and unenclosed lands." [12] The measure was limited, as Lord Lincoln put it, "to the object of enabling parties desirous of draining their own lands to carry their drains through other lands adjacent to their own, upon compensating the proprietors for the damage thereby done." [13]

Chief among agricultural improvements in the mid-nineteenth century, draining was to bulk large in the work of the Inclosure Commission. Lord Lincoln himself promised, on introducing the measure, that "in the course of a Session or two he hoped to be able to introduce a more extensive scheme of legislation in this respect." [14] That government might promote draining was not, however, an idea original to Lord Lincoln. Credit for it should go to agricultural reformers like Philip Pusey whose efforts in this cause go back to at least 1840.

Philip Pusey deserves particular notice here. His concern with agricultural improvement in the years 1840-45—and especially with legislation to enable limited owners to borrow for improvements—marks him out as one of the architects of the Inclosure Commission.[15]

He was a Berkshire squire who succeeded to the family estates in 1829, the elder brother of Edward Bouverie Pusey, the Oxford Tractarian, with whom he is sometimes confused. As an eldest son he entered Parliament; but the House of Commons proved to be not the sphere most suited to his abilities and personality. It would seem that he was a poor speaker. Also his opinions sometimes revealed a certain angularity which un-

[12] *Hansard*, 3rd S., vol. 80, p. 31.
[13] *Ibid.*
[14] *Ibid.*
[15] The first full-length biography of Philip Pusey is to be found in the unpublished doctoral dissertation (Johns Hopkins, 1961) of R. W. Linker: *Philip Pusey, Esq.: Country Gentleman 1799-1855.*

fitted him for party politics. Yet he was a dedicated man, anxious to serve some great cause. He was to find it in the cause of improved agriculture and rural welfare. His mind was both matter-of-fact and speculative: as his friend, Baron Bunsen once said of him, Pusey "was a most *unique* union of a practical Englishman and an intellectual German." [16] He was also humanely disposed to the laboring classes, especially in the countryside.[17]

By the late 1830's Pusey had turned his attention to the problems of English agriculture. Thereafter, until his death in 1855, he worked to promote agricultural improvement on two fronts: in Parliament and in the Royal Agricultural Society. In Parliament he was active not so much as a speaker in the House as a witness before parliamentary committees and, perhaps more important, as influential adviser to party leaders, especially to Gladstone and Peel. Sometime in the early 'forties he drew up for Gladstone a program of what ought to be done, particularly by the state, for English agriculture.[18] In the Royal Agricultural Society, in addition to serving as its president, Pusey was editor of the Society's *Journal;* and in this capacity he became acquainted with improving farmers and landowners in every corner of rural England, soliciting articles from them, often writing one himself. It was Sir Robert Peel who said to Pusey, "I know no one who has done more than yourself to enable the Country to enter into successful competition with other Countries in respect to agricultural produce." [19]

---

[16] Baroness Bunsen, *A Memoir of Baron Bunsen* (London, 1868), 2 vols., I, 613.

[17] As his brother, Edward Bouverie, once remarked to him: "I always felt glad in our rides together, to see your intercourse with the labourers: it gives an interest to what they do and makes them feel as fellow men, not mere instruments, and living machines"; see Pusey MSS, E. B. Pusey to Philip Pusey, Oct. 6, 1845, quoted in Linker, *Philip Pusey*, p. 531.

[18] Pusey refers to this memorandum in Add. MSS, 44,362, folio 299, P. Pusey to W. E. Gladstone, Sept. 4, 1845. Unfortunately the memorandum itself is not to be found in the Gladstone Papers in the British Museum.

[19] Add. MSS, 40,585, folio 297, Sir R. Peel to P. Pusey, Feb. 25, 1846.

It was the want of capital in agricultural enterprise which most concerned Pusey. "The misfortune is," he once wrote with some exaggeration, "that, according to an old remark, I forget by whom made, the capital and the soil of the country are not acquainted with each other." [20] Perhaps because he was something of a Tory humanitarian, the idea of using the state to help in financing agriculture may have come easily to him. It is plain that he held to the beneficence of state intervention as a matter of principle. In an illuminating article published in the *Quarterly*, entitled "Plato, Bacon and Bentham," Pusey declared, "Our own recent [political] systems . . . view man, we think, too much as a mere individual. They cannot of course lose sight altogether of his social relations but they treat him as if he were capable of maintaining his own powers of mind by his own efforts in a state of independent self-government." [21] In a letter to Gladstone early in 1843 he wrote, "I begin to think decidedly that some supervision on the part of government is necessary for giving energy to the present taste for improvements, and I think you will agree with me that in this country we carry to excess the practice of individual enterprise." [22]

In fact Pusey had already begun in a modest way to work at schemes of government intervention. In general what he sought was statutory reform of the legal position of limited owners of land, that is, of those who held their estates as tenants for life under strict family settlements. Since the aim of the strict family settlement was to insure so far as possible that a landed estate pass intact from eldest son to eldest son, it set out to limit the power of the "landowner" to sell or mortgage. Not surprisingly, observers often found it to be an obstruction to agricultural improvement. They pointed out that normally a

[20] P. Pusey, "On the Progress of Agricultural Knowledge during the last Four Years," *The Journal of the Royal Agricultural Society*, 1842.

[21] "Plato, Bacon, and Bentham." *The Quarterly Review*, April, 1838, quoted in Linker, *Philip Pusey*, p. 478.

[22] Add. MSS, 44,360, folio 62, P. Pusey to W. E. Gladstone, Feb. 12, 1843.

settlement allowed borrowing only for the purpose of raising specified sums for younger children's portions, that it rarely allowed mortgaging to effect improvements. Moreover, they alleged that it tended to render the landowner unwilling to improve out of income for he thus further aggrandized his eldest son at the expense of his younger children.

A note of caution should be sounded against exaggerating these difficulties. The common law in limiting the duration of a settlement inserted in practice a wide degree of freedom in the system of settlement, though this has seldom been recognized.[23] Normally, a landowner and his eldest son, upon the latter's coming of age, gained the power to disentail the estate, that is to bring the settlement to an end and to deal with the estate as they jointly saw fit. It is regularly assumed that they immediately divested themselves of this power and strictly resettled the estate. Reflection on human nature alone would suggest that this was not certain to be their course. It is not usually mankind's reaction to freedom and power to cast them immediately away. In practice fathers and sons often maintained their joint power for lengthy periods. Either they postponed resettling, or more likely, they resettled but maintained "a joint power of appointment" over their settlement. They would thus maintain their power for as long as they jointly lived. They might even extend such power by agreeing that it should inhere in the successor alone for his life. The Duke of Bedford was simply granted by his father an absolute power over his settlement. Clearly the subject of powers over settlements must qualify general statements about the effects of settlement.

When all is said, however, it must be concluded that settlement presented something of a barrier to agricultural improvement. Testimony to the fact is to be found in the private acts of Parliament, for the tenant for life might apply for such an act to free himself from the restraints of settlement. In the first

[23] See D. Spring, "English Landownership in the Nineteenth Century: A Critical Note," *The Economic History Review*, April, 1957.

decades of the nineteenth century these acts were numerous
and many of them dealt with the development of estates, prin-
cipally with urban and mining development but frequently
with agricultural development. What Pusey sought in effect
was a general act that would allow the tenant for life to borrow. So as to keep the institution of settlement intact he would
have his borrowing subject to a supervision insuring that the
estate and those who held future interests in it suffered no loss.
The supervisory power would thus be concerned to insure that
the improvements were properly executed; that they yielded
a profit, or at least, occasioned no loss; and that the charges
were amortized over a reasonable period.

The need for such legislation had presented itself to Pusey
on his own estate: as a tenant for life he had been confronted
by the expense and inconvenience met in obtaining a private
act of Parliament. Pusey had sought powers of selling an outlying part of the estate for the purpose of improving the rest,
and his own circumstances probably brought to mind the
general plight of tenants for life.[24] As he said a few years later
before a Select Committee of the House of Lords, "When I
look at the extent of land requiring drainage and the limited
means of the owners of it . . . I am perfectly convinced that
unless landlords are enabled to charge their estates for this purpose, it will be imperfectly done, if done at all." [25]

In 1840, with the assistance of Henry Handley, a Lincolnshire squire and agricultural improver,[26] Pusey brought forward a bill "to enable the Owners of Settled Estates to defray
the expenses of draining the same." [27] In its original form the

---

[24] It was estimated in the 1850's that private acts to obtain such powers
as that of sale cost £1,270 on the average; see *Hansard*, 3rd S., vol. 138,
p. 397.

[25] B.P.P., *Report of Select Committee (H. of L.) to enable Possessors
of Entailed Estates to charge . . . for the purpose of Draining* (1845,
XII), p. 119.

[26] Handley was prominent among agricultural improvers; in 1838 he
had raised the flag of improvement in *A Letter to Earl Spencer on the
Formation of a National Agricultural Institution* (London, 1838).

[27] B.P.P., *Public Bills* (1840, II).

bill proposed that life tenants in England and Wales be permitted to borrow for draining on the security of their estate, their applications to be heard either by the Court of Chancery or the Court of Exchequer. In its amended form the bill's provisions were extended to Irish landowners, and the Court of Chancery was given control in England and Wales, and the Court of Exchequer in Ireland.[28] In the House of Commons Sir Edward Sugden, an authority on the law of real property, denounced the bill as founded on a principle "which was without precedent in the law of Real Property in this country." [29] Although the bill was to pass, this criticism left its mark.

The Act in operation was a disappointment to Pusey. About five years later he described it as "a very imperfect bill indeed. In fact the principle was so much objected to that we fenced it round against possible abuse until we unfortunately made it impracticable." [30] Two things in particular made it so. First, resort to Chancery proved both protracted and expensive. John Bowes, a North Country landowner, testified that in order to borrow £8,000 under the Act his procedural costs amounted to £740.[31] Second, lenders found there were difficulties in the way of effecting their charges which diminished their security. Not surprisingly, by 1845, only eleven applications had been made under Pusey's Act.[32]

Still the principle had been established that tenants for life might borrow to undertake improvements. And once the gospel of agricultural improvement grew in popularity, as it did in the early 'forties, Pusey found allies in a renewed effort to provide adequate legislation. Support came particularly from the promoters of the Yorkshire Land Drainage Company, a company founded in 1843 whose directors included landed proprietors of the county and two draining engineers—the

[28] 3 & 4 Vict., c. 55.
[29] *Hansard*, 3rd S., vol. 52, p. 1219.
[30] B.P.P., *Rep. of S.C. (H. of L.) to enable . . . Entailed Estates to charge . . . for . . . Draining*, 1845, p. 123.
[31] *Ibid.*, p. 140.
[32] *Ibid.*, p. i.

renowned Smith of Deanston and Bailey Denton. The company failed to get under way "owing to the difficulties started by mortgagees and other claimants having interest in entailed estates"; [33] but learning from its difficulties it originated a bill to amend Pusey's Act, which Pusey himself volunteered to bring forward in the House of Commons.

This bill sought two objects: first, to simplify the procedure in Chancery and thereby to reduce expense; second, to give the improvement charge a priority over other charges on the estate and thereby to encourage the lender.[34] It would seem that Pusey himself proposed the latter as he wrote to Bailey Denton early in 1844, "I should even be disposed to try priority for such charges over existing mortgages." [35] This proposal, however, ran into difficulties in Parliament. The Solicitor-General, later Lord Chancellor Chelmsford, doubted that such priority would be just to previous lenders.[36] By August, when the bill had reached its second reading, Pusey was ready to abandon it, although only temporarily. The Duke of Richmond had shown himself friendly to the measure, as well as prepared to call for a committee of inquiry into the whole subject of agricultural improvements and the limited ownership of land. Such sponsorship was in itself something of a gain for the improvement party, especially as it would probably lead to a bill being started in the House of Lords where Chancery procedures would be discussed more knowledgeably than in the House of Commons.

The Duke of Richmond's Committee sat during April and May, 1845. Pusey was among its important witnesses, and his evidence (as well as that of other witnesses) disclosed some new ideas about estate improvements and their supervision. He confessed that since 1840 his notions of improvement had

[33] Denton, "On Land Drainage and Improvement by Loans from Government or Public Companies," *Journ. of R. Ag. Soc.*, 1868.
[34] B.P.P., *Public Bills* (1844, I).
[35] Denton, "On Land Drainage and Improvement by Loans from Government or Public Companies," *Journ. of R. Ag. Soc.*, 1868.
[36] *Ibid.*

widened, and that he was now anxious to obtain for limited owners the right to charge their estates not only for draining but also for new buildings. Draining waste land, as he pointed out, had little value if it was not followed by the erection of suitable buildings. Pusey admitted "there would be danger that persons might be disposed to charge their lands improperly with the expense of the repair of buildings which ought to fall upon themselves." He was hopeful, however, that this danger could be guarded against—although vague about the exact steps that should be taken. "We might," he declared, "put confidence in the Authority to be constituted by Parliament." [37]

The reformers were obviously uncertain about the nature of this authority. Bailey Denton and his legal adviser, Bellenden Ker, had been anxious to dispense with Chancery, but decided not to on the ground that the legal interests involved were very complex. Then they thought of having a Master in Chancery and a Tithe Commissioner act jointly, but abandoned this scheme too, on the ground that the Tithe Commission was not a permanent body.[38] Actually the most prescient of all suggestions came from a solicitor, Henry Lake. It had occurred to him

> that a Board of Commissioners, like the Tithe Commissioners, might be formed, to ascertain the Details of the proposed expenditures, by which great expense is incurred in Chancery. They might make inquiries as to the Necessity and Extent of Drainage required, and how the Money should be laid out, and so on.[39]

The Committee's report not surprisingly made no mention of a Board of Commissioners. The Court of Chancery, or some other "superior legal tribunal," was to be kept as the supervising body, although a number of recommendations were made by which its procedures might be simplified. The principle of

[37] B.P.P., *Rep. of S.C. (H. of L.) to enable . . . Entailed Estates to charge . . . for . . . Draining,* 1845, pp. 122–24.
[38] *Ibid.,* appendix C.
[39] *Ibid.,* p. 88.

Pusey's Act—namely, "the propriety and importance of enabling parties with limited estates to charge the inheritance" —was endorsed, with the forcible reminder added that "there never was a moment at which the extensive application of that principle, both in England and Ireland, would be more useful than the present." James Loch's evidence before the Select Committee on Public Works in Ireland (1835) was offered as confirmation of the beneficial results of the principle. Finally, the Committee declared that drainage works would fail to secure their full advantage "without the erection of farm buildings suitable to the improved state of the land drained." [40]

An Act soon followed, based on the Committee's report.[41] It provided for the continued use of the Court of Chancery, but expedited the Court's proceedings. It so defined permissible agricultural improvements as to include "any buildings of a permanent kind incidental or consequential to such draining." [42] Precisely what this meant was made clear in the House of Lords. The Marquis of Salisbury confessed to being uneasy about the power to mortgage for buildings, and Lord Beaumont assured him that the Act was intended to refer only to buildings of a rudimentary sort.[43] Finally, the Act introduced that innovation which Pusey and Bailey Denton had set their hearts on the previous year—namely the priority of the improvement charge. According to clause 6 of the Act, an improvement charge "shall have priority over other charges, except Tithe Commutation Rent-charges, and any Quit or Chief Rents incident to tenure."

Although the Act would appear to contain the revisions which were sought by the improvement party, it was never much used. Four years later, when an inquiry was held into its operation, learned witnesses disagreed as to why this was so. William Brougham, a Master in Chancery, testified to the pro-

---

[40] *Ibid.*, report.
[41] 8 & 9 Vict. c. 56, passed July 31, 1845.
[42] Clause 3.
[43] *Hansard*, 3rd S., vol. 82, pp. 54–55.

tracted procedures and the continued expense incurred under the Act.[44] James Murray, Secretary of Causes to the Master of the Rolls, declared that Brougham was referring to the Act of 1840, and that its amended version was in fact superior, both in speed of operation and in cheapness. It was still faulty, however, in the security offered to the lender. Murray provided the example of an insurance company which had refused to lend money under the Act because (as the company's solicitors put it) "it appears to us that the money must be advanced in some cases for a considerable time before the lender will get any security." [45]

It may be, however, that this Act would have found more use, if within the space of a year Parliament had not passed the Public Money Drainage Act, the first of two such statutes in aid of landowners' draining. A notable Act, it laid the foundations for the large place of the Victorian state in agriculture and estate administration. Its chief innovations were two. First, it advanced public money to landowners, the Treasury being authorized to make advances not exceeding two million pounds for Great Britain and one million pounds for Ireland. Second, to ensure that the money was properly laid out the administration of the Act was put under the control of the Inclosure Commissioners. The Commissioners thus took up a new task,

---

[44] B.P.P., *Report of Select Committee (H. of L.) to enable Possessors of Entailed Estates to charge . . . for the purpose of Draining* (1849, XII), pp. 11–19.

[45] *Ibid.*, p. 77. The rest of the solicitor's statement was as follows: "Before the security is complete, the Master in Chancery must be satisfied that the money has been fully expended in the improvements, and then he is to inquire into the costs, and give a certificate, and then, and not till then, the lands will become charged. By the 10th section, it is provided that upon the death of the person who borrowed the money, the inheritance shall remain chargeable with no more than six months' arrear of interest then due, and one-half of the last instalment then due, and the interest and instalments thereafter to become due, so that if one year's instalment and interest become due on the 29th of June, or before the payment is made, the lender would have a charge upon the land for only half the amount due, and must look to the representative of the tenant for life, probably a person without means, for the other half."

that of supervising improvements. Moreover, as the Act advanced money to owners of settled estates as well as absolute owners they in effect undertook that responsibility for protecting settlement which in the earlier legislation had been exercised by the Court of Chancery. Under the Public Money Act Chancery only came upon the scene in a case of disagreement between the tenant for life and the other heirs of the settlement.

The Public Money Drainage Act first came before the House of Commons at the end of May, 1846, but did not pass its third reading until August 13, after the fall of Sir Robert Peel's government.[46] It then came before the House of Lords, where it was amended slightly and became law in a fortnight.[47] Unfortunately the immediate background of the Act remains obscure. The memoirs are silent, and so is *Hansard*. In its parliamentary chronicle *The Times* reported a brief exchange between Lord Sandon and Sydney Herbert on the first reading of the bill in the House of Commons, the former asking for an outline of the proposed scheme, and the latter assuring him that "he trusted he would bring in an outline that evening." [48] On August 15, when the bill was first being debated in the House of Lords, *The Times* devoted a leading article to the Inclosure Commissioners, but in their old capacity as inclosers not in their new capacity as drainers.[49] The Public Money Drainage Act thus seems to have been little noticed, thrust into obscurity perhaps by the Corn Law drama.

That the Act was a *quid pro quo*,[50] intended by Sir Robert Peel to sweeten the bitter potion of repeal, may be an over-

[46] *Hansard*, 3rd S., vol. 86, p. 1421; vol. 88, p. 677. *The Times*, May 30, 1846. B.P.P., *Public Bills* (1846, II).

[47] *Journals of the House of Lords*, vol. 78, p. 1303. The Lords' chief amendment compelled the tenant for life to keep the drainage works intact and efficient during the period he was paying his charges.

[48] *The Times*, May 30, 1846.

[49] *Ibid.*, Aug. 15, 1846.

[50] Phrased used by O. R. McGregor in his introduction to Lord Ernle, *English Farming: Past and Present* (London, 1961), 6th ed., p. cxiii.

simplification. The improvement party, of which Peel was himself a notable member, had for some years been slowly moving towards a scheme such as that embodied in the Act. Perhaps in May, 1845, when Lord Lincoln promised the House of Commons to bring forward in a session or two a more extensive plan for the promotion of drainage works, Peel's government was then contemplating something like the Public Money Drainage Act.[51] Some months later Prince Albert, also an agricultural improver, proposed in a memorandum a law "enabling the state to advance money to the great proprietors for the improvement of their estates." [52] Perhaps the repeal of the Corn Laws did not so much force this legislation from the Peelites—or from the Whigs who eventually assumed its sponsorship—as present a welcome opportunity for the improvement party to fashion legislation on a subject which had deeply interested them for some time.

We may end our examination of the origins of the Board of Inclosure Commissioners at this point. In spite of some obscurity it is clear that at least two streams of effort joined in the creation of the Board as it took shape by 1846: the first came from those who were interested in inclosure; the second from those who were concerned to bring capital to agriculture, particularly to remove legal obstacles in the way. The Inclosure Act of 1845 brought the Board into existence; the Public Money Drainage Act of 1846 began its association with agricultural improvements, and made it, among other things, the surpervisor of limited owners who borrowed for them.

In a recent discussion concerning the nature of the administrative revolution in nineteenth-century England, some difference of opinion appeared as to the manner in which new administrative departments came to being, and the role of Ben-

---

[51] See earlier in this chapter.
[52] A. C. Benson and Viscount Esher, eds., *Letters of Queen Victoria: A Selection from Her Majesty's Correspondence between the years 1837 and 1861* (London, 1907), 3 vols., II, 79.

thamite doctrine in their creation.[53] The story of the origins of the Inclosure Commissioners would suggest that the precedent of the Tithe Commission set an instructive example which permitted the architects of the Inclosure Commission to go about their business with dispatch and to avoid the false starts characteristic of the growth of some administrative departments. As to the role of Benthamism, much depends on how this doctrine is defined. If it is defined as the principle of utility, it was plainly at work in the origins of the Inclosure Commissioners. At the same time the legislation administered by the Inclosure Commission sought to keep intact strict family settlement—an institution which would probably have ranked high among the iniquities of English society, in any list of those iniquities which Jeremy Bentham would have drawn up.

# II

Seventeen years after the passing of the first Public Money Drainage Act, *The Times* in a leading article on the Inclosure Commissioners observed that "every session some half-dozen new sets of duties are cast upon the Maid of All Work." [54] If there was some exaggeration in this statement, nonetheless it did justice to the steady growth in function and responsibility of the Inclosure Commissioners. They were concerned with the original inclosure business and the new business of tithe commutation acquired in 1851 when the two Commissions were amalgamated. They were also concerned with such miscellaneous business as facilitating the exchange of lands and enfranchising copyhold. At the same time the responsibility which the Commissioners had assumed in 1846 for the business of supervising agricultural improvements on individual estates

---

[53] O. MacDonagh, "The Nineteenth-Century Revolution in Government: A Re-appraisal," *The Historical Journal*, No. 1, 1958; H. Parris, "The Nineteenth-Century Revolution in Government: A Re-appraisal Reappraised," *The Historical Journal*, No. 1, 1960.

[54] *The Times*, April 20, 1863.

was one destined to grow and become more diversified and burdensome with the years.[55] The growth in this side of their business will concern us here.

The Private Money Drainage Act of 1849 might be noticed first in this period of expansion. It aimed at improving the Act of 1845 by extending to landowners who borrowed from private sources for the purpose of draining their estates the machinery of supervision as it operated under the Public Money Drainage Act. In short, it removed the Court of Chancery from the scene of private borrowing, and made the Inclosure Commissioners responsible for a new group of borrowers among landowners. As it turned out, the Act proved of limited usefulness, for reasons noted later in this chapter.

The following year saw a second Public Money Act—probably rendered inevitable by the unexpected use made of the first. That Act had caught English landowners napping, and they had been slow to make use of it. "In the first instance," according to William Blamire,

> the landowners generally entertained great fear of making applications where their property was subject to any encumbrance, upon the ground that the parties having those charges would object to an additional and a prior charge being imposed upon the property; many timid landowners hesitated; I had a great correspondence, and so had the office upon that point, and after a short time we completely disabused the minds of the landowners upon it by satisfying them that the only objections that would be taken would be, that they were not borrowing a sufficient sum of money for the improvement of their estates, because the party having the charge was a party to be very largely benefited.[56]

[55] G. W. Cooke, an Inclosure Commissioner, wrote in 1864: "the drainage and improvement jurisdiction of the Inclosure Commissioners has grown into an enormous machinery"; see G. W. Cooke, *The Acts for Facilitating the Inclosure of Commons in England and Wales with a Treatise on the Law of Rights of Commons . . . and on the Jurisdiction of the Inclosure Commissioners* (London, 1864), 4th ed., p. x.

[56] B.P.P., *Rep. of S.C. (H. of L.) to enable . . . Entailed Estates to charge . . . for . . . Draining*, 1849, p. 4.

This light, however, dawned first on the Scottish, not on the English landowners. It was the Scottish landowners who promptly came forward in such number and with such enthusiasm that of the two million pounds earmarked for landowners in Great Britain, they obtained £1,640,000.[57] According to James Caird this disproportion could be explained on the ground that the Scots had a larger experience of borrowing money on settled estates, being familiar for a long time with such legislation as the Montgomery Act.[58]

The second Act was therefore hedged about with precautions against Scottish, or for that matter English, alacrity.[59] The major part of two million pounds was earmarked for landowners in England and Wales, and steps were taken to apportion the sum fairly among English and Welsh counties. Under the first Act, even the sum of £360,000 which had gone to English landowners had gone mainly to landowners in the six northern counties.[60]

Unlike the first Act, the second finds some mention in *Hansard*. In the House of Commons the member for Tavistock, J. S. Trelawny, roundly denounced it.

> He looked upon the Bill as but the re-enactment of protection in a different shape . . . It was not discreet, wise or even honest, to dispose of the money of the nation to the landowners; and if this measure was intended to give them compensation for any loss they had sustained by free trade, the gain would be contemptible, while the principle would be utterly objectionable. Besides, it was an unnecessary increase of the functions of Government.[61]

This criticism found no support in the House. The Chancellor of the Exchequer, who took responsibility for explaining the

[57] *Ibid.*
[58] B.P.P., *Rep. of S.C. on Improvement of Land*, p. 376.
[59] *Hansard*, 3rd S., vol. 111, p. 882.
[60] Of this sum, £191,000 was granted to the six northern counties; see unsigned memorandum in Peel Papers: Add. MSS, 40,603, folio 139.
[61] *Hansard*, 3rd S., vol. 111, p. 879.

bill, merely replied that its principle was not new, and that its purpose was "to facilitate the change from one state of things to another." [62]

Both the Private Money Act of 1849 and the Public Money Act of 1850 fell short of obtaining what their original sponsors sought. Both had sought the power to charge estates for the cost of erecting farm buildings. The Private Money Act had been preceded by a committee of inquiry on entailed estates and draining charges of which the Duke of Richmond was again chairman; the Duke had pressed for this additional power, but to no avail. [63] The bill which ultimately became the second Public Money Act originally proposed such a power, [64] but met with the opposition of the Chancellor of the Exchequer. He maintained that if the interests of the remaindermen, that is, the heirs, were to be protected, constant supervision and inspection by the Inclosure Commissioners would be necessary in order to compel the tenant for life to keep the buildings in repair and to insure them—and this amount of interference by the government would be intolerable. "This difficulty in regard to the necessary interference constituted in his mind a great objection to the clause, although it might perhaps be got over." [65]

Despite the Chancellor's objections, what the bill sought had in fact already been obtained, although not in a public general act but in a private act. To explain this, we must go back to the early 1840's when a number of specialized lenders in the form of land improvement companies appeared. These companies amassed large capital sums, mainly by borrowing from insurance companies, which in turn they were prepared to lend to landowners. As the managing director of one of the leading companies put it, "the insurance companies would not

[62] *Ibid.*, p. 880.

[63] *Ibid.*, pp. 1113–14.

[64] B.P.P., *Public Bills* (1850, I). The clause ran: "Loans may be made for warping land in Great Britain and works for and connected with such warping and for the erection of farm buildings."

[65] *Hansard*, 3rd S., vol. 111, p. 885.

care to take the small charges which we take, and which we lump up into large amounts." [66] Some of the companies executed improvements as well as financed them; others were purely lenders.

The Yorkshire Land Drainage Company was the first of the land improvement companies. It had a very short life, although, as has been noted earlier, it played an important part in shaping legislation.[67] The second company was the Landowners' Drainage and Inclosure Company, founded in 1847, which also came to nothing.[68] It was the third, the West of England and South Wales Land Drainage Company, which in 1848 began the significant history of land improvement companies.

The West of England Company was formed by leading West Country landowners like Lord Clinton, Sir Thomas Dyke Acland, and Sir John Kennaway.[69] Its incorporating Act allowed the company to advance money to limited owners on the security of their estates for the following improvements: draining, irrigating, warping, embanking, and reclaiming land. It was believed originally that the company was empowered to erect farm buildings, but its Act was later interpreted so as to forbid this.[70] Unlike earlier legislation, the Act incorporating the West of England Company was not careful to protect the family estate against a wasteful tenant for life. The Inclosure Commissioners came onto the scene only when a remainderman made an objection, or the tenant for life was an infant or a lunatic. Otherwise the applicant need only advertise his proposals and obtain a certificate from the justices of the peace that such notice was served. No less unusual was the privilege granted the landowner of charging the estate in

[66] B.P.P., *Rep. of S.C. on Improvement of Land*, p. 96.
[67] *Ibid.*, p. 63.
[68] B.P.P., *Report of Select Committee (H. of L.) on Powers vested in Companies for the Improvement of Land* (1854-5, VII), p. 3.
[69] 11 & 12 Vict. c. 142.
[70] B.P.P., *Rep. of S.C. (H. of L.) to enable . . . Entailed Estates to charge . . . for . . Draining*, 1849, p. 66; B.P.P., *Rep. of S.C. on Improvement of Land*, p. 104.

perpetuity. As an Inclosure Commissioner described it, in tones that could only have been disapproving,

> a mortgage in fee is created by the owner of a limited interest without the intervention of any general authority to see that the works are those which should be executed or to ascertain that they have been efficiently executed, and in fact without any control at all.[71]

It is a matter for surprise that so unorthodox an Act became law, an Act so disrespectful of the institution of strict family settlement. Being so unusual, it might be best to relate its subsequent story here. The Inclosure Commissioners—particularly Darby and Blamire—were themselves highly distressed by this legislation. Darby felt so strongly about it that he appealed to the government on several occasions, and being told that he might use his discretion, refused to accept applications under the company's Act.[72] Fortunately for Darby's peace of mind, a Select Committee on the Powers of the Land Companies reported in 1855 that it was desirable to insure the redemption of any charge within twenty-five years, and to put no charge on an entailed estate without an order from the Inclosure Commissioners.[73] As it so happened, the West of England Company found its Act defective—the lack of a power to erect buildings had proved "a great obstacle." When it approached Parliament to seek an amendment, it was refused unless it surrendered its unusual powers.[74]

Untroubled by such difficulties was the story of the next company, the General Land Drainage and Improvement Company, which was incorporated by private act of Parliament in August, 1849,[75] shortly before the Private Money Act became law. It was capable of executing all the improvements undertaken by the West of England Company—and farm buildings

---

[71] B.P.P., *Rep. of S.C. on Powers vested in Companies,* p. 4.
[72] B.P.P., *Rep. of S.C. on Improvement of Land,* p. 54.
[73] B.P.P., *Rep. of S.C. on Powers Vested in Companies.*
[74] B.P.P., *Rep. of S.C. on Improvement of Land,* p. 110.
[75] 12 & 13 Vict. c. 91.

as well.[76] But as in the Private and Public Money Drainage Acts, the supervision of the Inclosure Commissioners was automatic; and the sums charged on the estate were amortized over a period of years. When Blamire first heard of this bill, although expressing some fear of its possible expense, he pronounced it at once "a great improvement upon the former Bills, that before a charge can be fixed upon the estate, the Company must satisfy the Inclosure Commissioners that the work has been duly and fitly executed." [77]

Inevitably the General Land Drainage and Improvement Company had its imitators. Of these the most active and successful—indeed the most successful of all the land companies judging by the total sum advanced—was the Lands Improvement Company, founded in 1853. At first restricted by its Act to lending only up to three-quarters of the amount requested for buildings, an amending Act of 1855 removed this limit.[78] Although empowered to execute improvement works, the Lands Improvement Company never did, confining itself instead to the lending of money. By 1873 its loans amounted to £3,004,392;[79] by 1880 they amounted to £4,192,241,[80] a sum exceeding that granted under the Public Money Acts.

The popularity of the private companies was founded on two things. First, the long list of improvements for which they were ready to lend money, a list which went beyond drainage and building to include many matters undreamt of by Pusey in the 'forties. Second, the longer period of time over which the improvement charge could be amortized. Under the Private Money Act of 1849 a landowner was required to extinguish the charge in 22 years which meant that when money was ob-

[76] B.P.P., *Rep. of S.C. on Powers Vested in Companies,* p. 3.

[77] B.P.P., *Rep. of S.C. (H. of L.) to enable . . . Entailed Estates to charge . . . for . . . Draining,* 1849, p. 8.

[78] B.P.P., *Rep. of R.C. on Depressed Condition of Agricultural Interests* (1881, XV), p. 63.

[79] B.P.P., *Rep. of S.C. on Improvement of Land,* p. 45; appendix F.

[80] B.P.P., *Rep. of R.C. on Depressed Condition of Agricultural Interests* (1882, XIV), p. 171.

tained at 4½ per cent his annual payment (of interest and capital) amounted to 7¼ per cent. The private companies, however, were empowered to charge for longer terms of years —25, 31 or (much less often) 50 years. In this way, when money was obtained at 4½ per cent, the companies charged something less than 6¾ per cent over a period of 25 years, and 6 per cent over a period of 31 years.[81] These lowered annual charges were of consequence to landowners, for they could more easily persuade their tenants to make the payments in the shape of a higher rent; or if they failed in this, as probably happened more often than the Inclosure Commissioners were ready to admit,[82] the lower charge might well prove attractive to the landowner himself.

The success of the land companies probably had much to do with the passing of the Improvement of Land Act in 1864, a general consolidating statute. This made it possible for landowners to borrow from any source under the supervision of the Inclosure Commissioners for a large number of improvements: drainage and irrigation, embanking, enclosing, and reclamation; the making of permanent farm roads, tramways, and railways for agricultural purposes; the clearing of land and the erection of farm houses and other buildings; the planting for shelter or for any beneficial purpose which would increase the permanent value of the land; the construction of enginehouses, waterwheels, saw and other mills, kilns, shafts, wells, banks, reservoirs, dams, watercourses, and bridges which would increase the value of the land for agricultural purposes; the erection of any engine or machinery of a permanent nature to effect improvements in drainage or irrigation; and finally the construction or improvement of jetties or landing places for the transport of cattle, sheep, and other agricultural stock and produce.[83]

This proliferation of landowners' powers to charge their

[81] Denton, "On Land Drainage and Improvement by Loans from Government or Public Companies," *Journ. of R. Ag. Soc.*, 1868.
[82] See below.
[83] 27 & 28 Vict. c. 114.

estates provoked a revealing debate. It began in 1863 with the proposal of the Lands Improvement Company to charge estates for investment in local railways—[84] a proposal which led to the appointment of a Select Committee to inquire into its feasibility.[85] George Darby, a witness before the Committee, doubted that the Inclosure Commissioners could accurately assess such a charge; and he stated his belief that "you have gone a very great length already in charging estates . . . I am every day alarmed respecting the charges which are being made on estates." [86] In the following year the Improvement of Land Act, which as we have seen sanctioned charges for agricultural railways, came before Parliament. Darby had little support except that which he probably would have wished to disavow—that of the venerable Lord St. Leonards who almost a quarter of a century before had (as Sir Edward Sugden) attacked Pusey's Act. Almost inaudible, he "was understood to object to many of the provisions of the Bill, and to say that in his opinion a more hazardous measure had never been brought forward." [87]

Times, however, had much changed since 1840, and the aged lawyer was rebuked as a reactionary. The Lord Chancellor declared that "if the law relating to landed property had been allowed to remain as it was sixty years ago that law would have operated as a continual drag upon the progress of society." [88] According to Earl Grey, "if the noble and learned Lord [St. Leonards] wished to abolish the whole system of settlement of landed estates, he had only to act upon the narrow principle of preventing improvements . . . It was only the relaxation of the old laws during the last twenty years, which had prevented the law of settled estates from being swept away as an intolerable nuisance to the country." [89]

This debate provoked a leading article which might well be

[84] B.P.P., *Report of Select Committee (H. of L.) on Charging of Entailed Estates for Railways* (1863, VII), p. 17.

[85] *Hansard*, 3rd S., vol. 169, p. 1216.

[86] B.P.P., *Rep. of S.C. on Charging . . . for Railways*, p. 36.

[87] *Hansard*, 3rd S., vol. 175, p. 1826.

[88] *Ibid.*, p. 1827.

[89] *Ibid.*, pp. 1827–28.

quoted at length. In it *The Times* burst forth in eloquent praise of the Inclosure Commissioners as the body responsible for this happy adaptation of family settlement and limited ownership to the needs of agricultural enterprise.

> The old notion was that, if you would prevent a possessor of land from squandering his property, you must debar him from the beneficial use of it. Therefore it was that the houses of wards in chancery fell into ruin, and their lands became desolate. It was for this reason that the fields of the church grew rank with weeds. . . . We have got rid of all this evil and odium by the simplest and most successful invention in modern legislation. The fear was that the man in possession would make light of the interest of the man who was to come after him; that the master of the Grammar School would leave the next master nothing to carry on with, that the rector would devour the benefice, that the tenant for life would eat up the inheritance. . . . The Legislature, therefore, some twenty years ago called into being a corporation which now represents . . . all the successors for all existing charity trustees, all future rectors and vicars and all the unborn heirs, and all people kept out of property which must in future become theirs. These yet-to-be born people of property now move about upon the earth incarnate in a corps of Parliament-created representatives; and they look on, and agree or disagree, while the present possessors build a new school-house . . . or round off the angles of a patch of glebe, or drain a great district of land, or build beast-houses or apportion encumbrances, or redeem rent-charges . . . setting everything, in fact, to rights, and in the most profitable condition for permanent enjoyment . . . [This] general guardian of all remaindermen [was] called the Enclosure Commission . . . This Commission, united to the person in possession, make up almost an ownership in fee, and by their joint action the intolerable shackles of the old Norman real property law become as soft as elastic bands.[90]

Appropriately enough, when some years later a young lord complained that he lacked freedom to manage his estates well, *The Times* publicly rebuked him for ignorance of his own

[90] *The Times*, April 20, 1863.

powers. At his audit dinner in 1879 Lord Carrington had declared that settlement so tied his hands that he was incapable of making improvements. *The Times* pointed out that Lord Carrington was in fact free "with the assistance of the Enclosure Commissioners [to do] anything . . . that is wanted to keep the estate in condition." [91]

## III

So far this account of the Inclosure Commissioners has been confined to tracing the growth of the Commissioners' functions. It might be appropriate now to turn to an examination of the Commissioners at work: to follow the inspectors in the field and to look more closely at the Commissioners who served in the London office.

In 1873 there were forty-six inspectors in the employ of the Inclosure Commissioners. As one Commissioner put it, the inspectors were men "who have been brought up . . . in the study and practice of all agricultural matters." [92] They were, however, something more than run-of-the-mill land agents and surveyors. If inspectors like H. W. Keary, Andrew Thompson, J. C. Morton, and James Fair were typical, they were leading land agents. In fact, it was suggested that employment under the Inclosure Commissioners was itself a sign that an agent had achieved a considerable reputation in his profession.[93]

The inspectors were part-time employees of the Inclosure Commissioners, paid by the day, and resident in different parts of the country. They were not, however, necessarily confined to inspecting estate improvements in their own localities. Andrew Thompson, for example, who resided at Keele in Staffordshire, journeyed widely in his tours of inspection, visiting estates in all the Midland counties and going as far afield as the East

[91] *Ibid.*, Oct. 30, 1879.
[92] B.P.P., *Rep. of S.C. on Improvement of Land*, p. 6.
[93] *Ibid.*, p. 21.

Riding of Yorkshire.[94] Improvement works varied greatly in their complexity and magnitude, and the Commissioners were inclined to send one of their best inspectors like Thompson to report on a special case wherever it happened to be located. Sometimes they were anxious to have a second opinion.[95]

In his application to the Inclosure Commissioners, the landowner specified his proposed improvements.[96] With this application in hand, the inspector made his first visit and his first report. If the landowner had applied for a loan to finance draining, the inspector—to judge from Thompson's reports—would inform the Board in London how much land needed draining; whether the proposed method was adequate; if not, how to make it so; the cost per acre; and the likely increase in the value of the land. If the landowner had applied for a loan to finance building, he would report in a similar way on the adequacy and likely profitability of what the landowner proposed. He was also concerned, however, to report upon the condition of the old buildings and whether they could be repaired—for normal estate repairs under the system of settlement were the sole responsibility of the tenant for life. Not infrequently the inspector made some mention of a landowner's idiosyncrasies—or of an agent's.

The following examples give some indication of the nature of Thompson's preliminary reports. On the Lancashire estate of Sir H. B. Houghton—of which Thompson declared "I have never in my experience inspected so large an Estate more in want of drainage"—there were 3,000 out of a total of 4,315 acres in need of draining. Thompson approved the owner's plan to erect his own tilery, for that would reduce costs. The draining, he predicted, would bring an increased value of thirteen shillings an acre.[97] On the Warwickshire estate of Lord

[94] In the Sneyd MSS, there are five volumes (numbered 4–8) of Andrew Thompson's reports to the Inclosure Commissioners, for the years 1857–68.

[95] B.P.P., *Rep. of S.C. on Improvement of Land*, p. 6.

[96] See appendix G, B.P.P., *Rep. of S.C. on Improvement of Land*, for examples of documents used.

[97] Sneyd MSS, Thompson's reports, vol. 4, Nov. 19, 1859.

Willoughby de Broke—where "the buildings are in a very dilapidated state"—the new farm houses would raise rents seven shillings an acre.[98] On Captain Byron's estate at Thrumpton Hall, Nottinghamshire, Thompson approved the building of thirteen new cottages in the place of thatched huts "only 10 feet square having one room below and one above in the roof. One could scarcely conceive anything more wretched." [99] He reported frequently on the Middleton estates in Lincolnshire and Nottinghamshire where the largest works in his inspection were under way. He informed the Inclosure Commissioners of the late Lord Middleton's aversion to improvements—he had left £300,000 for the purchase of land and not a penny for anything else—and of the late Lord's agent, Mr. Chowler, who was eighty and also an enemy to improvement.[100]

Sometimes an inspector like Andrew Thompson was sent to an estate, with the knowledge and consent of the Inclosure Commissioners, as a kind of consultant. This might happen when a landowner, new to the responsibilities of his property, was faced by the consequences of long neglect. Aware that much needed doing and that he would profit from good advice, he applied to the Inclosure Commissioners for the services of a first-rate inspector to make a survey of the estate and to advise him on what he should do and what proposals to make to the Inclosure Commissioners. The inspector then advised him generally, and an application followed.[101] It is not clear how much this consultant service of the Inclosure Commissioners was made available; in Thompson's reports there are not more than two cases of it.

Once the inspector gave his approval of the proposed works, the Inclosure Commissioners issued a provisional order whereby the applicant could obtain credit to get his works under way. If these involved drainage, they were inspected again on completion; if they involved buildings, they were inspected in

[98] Ibid., vol. 4, n.d., 1858.
[99] Ibid., vol. 5, May, 1860.
[100] Ibid., vol. 5, March 30, 1861.
[101] B.P.P., Rep. of S.C. on Improvement of Land, p. 21.

mid-course as well to make certain that the exact specifications ordered by the Inclosure Commissioners as to sizes and kinds of material were followed. Drainage therefore had two inspections, buildings three, generally by the same inspector.

Thompson's reports testify to his vigilance during these inspections. He refused to approve draining on Lord Forester's estate, represented at 4½ feet, but in fact only 3 feet.[102] He recommended that £300 be deducted from Sir Robert Gerard's charge for farm buildings on his Lancashire estate on the ground that they were unnecessarily ornamental.[103] He ordered the removal of insufficiently fired bricks used in the Earl of Shrewsbury's farm buildings.[104] And he was equally firm with C. W. Hoskyns, himself a writer on agricultural subjects, who had used young larch in his farm buildings: "I cannot pass roofs having the rafters made of the tops of larch trees." [105]

Once the inspector gave his approval of the completed works, the Inclosure Commissioners authorized a charge being placed on the estate for a fixed number of years. During this period no inspection was undertaken to ascertain whether the improvement was being satisfactorily maintained. The landowner had only to insure his buildings and to make an annual statement that his drainage was in working order. When the legislation of 1864 was under discussion, it was suggested that an inspection be made every two to four years. At least one of the Inclosure Commissioners approved this proposal, but nothing was done to implement it on the ground of expense to the state and annoyance to the landowner.[106]

Whenever landowner and inspector differed and the differences proved intractable, the Board of Inclosure Commissioners constituted the final court of appeal, and the landowner would probably be invited to visit the London office. When asked

[102] Sneyd MSS, Thompson's reports, vol. 4, Oct. 7, 1859.
[103] Ibid., vol. 5, Jan. 14, 1860.
[104] Ibid., vol. 8, Oct. 13, 1860.
[105] Ibid., vol. 4, Nov. 3, 1857.
[106] B.P.P., Rep. of S.C. on Improvement of Land, p. 17. Ridley was the Commissioner.

once what might happen on such an occasion, an Inclosure Commissioner declared that meetings of this sort passed off amicably enough: "we should certainly not force our view upon the landowner. I do not remember any case where we have done so." He then added a bit disconcertingly, "we may require alterations to be made." [107]

Who were these men who sat in authority over the land-owners of England? The Board of Inclosure Commissioners from the start had three members—a number which the Trevelyan–Northcote inquiry into government offices recommended on several grounds: first, that it made possible the deliberation and discussion which their business required; second, since their work demanded a full knowledge both of agriculture and the law, three officers were more likely to command such knowledge than one; and last, "a well-constituted Board" was more likely to gain the confidence of the public "than the unchecked authority of any individual." [108]

Apart from the aristocratic Commissioners of Woods and Forests, like Lords Lincoln and Morpeth, who were briefly members of the Board of Inclosure Commissioners, there were six other Inclosure Commissioners in the years 1845–80 whose membership was for the most part more lasting and whose contribution was more substantial. These men were George Darby (1798–1877), George Ridley (1819–80), H. C. Mules (1816–62), G. W. Cooke (1814–65), William Blamire (1790–1862), and James Caird (1816–92). The first four were barristers, the last two were practical agriculturists. All but Mules and Cooke were at some time Members of Parliament. At least five (of Mules there is very little known) came of families of varying gentility. Darby was educated at Westminster School and Cambridge, and married the daughter of a Member of Parliament. Ridley was a younger son of a well-known North Country family, and was educated at Christ Church, Oxford.

---

[107] *Ibid.*, p. 10. Ridley was the Commissioner.
[108] B.P.P., *Reports of Committees of Inquiry into Public Offices* (1854, XXVII), p. 253.

Cooke came of a respectable West Country family, and graduated from Jesus College, Oxford. Blamire was the son of a Cumberland landowner, nephew to John Christian Curwen, and was educated at Westminster School and Oxford. Caird was the younger son of the procurator fiscal for Wigtownshire, and attended Edinburgh University for about a year. Probably the most remarkable of these men were Blamire and Caird; although Cooke, who was a litterateur, traveler, and authority on the law of land tenures, is not without his interest. Fortunately, for Blamire and Caird we have more than a smattering of information.[109]

From his youth Blamire was a dedicated agriculturist. Influenced by his uncle who was a pioneer of agricultural improvement in the North Country, Blamire took a farm on his father's estate in preference to pursuing a more conventional career in the Church or the Law. He became known as a breeder of stock, and won a large popularity among the Cumberland "statesmen," which was eloquently testified to by his unseating Lord Lowther in the Cumberland election of 1831.[110] He sat in Parliament as a Whig from 1831 to 1836, speaking infrequently and for the most part briefly, usually on subjects connected with Cumberland. But when he spoke at some length, he commanded attention by combining an attractive diffidence of manner with an impressive and formidable array of information. In fact he made his parliamentary reputation by such a speech in 1836 on the subject of tithe commutation.

> Connected [as he said] . . . with a part of the country in many respects peculiarly circumstanced as to the payment of tithes, and having for a number of years had considerable experience in all rural matters, and having as a practical man, had ample opportunity of observing the working of the tithing system in

[109] See article on G. W. Cooke in *D.N.B.* Information about Darby, Ridley, and Mules has been pieced together from various works of reference. Darby was on the Commission 1845–77; Ridley, 1860–80; Mules 1852–62; Cooke 1862–65; Blamire 1845–60; Caird 1865–92.

[110] H. Lonsdale, *The Worthies of Cumberland: John Christian Curwen, William Blamire* (London, 1867), p. 246.

its various ramifications, he trusted he might be allowed to obtrude himself for a short time on the attention of the House.[111]

He obtruded himself so effectively as to become chief commissioner for the commutation of tithes and the major architect of a reform in the tenure of English land so vast and detailed as to have defied any historian's attempt at chronicling it. "Few reforms of such magnitude," it has been said, "involving so many interests, have given such universal satisfaction, and have stood the test of time so well." [112]

This was but the first, although the most remarkable, of Blamire's achievements as a public administrator. He also advised the government on the subject of copyhold enfranchisement, and was appointed commissioner for that purpose when legislation was framed to carry it out. His evidence before the Select Committee on Inclosures in 1844 was noted earlier in this chapter; a biographer described that evidence as "one of the most important sources of information concerning the tenure and incidents of commons." [113] He became of course an Inclosure Commissioner, and as has been noted, he did so while still a Tithe Commissioner. According to his biographer, he combined these offices without additional salary. We are told of Blamire's prodigious labors, all the more prodigious for being performed in a London office by a man bred to an out-of-doors life.[114] It has been said that these labors were "embodied in statutes and official reports." [115] But they did not end there. Like the efforts of Philip Pusey, they helped to re-make the face of rural England.

The name of James Caird is better known than that of William Blamire, for Caird was a publicist, the high priest of high farming. He came to farming, he once said, "after imbibing the principles from the Chair of Agriculture in the

---

[111] *Hansard*, 3rd S., vol. 32, pp. 607–15.
[112] *D.N.B.*, article on Blamire.
[113] *Ibid.*
[114] Lonsdale, *Worthies of Cumberland*, pp. 298–99.
[115] *Ibid.*

University of Edinburgh." [116] In the 1840's he took a clay farm on the Earl of Galloway's estate where he remained a tenant for two decades. In 1849 when it seemed as if free trade might provide too severe a climate for English farming, Caird came suddenly to public notice with a short pamphlet which assured farmers that their condition was far from hopeless. As he put it,

> a tenant-farmer, having no other occupation, and paying a money rent exceeding £1000 a year; and observing the fears of his brethren, particularly in the south, he is induced to lay before them, without argument, a simple narrative detailing a mode of management comparatively independent of foreign protection.[117]

The title of his pamphlet—*High Farming under Liberal Covenants, The Best Substitute for Protection*—summed up Caird's "mode of management." His program was essentially that of the improvement party—the party of Peel, Graham, Pusey, Earl Spencer, and the Duke of Richmond. Caird looked to landowners generally to lead the way, to invest in draining and farm buildings, to afford farmers security, and to spur them on. He believed that landowners would draw in increased rent "a fair interest upon the capital expended." [118] Caird's pamphlet quickly ran through eight editions, and was followed in 1850 by a reply to critics. Being a farmer and an educated man, Caird's casting of the protectionists in the role of the stupid party, blind even to opportunities and advantages that lay at hand, made a visible impression.

> Population [he wrote] may double for them; garden farming may spread itself over the country to supply the increasing demand; dairy produce may be sent in by the early trains every morning within a circuit of 40 or 50 miles of every one of our large towns; light portable manures, and cheap feeding stuffs may be conveyed from the remotest quarters, and the labour

[116] J. Caird, *High Farming Vindicated and Farther Illustrated* (Edinburgh, 1850), p. 25.

[117] J. Caird, *High Farming, under Liberal Covenants, The Best Substitute for Protection* (Edinburgh, 1849).

[118] Caird, *High Farming*, p. 26.

market be filled to overflowing; but all these advantages appear, from their own statements, to be unappreciated and unappropriated by them.[119]

Caird drove home his pamphleteering success in the next several years. In 1850 *The Times* set on foot an inquiry into the state of English farming, and hired Caird to conduct it. One of Sir Robert Peel's last acts was to encourage Caird to undertake the task. He urged on him the importance of reminding English farmers of the many examples of good farming to be found, and the moral to be drawn from those examples: namely that good farming was possible under free trade, and that poor farming was in all likelihood the consequence of protection.[120] Later Caird claimed that his "letters in the Times, continued from week to week for nearly two years, and embracing every county in England, were acknowledged to have supplied conclusive proof that 'protection had not stimulated improvement but had been the parent of neglect.' " [121] Although Caird was not the man to avoid self-praise, his letters no doubt were of importance in carrying the improvement party through some difficult years.[122] When published as a book, they provided the most notable general account of English farming since the days of Arthur Young and William Marshall.[123]

On one very important matter, however, Caird was not of

[119] Caird, *High Farming Vindicated*, p. 21.

[120] Caird, *English Agriculture*, pp. vii–viii.

[121] Add. MSS, 44,438, folio 112, Caird to W. E. Gladstone, March 21, 1873.

[122] Caird's correspondence with Gladstone, 1870–73, shows him in a not very pretty light, complaining that his services to English farming had not been adequately recognized.

[123] Caird described his work as the "only general account" of English farming since Arthur Young, and the *D.N.B.* described it as the "first." Mr. McGregor has rightly pointed to Henry Colman, *European Agriculture and Rural Economy from Personal Observation* (Boston, 1846), 2 vols., as being largely a general account of British farming which preceded Caird, but Colman is far less reliable than Mr. McGregor suggests; see Ernle, *English Farming*, p. xcvii.

the improvement party—at any rate, as led by Peel and Graham
and other landowners. For he was not in sympathy with the
social and political aims of the landowning class. He was, as
he later described himself to Gladstone, a close friend of Cob-
den and Bright—"with both of whom it has been my great
pride to have acted for many years on terms of intimate personal friendship." [124] As a Member of Parliament, he moved in
1858 to bring in a bill to assimilate the county franchise of
Scotland to that of England in order to reduce the political
power of the Scottish aristocracy. "The Government of Scotland," he declared, "was practically in the hands of the aristocracy, while the whole artisan and peasant population of Scotland were disfranchised." [125] In the same session f Parliament
he voiced an old complaint, that the cost of land transfer was
excessive—a complaint that often led to attack on the system
of settlement.[126] In his writings the Cobdenite hostility to strict
family settlement was made explicit: that "artificial system of
entail and settlement," he once called it; [127] and on another
occasion he declared that a simplified land law, with greater
freedom of sale, especially of encumbered estates, "would be
more beneficial to the owners and occupiers of land, and to
the labourers, in this country, than any question connected
with agriculture that has yet enjoyed the attention of the legis-
lature." [128]

# IV

In the light of Caird's opinions on settlement, there is a
certain appropriateness in his appointment to the Inclosure

[124] Add. MSS, 44,435, folio 33, Caird to W. E. Gladstone, Aug. 7, 1872.
[125] *Hansard*, 3rd S., vol. 150, p. 196. See also *Hansard*, 3rd S., vol. 158,
p. 385, for Caird's speech on the United States.
[126] *Ibid.*, vol. 150, p. 1494.
[127] J. Caird, *The Landed Interest and the Supply of Food* (London,
1878), p. 114.
[128] Caird, *English Agriculture*, p. 495.

Commission in 1865. By this time the Inclosure Commissioners
had reached the height of their powers. They were then filling
a large role as guardians of strict settlement. After 1865 they
became subject to increasing criticism, in large part because
settlement itself became subject to increasing criticism. The
years after 1865 were thus the years of decline in the history
of the Inclosure Commissioners—a decline which the final part
of this chapter will trace.

Shortly before Caird's appointment, criticism of the Inclosure
Commissioners made itself heard for the first time. The complaint was that limited owners, especially in Scotland, were too
closely supervised, that the Inclosure Commissioners were over-
bearing and arbitrary, inclined to impose uniform rules on
landowners, agents, and even resident inspectors. This was said
in the House of Commons, and some Scottish members were
indignant and vociferous. Caird among others urged upon the
Home Secretary "the propriety of impressing upon the Commissioners the importance of giving enlarged powers to the
resident Inspectors in Scotland." [129] It may have been his
knowledge of Scottish farming that in these circumstances
accounted for his appointment as Inclosure Commissioner.

The criticism of 1865 did not come to much. The Home
Secretary, Sir George Grey, himself a Northumbrian landowner, heeded it, but refused to believe in a tyranny exercised
by the Inclosure Commissioners. He declared that his office
had no power over the Commissioners, but promised the House
to request of them an answer to its criticism.[130] He therefore
requested that the Inclosure Commissioners inform him of what
rules they applied in sanctioning proposed improvements.[131]

The Inclosure Commissioners denied that their rules insisted
on absolute uniformity. As regards draining, it was the business

---

[129] *Hansard*, 3rd S., vol. 179, p. 1130.
[130] *Ibid.*, p. 1129.
[131] B.P.P., *A Copy of a Letter from the Secretary of State for the Home
Department to the Inclosure Commissioners, as to the Rules and Practice
of the Board, and of their Answer thereto* (1865, XLVII).

of each inspector to decide what was best, and there were no rules at all. As regards farmhouses, uniform specifications as to sound construction had been laid down by the London office in accordance with the best architectural opinion; but the plans for buildings were interfered with "as little as possible," and there was a great latitude allowed in the choice of materials. As regards cottages, the Commissioners declared themselves "willing to adopt any plan which affords a reasonable amount of accommodation, and provides for the separation of the sexes, and for health, comfort and decency."

Although the Commissioners may not have been as arbitrary as their critics judged them, it was inevitable that they exercised a large control. While avowing their desire to facilitate improvements, the Commissioners reminded Parliament "that they have also the responsible duty . . . of guarding the interests of those entitled in remainder or reversion to the estates proposed to be charged for the improvements." [132]

In 1872 Lord Salisbury brought forward a bill which was concerned to reduce in a particular respect the power of the Inclosure Commissioners. This was the Limited Owners' Improvement Bill. In the brief debate on its second reading Lord Salisbury pointed to the frequent "struggle in a limited owner's mind as to whether he should save his money for the younger children or should invest it in the improvement of the estate." [133] Under the Act of 1864, he continued, a limited owner could do both, but only under the supervision of the Inclosure Commissioners—that is, under what he described as "an amount of tutelage that very few landowners would submit to." [134] The result was, he argued, that the Act had been infrequently used in this way, and it was therefore necessary to limit the powers of the Inclosure Commissioners, if limited owners were to invest their own money in agricultural improvements.

[132] *Ibid.*
[133] *Hansard*, 3rd S., vol. 212, p. 7.
[134] *Ibid.*, p. 9.

It may well be that Lord Salisbury had more than this object in mind.[135] By the early 1870's settlement was under severe attack as a bulwark of aristocracy and an obstacle to agricultural improvement. When he introduced his bill, Lord Salisbury made a point of defending settlement, particularly on the ground that it "tended rather to the improvement of land than otherwise." [136] His bill, however, admitted to a defect in the working of settlement. In proposing a remedy [137]—one not without its risks—Lord Salisbury may have hoped to make settlement unexceptionable and thus outflank public criticism.

Whatever the motives of this enigmatic statesman his activities had at least one significant result—the Select Committee on the Improvement of Land. This Committee, impressive both in its witnesses and its members, proved something of a turning point in the history of the Inclosure Commissioners, marking out a kind of beginning of the end. Among other things, it recommended what Lord Salisbury had proposed, that the investment of a landowner's money should no longer be supervised by the Inclosure Commissioners.[138] Lord Salisbury ran a risk here. If Parliament was to begin relaxing the stringency of the Commissioners' supervision, where might that relaxation end? In short, what might become of the sanctions of family settlement?

The Committee in fact disclosed that the sanctions were already being undermined by economic forces. Several decades of experience had led to the conclusion that agricultural investment was risky. We have seen how modest were the Duke of Bedford's returns. There was no certainty, probably even little likelihood, that improvements would pay for themselves. It followed therefore that it was almost impossible to guarantee that an estate would not lose by undertaking them. In at-

---

[135] Earl Grey was not impressed by Salisbury's avowed object; see *Hansard*, 3rd S., vol. 215, p. 516.

[136] *Ibid.*, vol. 212, p. 7.

[137] *Ibid.*, p. 11.

[138] B.P.P., *Rep. of S.C. on Improvement of Land*, p. vii.

tributing responsibility for this state of affairs, the Committee put too much at the door of rising costs and interest rates, and too little at the door of an unwarranted confidence in new techniques.[139]

The Committee, however, brought this state of affairs forcibly to public attention by adducing a few, well chosen examples. Tenants, as it pointed out, sometimes paid the charge of 7 per cent on drainage improvements, but more often they paid 5 per cent. This meant for the landowner that at the end of 25 years, after a possible annual loss of 2 per cent, there would be a profit of 5 per cent—but only if the drains continued to work, an eventuality which was now looked upon as far from certain.[140] As to the profitability of farm buildings, an experienced agent testified that he never knew tenants to pay 5 per cent on the outlay, although he had known them sometimes to pay 3 per cent; [141] and as the report pointed out, "if for the sake of obtaining, even in perpetuity, without any cost of maintenance, an addition to his rent of 4 per cent on the effective outlay, the landowner accepts a charge of 7 per cent, he must inevitably be a loser." [142] As to the "balance sheet of cottage building," on it the report dolefully observed, "it is unnecessary to dwell." [143]

---

[139] According to B.P.P., *Rep. of S.C. on Improvement of Land,* p. 5: "Drainage which, 30 years ago, cost from £4 to £5 an acre, now costs £7 in some parts of the country, £10 in others. The cost of building has also risen very largely; so that cottages which could formerly have been built for £300 the pair, now cost from £360 to £400."

[140] *Ibid.,* p. iv. See Nicholson, *The Principles of Field Drainage,* chap. 9.

[141] B.P.P., *Rep. of S.C. on Improvement of Land,* p. 292.

[142] *Ibid.,* p. iv. As the report explained: "On a loan of £1,000 he would for 25 years pay £70 and receive £40; in other words he would annually lose £30. After the expiration of the term of 25 years, he would annually gain £40. But by the 4 per cent. tables, the value of an annuity at £30 for 25 years is £468, which is the sum that he would lose. The value of an annuity of £40, commencing 25 years hence, is £375, which is the sum that he would gain. He must, therefore, in such a case, be a loser of £93, even on the assumption that his farm building lasted without repair for ever."

[143] *Ibid.,* p. iv.

From the evidence presented to the Committee, it is plain that the Inclosure Commissioners, having willy nilly come to recognize this state of affairs, had relaxed their rule that the return on improvements must cover the charge.[144] Some years later, in testifying before the Royal Commission on Agricultural Depression, George Ridley removed whatever doubts may have still remained on the subject. He bluntly informed the Commission that loans for improvements were no longer conditional on bringing a sufficient profit. Asked whether this was an evasion of the Improvement Acts, Ridley replied, "we do not evade the Acts, we know the different set of circumstances." [145] Put another way, Ridley was admitting that if agricultural improvements were to go on, the old sanctions of family settlement would have to be jettisoned, and the future interests of the estate as a family property subordinated to the present condition of the land.

This was the doctrine that informed the revolutionary Act of 1882, the Settled Land Act. This legislation made it impossible to insure by a settlement that a particular landed property would remain in a particular landed family. It allowed a tenant for life for the first time to sell a part or all of the family estate although it required that the sales money remain subject to the family settlement. In short, it was the principle of the Settled Land Act to protect a capital sum, not a landed estate.

The Act further empowered the tenant for life who sold land to apply the sales money, if he chose, to the improvement of his estate. This provided him with an alternative method of improving that was cheaper and more convenient than the method used under the earlier Acts. Under the Settled Land Act he needed to obtain only the services of an approved sur-

[144] See Ridley's evidence on charges for buildings (B.P.P., *Rep. of S.C. on Improvement of Land*, p. 15). It may be significant that in describing the work of the Inclosure Commissioners, Caird (*The Landed Interest*, p. 85) merely observed that "some return seems always to be reckoned upon."

[145] B.P.P., *Rep. of R.C. on Depression of Agricultural Interests* (1881, XV), p. 53.

veyor. Having done this, he was under no obligation to submit
plans or to meet detailed specifications. The surveyor saw that
the improvements were "properly executed"—which presumably meant that they were neither frivolous in conception nor
wasteful in execution.[146]

Not surprisingly the work of the Land Commissioners—as
the Inclosure Commissioners were called under the Act of 1882
—declined markedly. In 1882, £151,923 was borrowed for
drainage and £150,721 for farm buildings under the Improvement of Land Acts. Twenty years later £1,950 was borrowed
for drainage and £54,438 for buildings.[147] As the old method
of financing improvement declined, the new one took its place.
Between 1893 and 1902 there was an annual outlay of £220,000
for agricultural improvements under the Settled Land Act.[148]
In this way the Land Commissioners, who became part of the
new Board of Agriculture in 1889, were bypassed.[149]

What was accomplished by the Inclosure Commissioners
before 1882? The expenditure on agricultural improvements
sanctioned by the Inclosure Commissioners between 1846 and
1881 amounted to £13,597,620. Of this sum £8,259,404 had
been spent on drainage (inclusive of the 4 million spent under
the Public Money Drainage Acts), £3,397,133 on farm buildings, £823,190 on cottages.[150] In 1873 James Caird, calculating
what had been done up to that date, had speculated on its significance. He guessed that drainage worth eight million pounds
would lay dry two million acres, and guessing at a modest
estimate that ten million acres had needed draining he con-

[146] For undertaking agricultural improvements under the Settled Land
Act, see *Public General Statutes*, 1882, pp. 123–24; also B.P.P., *Rep. of R.C.
on Agricultural Depression* (1895, XVI, Part III), pp. 319–20.

[147] B.P.P., *Rep. of R.C. on Agricultural Depression* (1895, XVI, Part
III) appendix 29; B.P.P., *Board of Agriculture: Annual Report of Proceedings under the Tithe Acts*. . . . (1903, XVII), table 12.

[148] B.P.P., *Board of Agriculture Rep.* (1903, XVII), table 13.

[149] For the new Board, see F. L. C. Floud, *The Ministry of Agriculture
and Fisheries* (London and New York, 1927), *passim*.

[150] B.P.P., *Rep. of R.C. on Depressed Condition of Agricultural Interests* (1882, XIV), paper submitted by James Caird. See Appendix VIII.

cluded that about one fifth of what needed doing had been done by means of investment issuing directly from the state or from land companies chartered by the state. If Caird's guesses were something like the truth of the matter, the English state in the nineteenth century may be said to have given a strong impulse to agricultural improvement.[151]

Since the intervention of the state was in large part intended to adapt strict family settlement to the agricultural needs of nineteenth-century England, the critics of settlement looked upon that intervention as artificial and superfluous. They would have preferred simply to abolish the settlement of land. Eventually this became the policy of the state. Nevertheless, the work of the Inclosure Commissioners, only part of which has been closely examined here, constituted a notable chapter in the history of nineteenth-century agriculture and estate administration.[152]

[151] B.P.P., *Rep. of S.C. on Improvement of Land*, p. 344. It should be added that other experts like Bailey Denton seem to have been less optimistic than Caird, although Denton's remarks on the subject were unfortunately vague (see p. 67).

[152] See Appendix IX for a summary of the legislation dealing with agricultural improvements.

# ✍ CONCLUSION

IT MIGHT BE USEFUL to devote this brief conclusion to the question, were the administrators of English landed estates businesslike? If we are to believe some observers they were utterly lacking in this quality. A recent opinion, for example, has made much of the strength of the political imperatives of the landed society. It has argued that the economic functions of landowners were severely subordinated to their political functions, that landowners exerted a kind of political tyranny over their dependants, that they were far more interested to know how their tenants voted than how they farmed.[1]

If this were true, one would expect nineteenth-century land agents to have spent a great deal of time looking into the political opinions of those who applied for farms. But little if any evidence has turned up that they did so. Their chief concern was to find if tenants could farm well. Perhaps they rarely concerned themselves with the political opinions of tenants for the simple reason that they could count on tenants' showing a considerable malleability in their opinions. That English farmers did not display so intense an interest in politics as frequently to insist on having opinions of their own seemed natural enough even to an American observer.[2] In short, as Professor Gash has put it,

[1] O. R. McGregor in Ernle, *English Farming*, pp. cxxix–cxxx.
[2] Colman, *European Agriculture*, I, 168.

178

in the country districts . . . the situation was semi-feudal, and the tenant followed the political tenets of his landlord as a kind of political service due to the owner of the land from the occupier. It would be a mistake to attribute this entirely or even mainly to coercion.[3]

The theory of a landowner's tyranny goes on to allege that landowners found the means of coercing their tenants by denying them leases and security of tenure. Tenants went without leases because in return they obtained lower rents; and landowners were content to accept lower rents and slovenly farming because they preferred to maintain their political power.

As the history of the game laws demonstrates only too brutally [this theory concludes] landlords never hesitated to coerce their tenantry to accept practices which increased the amenities of their estates; among these good farming did not figure importantly.[4]

This is melodrama. It is a ticklish matter to generalize about the prevalence and significance of the long lease. But it might be suggested that the long lease was far from unknown; that it was commoner on the great estates than elsewhere; that when it was criticized, as it was after 1815, the reasons were economic rather than political; that good farming was sometimes practiced without it; and that its prevalence did not necessarily put an end to political subordination, as the example of the Scottish farmers might indicate. The subject of leases clearly needs detailed study, but in an economic not a political context.[5]

It needs no further research, however, to be sceptical of the implied backwardness of English farming in the nineteenth century. No doubt landowners can be found who heeded nothing but their political functions. Yet it may be asked what

[3] N. Gash, *Politics in the Age of Peel* (London, 1953), p. 177.
[4] O. R. McGregor in Ernle, *English Farming*, p. cxxxi.
[5] See the useful review of Mr. McGregor's essay by G. Mingay in *The Agricultural History Review*, vol. X, 1962.

nation farmed better than the English? According to Sir John Clapham, "in no country at any time has the combination of arable farming and sheep farming been so successfully carried out as in nineteenth-century Britain." [6] In fact the mid-nineteenth century saw, as Caird once said, a vast improvement in farming methods; [7] and of all the forces responsible for this transformation none was more important than that exerted by English landowners and their agents.

Another opinion—a nineteenth-century opinion—had it that English farming was backward and that English landowners were poor managers for social rather than political reasons. What was held to be at fault was the institution of strict family settlement. Admittedly landowners were passionately concerned to keep their estates in their families. No one has put this better than the Psalmist: "Their inward thought is, that their houses shall continue for ever, and their dwelling places to all generations; they call their lands after their own names." Admittedly a device that was useful to this end was frequently employed. To what degree, however, settlement affected agriculture is not certain.

It was argued that because landowners were limited in their powers of borrowing they failed to invest sufficiently in agricultural improvements. In the early years of the century there was truth in this. But even here a qualification needs making. Settlement in practice was probably never as restrictive of a landowner's powers as it has been made out. This is a subject that needs detailed investigation; but it can be said with some confidence that the inherent freedoms of the system—which have been noted in the previous chapter—inevitably tended to considerable flexibility in practice. It can also be said with confidence that as the nineteenth century progressed settlement came to be flexibly practiced with increasing frequency. The Duke of Bedford, for example, might have chosen to improve by borrowing, for he was not the prisoner of his family settlement. In any case, as we have seen, by the middle of the

[6] Quoted in Chambers, *The Workshop of the World*, p. 85.
[7] Caird, *The Landed Interest*, p. 29.

century the state had set about removing the difficulties of the landowner whose settlement did interfere with the proper management of his estates. One must hesitate therefore to make a case for a shortage of landowner's capital in English agriculture. In fact a scholar has recently gone on to make the opposite case, that English agriculture came to suffer from overcapitalization.[8]

It was also not uncommon in the nineteenth century to find in settlement—because it passed on estates from eldest son to eldest son—a source of administrative ineptitude on landed estates. It was argued that landowners, owing their position to biology rather than to innate capacity, and being assured of great wealth, were likely to be lacking in habits of business. Again there was some truth in this. Not all eldest sons proved adequate administrators. But a surprising number of them did, perhaps because it was hard to escape the contagion of business in the nineteenth century. Moreover, if they knew nothing about business, it was not difficult for them to find efficient agents. The result was that a landowner like the second Duke of Buckingham, who did only harm as the manager of his estates, was highly unusual.

All this should not surprise us. With a long history of political and economic success, English landowners were scarcely bereft of such humdrum qualities as practicality and prudence. Of all the qualities associated with aristocracy these are often the least recognized although they may be the most consistently displayed. Somehow they tend to be obscured, perhaps by the bourgeois censoriousness that lurks in most of us. The truth of the matter may be that English landowners differed little from industrialists, that they were reasonably businesslike in their procedures, that they rationally maximized their incomes.

Unfortunately this description does not fit a great landowner like the Duke of Bedford. As we have seen, he would probably have done better for himself if he had not invested so heavily in agriculture. Whether this level of investment was confined to the leviathans among landowners and whether it was typical

[8] Thompson, "English Great Estates . . . ," *Contributions*, p. 394.

of them are matters that need looking into. How long they persisted in such investment also needs investigation. It is to be noted that the Duke of Bedford's successor reduced his investment on the Woburn estate sharply in 1869.[9]

It may be that this phenomenon of uneconomic investment among great landowners should be looked on as something of an aberration, the product of peculiar circumstances. It went hand in hand with method and system in the administration of great estates. Agents were likely to be imbued with the professional spirit, bringing informed and vigorous minds to bear on the problems of increased productivity. The best techniques plainly fascinated them. Indeed they may have been too enthusiastic, too ready to believe that universal remedies were at hand, and perhaps too ready to cling to them once they thought they had found them. In short, the blandishments of the new scientific agriculture probably help to explain the large expenditure.

By the 1850's, moreover, it was likely that the finances of a great landowner were prospering. In all probability there had been a period of retrenchment in which old forms of wasteful expenditure were eliminated or reduced. At the same time there may well have emerged new sources of income, like mines or urban ground rents, which came to account for an increasing proportion of gross income. These financial circumstances may have bred a tolerance of large expenditure on permanent agricultural improvements.

Finally there is the elusive matter of social leadership, the traditional role of the great landowner. It is not unknown, of course, for industrialists to be influenced by social considerations.[10] But it may be that the great landowner was especially vulnerable in the nineteenth century. On the defensive generally, he may have found a peculiar relish and satisfaction in so vigorously taking the lead in agricultural affairs.

[9] Duke of Bedford, *A Great Estate*, p. 223.
[10] See C. F. Carter and B. R. Williams, *Investment in Innovation* (London, 1958), chap. 4.

# APPENDIX I

## THE DUKE OF NORTHUMBERLAND'S
## BAILIWICKS, 1848

[ALNWICK CASTLE MSS]

| Name of Bailiwick | Quantity | | | Number of Farms | Total Rental |
|---|---|---|---|---|---|
| | A | R | P | | |
| Alnwick | 7,791 | 0 | 25 | 32 | £11,157/10/1½ |
| Barrasford | 8,034 | 1 | 33 | 37 | 5,393/10/8½ |
| Chatton | 18,619 | 2 | 0 | 26 | 8,988/6/5½ |
| Lucker | 9,052 | 0 | 0 | 24 | 8,096/15/9 |
| Lesbury | 5,560 | 0 | 0 | 28 | 9,294/7/1½ |
| Newburn | 3,147 | 2 | 17 | 20 | 5,613/2/10 |
| Prudhoe | 5,039 | 0 | 14 | 31 | 5,128/12/7½ |
| Rothbury | 14,825 | 2 | 30 | 33 | 4,915/12/0 |
| Redsdale | 57,615 | 1 | 20 | 26 | 6,833/18/11½ |
| Shilbottle | 5,809 | 0 | 0 | 29 | 4,821/11/4½ |
| Tynemouth | 4,860 | 3 | 5 | 52 | 14,419/18/3 |
| Warkworth | 4,360 | 0 | 0 | 23 | 5,458/2/10 |
| Wark | 1,382 | 0 | 29 | 11 | 952/8/9 |
| Berwick | 190 | 0 | 0 | | 934/2/6 |
| | 146,286 | 3 | 13 | 372 | £92,008/0/3½ |

# APPENDIX II

## PERSONS EMPLOYED IN MANAGEMENT OF BEDFORD ESTATES, 1861

[BEDFORD MSS, ANNUAL REPORTS, 1861]

| Estate | Employment | Annual Salary |
|---|---|---|
| 1. *General* | Auditor | |
| T. T. Wing | | £1,000 |
| 2. *Middlesex* | | |
| C. Parker | Agent | House and £800 |
| H. Bailey | Receiving Clerk | £300 |
| W. F. Clarke | Clerk | £210 |
| T. Hardy | Porter, Bedford Office | £92 |
| | 1 Laundress | £12/12/ |
| | 8 Gatekeepers | £40–£52 each |
| 3. *Covent Garden Market* | | |
| W. Gardener | Superintendent and Collector | £450 |
| J. Stace | Assist. Superintendent and Collector | £200 |
| T. Bech | Assist. Collector | £150 |
| | 2 Beadles | £72 each |
| | 3 Watchmen | £54–£59 each |
| | 1 Engineman | £54 |
| 4. *Bedfordshire and Buckinghamshire* | | |
| T. Bennett | Agent | House and £760 |
| C. Hacker | Surveyor | House and £320 |
| | 5 Clerks | £52–£196 each |
| | 1 Woodsman | House and £120 |
| | 1 Gardener | House and £170 |
| | 1 Park keeper | £260 |
| | Chief Woodsman | House and £200 |

184

| Estate | Employment | Annual Salary |
|---|---|---|
| J. Coleman | Bailiff, Woburn Park Farm | House and £200 |
| | 1 Gamekeeper | House and £100 |
| | Bailiff, Chenies | House and £62 |
| **5. Devonshire** | | |
| J. Benson | Agent | House and £750 |
| E. Rundle | Surveyor | House and £200 |
| | 4 Clerks | £18–£160 each |
| | Asst. Mining Toller | £50 |
| | Superintendent of Quays | House and £120 |
| J. Manning | Superintendent of Buildings in Progress | £78 |
| | 1 Woodsman | House and £180 |
| | Superintendent of Mines | £120 |
| | Inspector of Mines | £100 |
| | Hundred Bailiff for Tavistock | £16 |
| | 5 Reeves | £1–£16 each |
| | Endsleigh Gardener | £80 |
| **6. Thorney** (Cambridgeshire) | | |
| R. Mein | Agent | House and £800 |
| J. Edwards | 1st Clerk | House and £125 |
| | 2nd and 3rd Clerks | House and £80 each |
| | Surveyor | House and £150 |
| | 2 Clerks | £47–£62 each |
| | Surveyor | House and £150 |
| | 2 Clerks | £47–£62 each |
| | Superintendent of Laborers | House and £80 |
| | Works Manager | £130 |
| | Collector of Tolls at Dog in a Doublet Sluice | £20 |
| | 1 Woodsman | House and £36 |
| **7. Wansford** | | |
| | Resident Clerk | House and £110 |
| | Woodsman and Nurseryman | House and £54 |
| | Gamekeeper | House and £52 |
| | Under Gamekeeper | House and £44 |
| **8. Dorsetshire** | | |
| H. A. Templer | Agent | £52 |

APPENDIX II (*Continued*)

| Estate | Employment | Annual Salary |
|---|---|---|
| 9. *Exeter* | | |
| Messrs. Dymond | Agent | £5 |
| 10. *Summary of Management Expenses* | | |
| Auditor | | £1,000 |
| Middlesex | | £2,945 |
| Bedfordshire and | | |
| Buckinghamshire | | £2,706 |
| Devonshire | | £2,197 |
| Thorney | | £1,550 |
| Wansford | | £261 |
| Dorsetshire | | £52 |
| Exeter | | £5 |
| | Total | £10,719 |

# APPENDIX III

## THE DUKE OF BEDFORD'S TOTAL HOUSEHOLD EXPENDITURE 1839–41, AT HIS HOUSES AT WOBURN, OAKLEY, ENDSLEIGH, AND LONDON

[BEDFORD MSS, ANNUAL REPORTS, 1841]

|  | 1839 | 1840 | 1841 |
|---|---|---|---|
| Household (strictly) | £20,010/2/6 | £9,545/6/10 | £11,606/17/4 |
| Stables | 3,931/5/4 | 3,446/5/11 | 3,488/6/1 |
| Taxes and Rates | Not mentioned | 855/0/10 | 920/12/5 |
| Rent | "          " | 1,140 | 1,170 |
| Insurance | "          " | 290/15/0 | 289/12/6 |
| Renewal and Repair of Abbey furniture | "          " | 294/5/5 | 276/7/9 |
| Librarian's Salary | 200 | 200 | 200 |
| Game | 809/15/4 | 998/8/0 | 1,043/9/3 |
| Gardens | 3,371/4/9 | 2,363/18/3 | 2,078/14/0 |
| Aviary | 168/16/0 | 91/1/11 | 105/14/9 |
| Nursery | 450/6/7 | discontinued | |
| Park | 1,398/12/10 | 1,595/6/6 | 1,958/8/4 |
| Deer Park | 356/8/1 | 510/16/4 | 712/18/6 |
| Charities | 933/16/0 | 828/10/8 | 1,069/19/6 |
| Pensions | 1,065/5/0 | 1,118/13/6 | 1,544/8/3 |
| Voluntary Payments | 2,297/14/0 | 1,209/15/4 | 1,227/6/10 |
| Total | 34,936/1/7 | 24,488/5/5 | 27,692/15/7 |

187

# APPENDIX IV

## WOBURN HOUSEHOLD BILLS, 1841
### (FOOD, FUEL, FURNITURE, SERVANTS, AND STABLES)

[BEDFORD MSS, ANNUAL REPORTS, 1841]

| Item | Cost |
|---|---|
| Baker | £435/9/7 |
| Butterman, Cheesemonger | 215/8/2 |
| Dairyman | 68/18/10 |
| Butcher | 556/19/16 |
| Venison | 63/19 |
| Poulterer | 140/4/5 |
| Game | 44/17/0 |
| Fishmonger | 77 |
| Confectioner | 30/2/0 |
| Grocer and Tea Man | 286/11/5 |
| Furniturer and Greengrocer | 368/5/7 |
| Italian Warehouseman | 107/8/4 |
| Oilman and Tallow Chandler | 351/7/11 |
| Wax Chandler | 104/15/4 |
| Malt Hops and Brewing | 412/10/4 |
| Wine, Spirits | 168/13/3 |
| Fuel | 780/11/3 |
| Perfumer | 29/9/8 |
| Watch and Clock Maker | 17/0/6 |
| Upholsterer and Dyer | 311/6/8 |
| Linendraper and Haberdasher | 291/3/5 |
| Turner | 85/3/6 |
| Brazier and Ironmonger | 245/11/12 |
| Glass, China and Earthenware | 130/12/9 |
| Stationer | 56/10/10 |
| Apothecary | 97/6/3 |
| Liveries | 516/17/4 |
| Carrier | 71/8/5 |
| Chimney sweeper | 17/6/6 |
| Assist. Servants | 73/11/0 |
| Sundries | 50/12/9 |
| Total | 6,207/3/0 |
| Servants | 2,137/13/2 |
| Stable | 1,221/12/0 |
| Total | £9,566/8/2 |

# APPENDIX V

## DUKE OF BEDFORD'S INDEBTEDNESS, 1839

[BEDFORD MSS, ANNUAL REPORTS, 1848]

| To Whom Due | Amount |
|---|---|
| **1.** *Mortgages and Family Charges* | |
| Trustees of Lord and Lady G. W. Russell's Marriage Settlement | £40,000 |
| Trustees of Lord and Lady G. W. Russell's Marriage Settlement | 7,000 |
| Trustees of Lord John Russell's First Marriage Settlement | 20,000 |
| "      "      " Second " " | 20,000 |
| Trustees of Lord and Lady Wriothesley Russell's Marriage Settlement | 12,000 |
| Lord Edward Russell | 12,000 |
| Trustees of Lord and Lady C. J. Fox Russell's Marriage Settlement | 12,000 |
| Trustees of Lord and Lady F. J. Russell's Marriage Settlement | 12,000 |
| Trustees of Lady G. E. Russell and Mr. Romilly's Marriage Settlement | 12,000 |
| Trustees of Lady Henry Russell's Marriage Settlement | 12,000 |
| Lord Cosmo George Russell | 12,000 |
| Trustees of Lord and Lady A. G. Russell's Marriage Settlement | 12,000 |
| Lady Rachel Evelyn Russell | 12,000 |
| Trustees of Lord William Russell's Marriage Settlement | 45,000 |
| Trustees of the Baroness de Clifford's Marriage Settlement | 43,910 |
| Arthur Craven, Esq. | 34,000 |
| Henry Craven, Esq. | 26,000 |
| F. P. Delme Radcliffe, Esq. | 22,000 |
| Sun Fire Office | 20,000 |
| "      "      " | 20,000 |
| Messrs. Child and Co. | 55,000 |
| Messrs. Barclay and Co. | 22,000 |
| Thornhaugh Parish | 60 |
| Total | £482,970 |

APPENDIX V *(Continued)*

| To Whom Due | | Amount |
|---|---|---|
| **2. *Bonds*** | | |
| The Duchess of Bedford | | 5,500 |
| Lady G. W. Russell | | 1,000 |
| Lord F. J. Russell | | 850 |
| Trustees for Mrs. Randolph and Lord Wriothesley Russell | | 6,300 |
| Mrs. Hunter's Trustees | | 4,000 |
| Miss Mary Sophia Ansell | | 20,000 |
| Thomas Mason | | 2,300 |
| Colonel Bray's Executors | | 70 |
| John Forrester | | 300 |
| S. Bellamy | | 200 |
| | Total | £40,520 |
| | | |
| **3. *Notes at Hand*** | | |
| W. Ingram and wife | | £120 |
| W. Wood | | 100 |
| | Total | £220 |
| | | |
| **4. *Legacies bequeathed by the late 6th Duke*** | | |
| Lord G. W. Russell | | £10,000 |
| Lord John Russell | | 10,000 |
| Lady Wriothesley Russell | | 1,000 |
| Sir Robert Adair | | 5,039 |
| Servants | | 2,190 |
| | Total | £28,230 |
| Total | | £551,940 |

# APPENDIX VI

## NET INCOME OF THE BEDFORD ESTATES, 1832–38 [Bedford MSS, Annual Reports, 1839]

| | 1832 | 1833 | 1834 | 1835 | 1836 | 1837 | 1838 |
|---|---|---|---|---|---|---|---|
| **1. Middlesex** | | | | | | | |
| Bloomsbury | £34,500 | 39,100 | 39,200 | 39,900 | 40,400 | 40,400 | 40,400 |
| Covent Garden | 24,100 | 24,100 | 24,100 | 24,200 | 24,710 | 24,710 | 24,710 |
| St. Martin's | 8,700 | 8,700 | 8,700 | 8,700 | 7,490 | 7,490 | 7,500 |
| **2. Bedfordshire** | | | | | | | |
| Woburn and Bedford | 6,500 | 7,000 | 8,200 | 10,000 | 11,000 | 9,500 | 8,500 |
| Ampthill Honor | — | 340 | 320 | 290 | 250 | 250 | 200 |
| Bedford Woods | 1,500 | 1,747/8/9 | 1,626/11/10 | 1,036/19/0 | 1,251 | 1,341/11/12 | 1,464/12/10 |
| Woburn Woods | 4,000 | 5,108/17/4 | 5,126/6/10 | 4,336/11/0 | 5,281/1/0 | 6,758/13/7 | 6,354/3/2 |
| Woburn Farms | — | 400 | — | 1,724/7/4 | 1,309/18/6 | — | 500 |
| **3. Buckinghamshire** | | | | | | | |
| Chenies | — | 500 | 800 | 500 | 1,500 | 1,205/10/11 | 500 |
| **4. Cambridgeshire** | | | | | | | |
| Thorney | 7,270/0/1 | 8,400 | 6,300 | 8,800 | 9,400 | 8,800 | 8,800 |
| **5. Northamptonshire** | | | | | | | |
| Thornhaugh | 1,600 | 1,200 | 1,200 | 1,200 | 600 | 1,200 | 1,200 |
| **6. Dorset** | | | | | | | |
| Kingston Russell | 1,100 | 1,012 | 1,135 | 910 | 1,120 | 1,180 | 1,140 |
| **7. Devon and Cornwall** | | | | | | | |
| Tavistock Borough | 4,500 | 3,500 | 4,000 | 4,000 | 6,000 | 5,000 | 5,000 |
| Bedford Circus | 203 | — | 30/18/6 | 109/11/0 | 101/11/3 | — | 74/11/3 |
| **8. Total** | 94,507/4/9 | 101,388/5/5 | 101,233/14/4 | 106,197/3/1 | 111,795/0 | 188,676 | 109,549 |

# APPENDIX VII

## GROSS RENTALS AND EXPENDITURE ON PERMANENT IMPROVEMENTS ON BEDFORD ESTATES, 1842–61

[BEDFORD, A GREAT AGRICULTURAL ESTATE, PP. 220–23]

| Bedfordshire | Gross Rent | Permanent Improvements |
|---|---|---|
| 1842 | £34,117 | £6,638 |
| 1843 | 35,041 | 12,272 |
| 1844 | 35,408 | 10,414 |
| 1845 | 35,898 | 13,413 |
| 1846 | 35,408 | 12,477 |
| 1847 | 35,514 | 14,909 |
| 1848 | 36,384 | 14,254 |
| 1849 | 35,836 | 11,548 |
| 1850 | 36,932 | 17,249 |
| 1851 | 34,816 | 15,387 |
| 1852 | 33,707 | 14,181 |
| 1853 | 33,359 | 16,049 |
| 1854 | 34,749 | 11,063 |
| 1855 | 37,002 | 13,728 |
| 1856 | 38,597 | 14,445 |
| 1857 | 41,113 | 11,892 |
| 1858 | 42,603 | 15,803 |
| 1859 | 41,837 | 17,841 |
| 1860 | 40,548 | 16,517 |
| 1861 | 41,822 | 15,723 |

# APPENDIX VIII

## AMOUNTS CHARGED ON ESTATES IN ENGLAND AND SCOTLAND BY SANCTION OF INCLOSURE COMMISSIONERS TO DEC. 31, 1881

[B.P.P., Rep. of R.C. on Depressed Condition of Agricultural Interests (1882, XIV), appendix]

| | |
|---|---|
| Drainage | £ 8,259,404/8/4 |
| Farm Buildings | 3,397,133/15/10 |
| Cottages | 823,910/2/6 |
| Embanking | 112,830/13/6 |
| Roads | 124,202/11/5 |
| Reclamation | 61,913/9/0 |
| Clearing | 79,468/5/5 |
| Planting | 70,254/17/0 |
| Inclosing | 237,846/10/1 |
| Other Agricultural Improvements | 171,385/8/1 |
| Subscriptions to Railways | 63,333/1/1 |
| *Owners' Residences | 196,657/16 |
| Total | £ 13,597,620/18/9 |

* Under the Limited Owners' Residence Acts of 1870–1.

# APPENDIX IX

## LEGISLATION CONCERNING IMPROVEMENTS ON LANDED ESTATES

1. *Companies Acts:* under which money was advanced by the companies and made a charge on the land by the Inclosure Commissioners.
   - 1848   11 and 12 Vict. c. 142:   The West of England and South Wales Land Drainage and Inclosure Co.
   - 1849   12 and 13 Vict. c. 91:   General Land Drainage and Improvement Co.
   - 1853   16 and 17 Vict. c. 154 ⎫
     18 and 19 Vict. c. 84  ⎬   The Lands Improvement Co.
     22 and 23 Vict. c. 82  ⎪
     26 and 27 Vict. c. 140 ⎭
   - 1860   23 and 24 Vict. c. 169 and c. 194:   The Land Loan and Enfranchisement Company

2. *Public Money Drainage Acts:*
   - 1846   9 and 10 Vict. c. 101:   First Act
   - 1850   13 and 14 Vict. c. 31:   Second Act
   - 1847   10 Vict. c. 11 ⎫
     1848   11 and 12 Vict. c. 119 ⎬ altering and amending
     1856   19 Vict. c. 9 ⎭

3. *Public Acts:* under which the money for Improvements to be made a charge on Land by the Inclosure Commissioners was provided from private sources or from the companies.
   - 1849   12 and 13 Vict. c. 100:   Private Money Drainage Act
   - 1864   27 and 28 Vict. c. 114:   The Improvement of Land Act
   - 1870   33 and 34 Vict. c. 56 ⎫ The Limited Owners' Residences Acts
     34 and 35 Vict. c. 84 ⎭
   - 1877   40 and 41 Vict. c. 31:   The Limited Owners' Reservoirs and Water Supply Further Facilities Act

4. *Acts of Parliament:* under which charges were made on Land but not through the Inclosure Commissioners.
   - 1840   3 and 4 Vict. c. 55:   Pusey's Act
   - 1845   8 and 9 Vict. c. 56

194

# ⚰ BIBLIOGRAPHY

This is not an exhaustive bibliography, but cites only those materials and works referred to in the footnotes.

## A. MANUSCRIPT SOURCES

The following manuscripts have been consulted for the general subject of landownership in nineteenth-century England, and have in varying degree offered information relevant to this study. Portions of these manuscripts which have proved especially useful are noted.

ALNWICK CASTLE MSS. In the possession of the Duke of Northumberland, Alnwick Castle, Northumberland. Especially the Business Minutes, 1847–80, drawn up by the Duke's Commissioner.

ALTHORP MSS. In the possession of Earl Spencer, Althorp, Northamptonshire. Especially the correspondence of John Beasley, the Spencer agent.

BEDFORD MSS. In the Bedford Estate Office, London. This has been the most important manuscript source for this study. The annual reports, beginning in 1839, and the correspondence between Christopher Haedy and the 7th Duke of Bedford were especially useful.

BROUGHTON MSS. In the British Museum Additional Manuscripts.

CHATSWORTH MSS. In the possession of the Duke of Devonshire, Chatsworth, Derbyshire.

CRUWYS MORCHARD MSS. In the possession of Mrs. M. C. Cruwys, Cruwys Morchard House, Tiverton, Devon.

ELLESMERE MSS. In the possession of the Northamptonshire Record Office, Delapre Abbey, Northampton. Especially the letters of James Loch to Lord Francis Egerton, 1837–46.

GLADSTONE MSS. In the British Museum Additional Manuscripts. These were consulted for the useful correspondence of Philip Pusey and James Caird.

HOLKHAM MSS. In the possession of the Earl of Leicester, Holkham, Norfolk. Especially the letter books of Francis Blaikie.

KIMBOLTON MSS. In the Huntingdonshire County Record Office, Huntingdon. The letters of Alexander Haldane to Lady Olivia Sparrow and to various members of her family are useful; and so are the reports of Chancery proceedings between Haldane and Lady Sparrow.

LAMBTON MSS. In the possession of Lord Lambton, Lambton Castle, county Durham. Especially Henry Stephenson's annual reports and Henry Morton's letters to the first and second Earls of Durham.

LEGH MSS. In the John Rylands Library, Manchester.

LIVERPOOL MSS. In the British Museum Additional Manuscripts. These were consulted for James Loch's correspondence.

MILTON MSS. In the Northamptonshire Record Office, Delapre Abbey, Northampton. Especially the letters of Daniel Maude to Earl Fitzwilliam.

MONSON MSS. In the Lincolnshire Record Office, Lincoln. The 6th Lord Monson's letters to his son in the 1840's and 1850's are useful.

NETHERBY MSS. There are two collections which bear this title. The first is in the possession of Sir Fergus Graham, Netherby, Cumberland, and it contains the letter-books of John Yule. The second is the microfilm copy of the public papers of Sir James Graham, and is deposited in the Library of the Johns Hopkins University.

NEWCASTLE MSS. In the Library of the University of Nottingham, Nottingham. Especially the letters of the agent, Henning.

PAGET MSS. In the Library of the University of Bristol, Bristol. The diaries of J. M. Paget of Cranmore Hall, Somerset, 1838–66 are useful for the understanding of a small estate's administration.

PANSHANGER MSS. In the Hertfordshire Record Office, Hertford. Especially the letters of F. F. Fox to Lord Melbourne.

PEEL MSS. In the British Museum Additional Manuscripts. These were consulted for Sir Robert Peel's correspondence on agricultural subjects.

PORTLAND MSS. In the Library of the University of Nottingham, Nottingham.

RICARDO MSS. In the Library of the University of Cambridge, Cambridge.

SACKVILLE MSS. In the Kent County Record Office, Maidstone, Kent.

SNEYD MSS. In the Library of the University College of North Staffordshire, Keele, Staffs. Especially the letters of Andrew

Thompson, both to Ralph Sneyd and to the Inclosure Commissioners.
STOWE MSS. In the Huntington Library, San Marino, California.
WENTWORTH WOODHOUSE MSS. In the Central Library, Sheffield.
WHARNCLIFFE MSS. In the Central Library, Sheffield.

## B. PARLIAMENTARY PAPERS

### 1. Reports of committees and commissions

The evidence brought before these committees and commissions is indispensable for the story of the Inclosure Commissioners. Reference has been made to the following reports:

1821, IX: *Report from the Select Committee on the Petitions complaining of the depressed state of agriculture of the United Kingdom.*

1828, VII: *Report from the Select Committee on the Bill for altering the Law Concerning Entails.*

1836, XI: *Report of the Select Committee on the State of the Coal Trade.*

1844, V: *Report of Select Committee on Commons' Inclosure.*

1845, XII: *Report of Select Committee (H. of L.) to enable Possessors of Entailed Estates to charge . . . for the Purpose of Draining.*

1847-8, VII: *Report of Select Committee on Agricultural Customs.*

1849, XII: *Report of Select Committee (H. of L.) to enable Possessors of Entailed Estates to charge . . . for the Purpose of Draining.*

1854, XXVII: *Reports of Committees of Inquiry into Public Offices.*

1854-5, VII: *Report of Select Committee (H. of L.) on Powers vested in Companies for the Improvement of Land.*

1856, XVI: *Report from Select Committee on Rating of Mines.*

1860, XXX: *Report of the Commissioners appointed to inquire into Greenwich Hospital.*

1862, VIII: *Report of Select Committee on the Ecclesiastical Commission.*

1863, VII: *Report of Select Committee (H. of L.) on Charging of Entailed Estates for Railways.*

1873, XVI: *Report of Select Committee (H. of L.) on the Improvement of Land.*

1881, XV, XVII:⎫ *Report of the Royal Commission on the De-*
1882, XIV:    ⎬ *pressed Condition of the Agricultural In-*
          ⎭ *terests.*

1890–1, XLI: *Second Report of Royal Commission on Mining Royalties.*

1894, XVI Pt. III: *First Report of Royal Commission on Agricultural Depression.*

1896, XVII: *Second Report of Royal Commission on Agricultural Depression.*

1896, XXXIV: *Second Report of Royal Commission on Land in Wales and Monmouthshire.*

1903, XVII: *Board of Agriculture, Annual Report of Proceedings under the Tithe Acts . . . The Draining and Improvement of Land Acts . . . for the year 1902.*

## 2. Other Parliamentary Publications.

*Journals of the House of Commons and House of Lords*
*Statutes at Large*
Hansard's *Parliamentary Debates*, 3rd Series

## C. NEWSPAPERS, PERIODICALS, AND PAMPHLETS

### 1. Newspapers

*The Farmers' Journal*
*Mark Lane Express*
*The Times*

### 2. Periodicals

*Annual Register*
*Edinburgh Review*
*Journal of the Royal Agricultural Society*
*Quarterly Review*
*Saturday Review*

### 3. Pamphlets

BEASLEY, J., *The Duties and Privileges of the Landowners, Occupiers and Cultivators of the Soil* (London, 1860).

CAIRD, J., *High Farming, under Liberal Covenants, The Best Substitute for Protection* (Edinburgh, 1849).

——, *High Farming Vindicated and Farther Illustrated* (Edinburgh, 1850).

HANDLEY, H., *A Letter to Earl Spencer on the Formation of a National Agricultural Institution* (London, 1838).
STURGE, W., *The Education of the Surveyor* (London, 1868).


D. WORKS OF REFERENCE


BATEMAN, J., *The Great Landowners of Great Britain and Ireland* (London, 1883), 4th ed.
BATHURST, C. and KINCH, E. (eds.), *Register of the Staff and Students of the Royal Agricultural College* (Cirencester, 1897).
BOASE, F., *Modern English Biography*.
COOKE, G. W., *The Acts for Facilitating the Inclosure of Commons in England and Wales with a Treatise on the Law of Rights of Commons . . . and on the Jurisdiction of the Inclosure Commissioners* (London, 1864), 4th ed.
*Dictionary of National Biography*.
FORDYCE, T., *Local Records or Historical Register of Remarkable Events*, 2 vols. (Newcastle-upon-Tyne, 1867).
FOSTER, J., *Pedigrees of the County Families of Yorkshire* (London, 1874).
*Law Reports*.
VENN, J. and J. A., *Alumni Cantabrigienses* (Cambridge, 1922–53).
WELFORD, R., *Men of Mark 'Twixt Tyne and Tweed*, 3 vols. (London, 1895).


E. BOOKS, ARTICLES, AND OTHER SOURCES


1. Manuals on Land Agency

DEAN, G. A., *The Land Steward* (London, 1851).
KENT, N., *Hints to Gentlemen of Landed Property* (London, 1799).
LAURENCE, E., *The Duty and Office of a Land Steward* (London, 1736).
LAWRENCE, J., *The Modern Land Steward* (London, 1801).
LOW, D., *On Landed Property and the Economy of Estates* (London, 1856).
MACDONALD, D. G. F., *Estate Management* (London, 1868).
MARSHALL, W., *On the Landed Property of England, An Elementary and Practical Treatise; containing the Purchase, the Im-*

*provement, and the Management of Landed Estates* (London, 1804).

MORTON, J. L., *The Resources of Estates* (London, 1858).

SMITH, H. H., *The Principles of Landed Estate Management* (London, 1898).

2. Biographies of Agents

BUTLER, J. E., *Memoir of John Grey of Dilston* (Edinburgh, 1869).

DRIVER, C. H., *Tory Radical: The Life of Richard Oastler* (New York, 1946).

HUSSEY, S. M., *Reminiscences of an Irish Land Agent* (London, 1904).

PETRE, L., *The Life of the Hon. Henry W. Petre* (1907, privately printed).

RICHARDSON, B. W., *Thomas Sopwith* (London, 1891).

STURGE, E., *Reminiscences of My Life* (1928, privately printed).

3. Nineteenth-Century Works on Agriculture

BEDFORD, DUKE OF, *A Great Agricultural Estate* (London, 1897), 3rd ed.

CAIRD, J., *English Agriculture in 1850–51* (London, 1852), 2nd ed.

———, *The Landed Interest and the Supply of Food* (London, 1878).

COLMAN, H., *European Agriculture and Rural Economy from Personal Observation*, 2 vols. (Boston, 1846).

LOCH, J., *An Account of the Improvements on the Estates of the Marquess of Stafford* (London, 1820).

4. Learned Articles and Essays

BREBNER, J. B., "Laissez Faire and State Intervention in Nineteenth-Century Britain," *The Journal of Economic History*, Supplement VIII, 1948.

HABAKKUK, H. J., "Economic Functions of English Landowners in the Seventeenth and Eighteenth Centuries," *Explorations in Entrepreneurial History*, no. 2, 1953–4.

HUGHES, E., "The Eighteenth Century Estate Agent," in *Essays in British and Irish History in Honour of James Eadie Todd*, eds. H. A. Cronne, T. W. Moody, and D. B. Quinn (London, 1949).

———, "The Professions in the Eighteenth Century," *Durham University Journal*, March, 1952.

KITSON Clark, G., "The Electorate and the Repeal of the Corn

Laws," *Transactions of the Royal Historical Society,* 1951.

LARGE, D., "The Third Marquess of Londonderry and the End of the Regulation 1844-5," *Durham University Journal,* December, 1958.

MACDONAGH, O., "The Nineteenth-Century Revolution in Government: A Reappraisal," *The Historical Journal,* No. 1, 1958.

MINGAY, G. E., "The Size of Farms in the Eighteenth Century," *The Economic History Review,* April, 1962.

MITCHELL, A., "The Association Movement of 1792-3," *The Historical Journal,* No. 1, 1961.

PARRIS, H., "The Nineteenth-Century Revolution in Government: A Re-Appraisal Reappraised," *The Historical Journal,* No. 1, 1960.

SPRING, D., "The Earls of Durham and the Great Northern Coal Field, 1830-1880," *The Canadian Historical Review,* September, 1952.

———, "Earl Fitzwilliam and the Corn Laws," *The American Historical Review,* January, 1954.

———, "A Great Agricultural Estate: Netherby under Sir James Graham, 1820-1845," *Agricultural History,* April, 1955.

———, "Ralph Sneyd: Tory Country Gentleman," *Bulletin of John Rylands Library,* March, 1956.

———, "English Landownership in the Nineteenth Century: A Critical Note," *The Economic History Review,* April, 1957.

———, "Agents to the Earls of Durham in the Nineteenth Century," *Durham University Journal,* June, 1962.

SPRING, D. and E., "The Fall of the Grenvilles, 1844-1848," *Huntington Library Quarterly,* February, 1956.

SPRING, D. and CROSBY, T. L., "George Webb Hall and the Agricultural Association," *The Journal of British Studies,* November, 1962.

STURGESS, R. W., "A Study of Agricultural Change in the Staffordshire Moorlands, 1780-1850," *North Staffordshire Journal of Field Studies,* No. 1, 1961.

THOMPSON, F. M. L., "The End of a Great Estate," *The Economic History Review,* August, 1955.

———, "Agriculture since 1870," in *A History of Wiltshire,* ed. E. Crittall (London, 1959), vol. 4.

———, "English Great Estates in the Nineteenth Century (1790-1914)," in *Contributions to First International Conference of Economic History* (Paris, 1960).

WARD, J. T., "The Earls Fitzwilliam and the Wentworth Woodhouse Estate in the Nineteenth Century," *Yorkshire Bulletin of Economic and Social Research,* March, 1960.

## 5. Novels

Austen, J., *Persuasion.*
Eliot, G., *Middlemarch.*
Forster, E. M., *The Longest Journey.*
Hardy, T., *Desperate Remedies.*
Surtees, R. S., *Hillingdon Hall.*
———, *Ask Mama.*
———, *Plain or Ringlets.*
Trollope, A., *Doctor Thorne.*
———, *The Eustace Diamonds.*

## 6. Miscellaneous Autobiography, Biography, and Correspondence

Annan, N. G., *Leslie Stephen: His Thought and Character in relation to his Time* (London, 1951).
Aspinall, A. (ed.), *Three Early Nineteenth Century Diaries* (London, 1952).
Brougham, Lord, *The Life and Times of Henry Lord Brougham,* 3 vols. (New York, 1871).
Broughton, Lord, *Recollections of a Long Life,* ed. Lady Dorchester, 6 vols. (London, 1910–11).
Buddle Atkinson, R. H. M. and Jackson, G. A., *Brougham and His Early Friends: Letters to James Loch 1798–1809,* 3 vols. (London, 1908).
Bunsen, Baroness, *A Memoir of Baron Bunsen,* 2 vols. (London, 1868).
Charlton, L. E. O. (ed.), *The Recollections of a Northumbrian Lady 1815–66* (London, 1949).
*Creevey Papers,* ed. Sir H. Maxwell, 2 vols. (New York, 1903).
Cross, J. W. (ed.), *George Eliot's Life,* 3 vols. (New York, n.d.).
*Dudley, Letters of the Earl of, to the Bishop of Llandaff* (London, 1841).
Estrange, A. G. L., *The Life of Mary Russell Mitford,* 3 vols. (London, 1870).
Falk, B., *The Bridgewater Millions* (London, 1942).
Fitzmaurice, Lord Edmond, *The Life of William, Earl of Shelburne,* 2 vols. (London, 1912).
*Greville Memoirs 1814–60,* ed. L. Strachey and R. Fulford, 7 vols. (London, 1938).
Haldane, A., *The Lives of Robert Haldane of Airthrey and his brother James Alexander Haldane* (Edinburgh, n.d.).
Heron, Sir R., *Notes* (Grantham and London, 1851), 2nd ed.

HINE, R. L., *Hitchin Worthies* (London, 1932).

HODDER, E., *The Life and Work of the Seventh Earl of Shaftesbury*, 3 vols. (London, 1886).

LEADER, R. E. (ed.), *Life and Letters of John Arthur Roebuck* (London, 1897).

LONSDALE, H., *The Worthies of Cumberland: John Christian Curwen, William Blamire* (London, 1867).

LYSTER, G. (ed.), *A Family Chronicle* (London, 1908).

MARCHANT, D. LE, *Memoir of Viscount Althorp* (London, 1876).

MAXWELL, SIR H., *The Life and Letters of the Fourth Earl of Clarendon*, 2 vols. (London, 1913).

O'CONNOR, I., *Edward Gibbon Wakefield* (London, 1929).

PÜCKLER-MUSKAU, PRINCE, *Tour in Germany, Holland and England*, 4 vols. (London, 1832).

*Russell, Letters to Lord George William, 1817–45*, 2 vols. (London, 1915, privately printed).

*Schreiber, Lady Charlotte: Extracts from her Journal, 1853–91*, ed. EARL OF BESSBOROUGH (London, 1952).

*Scott, The Letters of Sir Walter*, ed. H. J. C. GRIERSON, 12 vols. (London, 1932–37).

STIRLING, A. M. W., *Coke of Norfolk and his Friends*, 2 vols. (London, 1908).

———, *The Letter-Bag of Lady Elizabeth Spencer-Stanhope*, 2 vols. (London, 1913).

SURTEES, R. S. and CUMING, E. D., *Robert Smith Surtees (Creator of 'Jorrocks') 1803–64* (Edinburgh and London, 1924).

TILBY, A. WYATT, *Lord John Russell: A Study in Civil and Religious Liberty* (New York, 1931).

TWISS, H., *The Public and Private Life of Lord Chancellor Eldon*, 2 vols. (Philadelphia, 1844).

*Victoria, Queen, Letters of: A Selection from Her Majesty's Correspondence between the Years 1837 and 1861*, eds. A. C. BENSON and VISCOUNT ESHER, 3 vols. (London, 1907).

7. Miscellaneous Books

APPLEMAN, P., MADDEN, W. A. and WOLFF, M. (eds.), *1859: Entering an Age of Crisis* (Bloomington, 1959).

ASHWORTH, W., *An Economic History of England: 1870–1939* (London, 1960).

BAGEHOT, W., *The English Constitution*, (World's Classics ed.)

CARR-SAUNDERS, A. M. and WILSON, P. A., *The Professions* (Oxford, 1933).

CARTER, C. F. and WILLIAMS, B. R., *Investment in Innovation* (London, 1958).

CHAMBERS, J. D., *The Workshop of the World* (London, 1961).

CLAPHAM, A., *A Short History of the Surveyor's Profession* (London, 1949).

CLAPHAM, J. H., *An Economic History of Modern Britain*, 3 vols. (Cambridge, 1926–38).

ERNLE, LORD, *English Farming: Past and Present*, with introductions by G. E. Fussell and O. R. McGregor (London, 1961), 6th ed.

FLOUD, F. L. C., *The Ministry of Agriculture and Fisheries* (London and New York, 1927).

GASH, N., *Politics in the Age of Peel* (London, 1953).

HARVEY, N., *The Farming Kingdom* (London, 1955).

HOLDSWORTH, SIR W., *A History of English Law*, 13 vols. (London, 1903–52).

HUGHES, E. C., *Men and their Work* (Glencoe, Illinois, 1958).

JEFFERIES, R., *Hodge and His Masters* (London, 1937).

McCLATCHEY, D., *Oxfordshire Clergy 1777–1869: A Study of the Established Church and of the Role of its Clergy in local society* (Oxford, 1960).

MARSHALL, T. H., *Citizenship and Social Class and other essays* (Cambridge, 1950).

MILL, J. S., *Principles of Political Economy*, ed. Sir W. J. Ashley (London, 1929).

NICHOLSON, H. N., *The Principles of Field Drainage* (Cambridge, 1942).

PARES, R., *King George III and the Politicians* (Oxford, 1953).

ROBERTS, D., *Victorian Origins of the British Welfare State* (New Haven, 1960).

ROBSON, R., *The Attorney in Eighteenth Century England* (Cambridge, 1959).

STEPHEN, SIR G., *Adventures of an Attorney in Search of Practice*, 2 vols. (Philadelphia, 1839).

TITMUSS, R. M., *Essays on 'The Welfare State'* (London, 1958).

TOCQUEVILLE, A. DE, *Democracy in America*, 2 vols., translated by H. Reeve.

TRILLING, L., *The Opposing Self* (New York, 1955).

YOUNG, G. M., *Last Essays* (London, 1950.).

8. Unpublished Dissertations

LINKER, R. W., *Philip Pusey, Esq., Country Gentleman 1799–1855* doctoral dissertation deposited in the Library of the Johns Hopkins University, 1961.

# ⚰ INDEX